# Before Before

# Law, Meaning, and Violence

The scope of Law, Meaning, and Violence is defined by the wide-ranging scholarly debates signaled by each of the words in the title. Those debates have taken place among and between lawyers, anthropologists, political theorists, sociologists, and historians, as well as literary and cultural critics. This series is intended to recognize the importance of such ongoing conversations about law, meaning, and violence as well as to encourage and further them.

Series Editors:     Martha Minow, Harvard Law School
                    Austin Sarat, Amherst College

RECENT TITLES IN THE SERIES

# Before Before

## A Story of Discovery and Loss in Sierra Leone

BETSY SMALL

University of Michigan Press
Ann Arbor

For questions or permissions, please contact um.press.perms@umich.edu

Published in the United States of America by the
University of Michigan Press
Manufactured in the United States of America
Printed on acid-free paper
First published March 2025

A CIP catalog record for this book is available from the British Library.

*Library of Congress Cataloging-in-Publication data has been applied for.*

ISBN 978-0-472-07729-8 (hardcover : alk. paper)
ISBN 978-0-472-05729-0 (paper : alk. paper)
ISBN 978-0-472-90490-7 (open access ebook)

DOI: https://doi.org/ 10.3998/mpub.14373970

The University of Michigan Press's open access publishing program is made possible
thanks to additional funding from the University of Michigan Office of the Provost and
the generous support of contributing libraries.

*For my children, Lillian, William, and Lucas.*
*And for the children of Tokpombu.*

To those peoples in the huts and villages of half the globe struggling to break the bonds of mass misery, we pledge our best efforts to help them help themselves, for whatever period is required—not because the communists may be doing it, not because we seek their votes, but because it is right. If a free society cannot help the many who are poor, it cannot save the few who are rich.

—PRESIDENT JOHN F. KENNEDY, 1961

Why are we having all these people from shithole countries come here?

—PRESIDENT DONALD J. TRUMP, 2018

# Contents

# Preface

I first encountered Tokpombu village as a Peace Corps volunteer in 1984. It existed in a narrow opening in the rainforest where forty rice farming families, Christians and Muslims, were intermarried and had long lived together harmoniously, educating their children and working toward a better standard of life. My assignment was to work with the community to improve their rice yields using new agricultural methods including hybrid varieties according to the precepts of the Green Revolution of the 1970s, which promised to feed the world.

At the time, the Cold War was waning and Ronald Reagan was reelected as president on a platform that proclaimed a "new morning in America." The U.S. seemed to be coming back from its travails in Vietnam and the scandal of Watergate. It was the year of the first Apple Mac, the first SUV, and Arnold Schwarzenegger's first *Terminator* film and Prince's "Purple Rain." And whereas the Peace Corps volunteers who served in Sierra Leone in the sixties and seventies came from the era of Presidents John F. Kennedy and Lyndon Johnson when liberal idealism could feel pride in the collective achievements of the civil rights movement, my generation of the eighties and nineties came from a culture that championed individualism and the attainment of wealth. Yuppies had long since replaced the hippies, and the number-one TV show was *Dynasty*, which followed the endless feuding between two oil-rich Texas families. McMansions had replaced ranch houses in the ever-expanding suburbs, followed by luxurious suburban malls with their high-rise atriums, glass elevators, multiplex cinemas, food courts, and a venue for beauty pageants.

The Peace Corps was launched as a new agency within the Department of State in 1961 at a time of great social and political upheaval when student activists known as the Freedom Riders joined African Americans in the fight against segregation, the Cuban Missile Crisis erupted, and

Berlin was a capital city divided by a wall. The vision of the Peace Corps was both principled and pragmatic. It addressed the social and economic inequities of a postcolonial world, and showcased American democratic values during an escalating Cold War. The ideals of the Peace Corps were to advance the cause of universal civil rights and human rights abroad and, in its ideal, to bring those lessons home. It sought to fulfill three core tenets: to help other countries meet the need for trained workers, to promote a better understanding of Americans in the countries where volunteers serve, and to encourage Americans to better understand citizens of other nations. This revolutionary approach supported nation-building and self-determination. It disrupted the imposition of outsized colonial powers that had defined the modern world for centuries.

Forty percent of the countries on the initial Peace Corps roster were African countries although no African American country directors were appointed until 1977. The agency hoped that the experiences of the disproportionately white volunteers would generate a reevaluation of their ethnocentric beliefs and also America's acceptance of the "color line." From the start, it was required that stateside trainings take place only in desegregated spaces, which precluded the participation of some American universities that still practiced segregated policies.

The Peace Corps' pioneering Cold War era efforts was effective because the organization pushed new boundaries and filled its ranks with Americans who sought to bring their idealism to the wider global stage. But in the eighties, the vision of President Kennedy and Sargent Shriver, the first director of the Peace Corps, and of the agency as an exuberant youth contingent had lost its high profile and luster. Not only were emerging nations increasingly able to rely on their own skilled workers, but among the volunteers a cultural shift was also taking place. Increasingly, recruits for the Peace Corps reflected the nation's new conservatism. Not surprisingly, even the Peace Corps attracted those with degrees in business and technology over the liberal arts generalists, the category into which I fell. I was still welcomed to Sierra Leone as one of "Kennedy's children," but back home, government deregulation—"Reaganomics"—and its meritocratic aspirations championed the day.

Sierra Leone became an independent nation the same year that the Peace Corps was inaugurated, and in the following year, when I was born, the country welcomed its first cohort of thirty-two American Peace Corps volunteers. Over time, more than 3,500 have served there. When I arrived in 1984, the zeitgeist was one of pervasive lament and a sense of powerlessness. It had become evident that the country's first executive president, Siaka Stevens, had suppressed all opposition, establishing a one-party state under his own party, the All-People's Congress. It also seemed clear that he would never deliver the promised economic and social growth many Sierra Leoneans had hoped for after independence in 1961 and again in 1980 when the country proudly hosted the Pan-African Organization of African Unity summit. The ongoing struggle for independence from colonial rule drove the OAU's prestigious alliance, and it had been Sierra Leone's moment to further establish itself among the newly emerging nations of Africa. But in a frenzy of preparation, President Stevens drained the government's treasury and international credit to build a state-of-the-art infrastructure to accommodate the international delegations. New hotels, road improvements that included the country's first traffic light, and, most lavishly, a new conference center and Heads of State Village were all intended to trumpet Sierra Leone's national pride. But in the years that followed, these buildings stood as mostly abandoned white elephants—even the traffic light stopped working. Rather than conceiving policies promoting economic and social stability and modernizing the country, this mismanaged summit led to a national debt crisis.

I hardly knew any of this when I arrived in Tokpombu, 250 miles from the country's Atlantic coastline. The only Western technology in this rainforest valley was an occasional radio, watch, or kerosene refrigerator. Its collection of mud homes, small streams, and swamps, and the well-trodden footpaths through nearly impenetrable tropical undergrowth were made accessible by the craggy laterite road that mostly washed away during the rains. What I couldn't understand at the time was how the people living there seemed to embody both their distant and more recent past but with no secure footing in their future.

Beyond the political and economic reality that I could only tenuously grasp flowed a complex history that stretched back well beyond the country's independence. I could not see at that time all that had taken place in this region. How, for generations, farmers labored to clear dense rainforests to establish their towns and cultivate their crops. How, hundreds of years earlier, African traders raided villages, often in the middle of the night, abducting innocent farmers and their families. How they led these captives away—men, women, and children bound to each other at the neck and ankles trudging along footpaths, toward the coast, passing through a succession of kingdoms where it was typical for a king (or sometimes queen) flanked by heavily armed men to require a tax to pass through their section of the river. And then, closer to the coast, at the headwaters of the country's major rivers, the large markets where African traders could buy gold dust, ivory tusks, cowhides, beeswax, spices, and camwood for dying textiles. How, at these markets, African traders paid for the boat passage of their material and human bounty to the harbor, where British traders were on wait to pay them with cloth, brandy, rum, gin, guns, and ammunition. Light sailing vessels then delivered the human cargo five more miles upstream along Africa's largest natural harbor, the Sierra Leone River, to Bunce Island.

Since the fifteenth century, Sierra Leone's vast harbor, formed by two rivers that flow down from the interior, served as a crossroads of commerce where, at various times, the Portuguese, English, French, and Dutch, and to a lesser extent Danes and the German Baltic states, competed for trade. A Portuguese navigator, Pedro de Cintas, gave the country its name in 1462: *Sierra Leone,* or "Mountain Lion." One can imagine the connection between the name and the thunderous roll of storms across the mountainous peninsula, which rises at the entrance to the great harbor, looking and sounding like a roaring lion during the rainy season.

The unimpressive land mass of Bunce Island, less than one-third of a mile long, was strategically located for all kinds of commercial sailing vessels along Africa's west coast. But over the course of the eighteenth century, when nearly 30,000 people were transported from Senegal to the Gambia to Sierra Leone, Bunce emerged as a premier location where Europeans could control large numbers of trafficked Africans. Marched onto ships anchored beneath Bunce's fortress cannons, chained captives were crammed two hundred or more to a ship and endured unimaginably brutal conditions as they were transported across the Atlantic. Plantation owners quickly recognized the economic opportunity for rice to grow along America's southeast coast, specifically the Carolinas and Georgia. But with no knowledge of its farming techniques and little immunity to malaria and yellow fever, the enslavers came to rely on the competence of farmers from the Rice Coast of Africa, of which Sierra Leone was a part. The expertise of these captives in developing and building swamp-rice irrigation systems, as well as their relative resistance to the region's infectious diseases, created America's own lucrative Rice Coast. Slave merchants were willing to pay higher prices for these skilled farmers, as well as organize and advertise their sale. With a growing demand for rice in Europe, rice cultivation, not cotton, held preeminence in the early Americas.

Many African descendants in the U.S. have traced their ancestral past, but the rice farmers of America's southeastern plantations are the only group who can directly tie their lineage to Sierra Leone. This intact community, known as the Gullah, have retained much of their language and cultural heritage through songs, dances, stories, basket-making, and rice-eating traditions. At the start of the American Revolutionary War in 1775, the British recruited enslaved African farmers into their regiments, promising them freedom and citizenship. When the war concluded, they evacuated 3,000 of these "Black Loyalist" refugees from southern ranks, many of whom were from South Carolina and Georgia, and provided them asylum along with other white Loyalists in the Maritimes and Nova Scotia. However, these formerly enslaved farmers found it difficult to thrive in the hostile climate—it was hard to grow crops in rocky soil with such a short growing season, and Black Loyalists were shut out of a racist labor market, precluding any real opportunity for integration into their communities. A decade later, in 1787, one of Britain's philanthropic antislavery companies financed by British citizens and aided by Protestant churches, the Sierra Leone Company, orchestrated North America's most extensive back-to-Africa voyage. The company offered Black Loyalists the opportunity to return to their ancestral continent. A third of the original group registered for this free passage to Sierra Leone, to what was called the "Province of Freedom."

For the British government, the Black Loyalists proved good candidates for the new colonial authority. They were skilled farmers, tradesmen, and former soldiers, and their allegiance tilted westward, not inland. Not surprisingly, this created early tensions between upcountry Sierra Leone and its new coastal "elite" who prospered as dutiful citizens administering to the ambition of British trade, including the horrors of the Bunce Island fort. Many took up their benefactor's cause of Christian evangelization.

This early settlement and subsequent waves of formerly enslaved returnees to Freetown—what Loyalists renamed their new home—also cleaved a class and cultural divide based on racial hierarchy and institutionalized exploitation, despite the original altruism of the project. Freetown marked the beginning of a new era of colonization in Sierra Leone, one that culminated with the West Africa Conference (or Berlin Conference) a century later when trade between Europe and Africa, even after the Atlantic slave trade was outlawed, ushered in a new imperial era.

The ties that bind North America to Sierra Leone, its traceable links, and its agricultural foundations are the point at which all Americans and West Africans meet. Everyone of us inhabits complicated relationships with the past—we reckon at our own pace and in our own language and within our own families. This book is my journey to create a shared reality between the Sierra Leonean farmers who became my friends, the story they told, the story I now know, and how we bridge the abyss. The farmers I met when I lived in Tokpombu enlightened me about how the passage of time in one place transmits a continuation—a home into which you can be born, learn, come of age, make a livelihood, make your family, and bury your dead.

It may have been too simplistic to think that sending mostly white Americans to "serve" for two or, in my case, three years, among people so vastly different from our own on their soil and terms would chip away at poor governance and economic and racial injustice. And it was certainly ironic that the Peace Corps sent me to grow rice in Sierra Leone.

As an agriculture volunteer in a new postcolonial state dealing with food insecurity, I learned astonishing depths of trust and courage amid a culture of disease, infant mortality, corruption, and unfamiliar cultural practices. Working in swamps and growing rice alongside members of this community, I shared the anguish of their illness and grief over the loss of children and elders, as well as the joyful cadences of their daily lives informed by their ties to the land, which brought them connection and dignity.

The farmers in Tokpombu between 1984 and 1987 recognized that official corruption was accelerating and making their lives more difficult year by year, as did many others I encountered in the country then. But they were discreet about sharing their political views, speaking only privately among family and friends out of fear of reprisal. Everyone understood this rampant corruption would result in some terrible upheaval. However, no one knew how or when it would occur and no one could have imagined they were on the precipice of a period of horrendous violence and on an unprecedented scale. Living in a community that became ground zero for one of the world's most vicious and ignored bloodbaths taught me that the best way to care for one another is to listen and speak when we can.

Forty years ago, the Peace Corps' mission was to teach an uneasy country a better way to live. Now, the question is whether we know what that better way looks like and what Sierra Leone's culture and tragedy can teach us about how to peacefully coexist and develop sustainable environmental practices and economic development governed by uncompromising adherence to the rule of law.

I wrote this story because understanding and imagining what we lose or gain in each turn of our personal journeys tells a larger story of power and exploitation and survival, but also connection. I was the stranger tenderly held in a community and inside people's homes before the onset of the eleven-year Blood Diamond War that began in 1991 and took an estimated 70,000 lives and displaced 2.6 million people, and then the Ebola outbreak and the deaths of 12,000 more. This book is the time of Before Before, my present reminiscences and the interwoven history of North America and Sierra Leone that opened the door to a wider understanding of our clashing lives with its unsettled scores.

For over six decades, this sometimes-overlooked agency of the Peace Corps—though far from perfect—has been actively engaged in nonviolent, collaborative international projects, building new and sustainable systems, often within environments that challenge models of domination. At the same time, it is necessary to acknowledge that the experience I had as a Peace Corps volunteer in Sierra Leone may be different from those of other volunteers. There is great diversity in our collective experience.

It is my hope that *Before Before* will amplify what it means to exert our humanity in the first half of the twenty-first century at a time when our climate and democratic values hang in the balance. Our greatest responsibility to the next generation is to belong to each other's futures.

# Acknowledgments

The idea for this book came during the early years of the violence in Sierra Leone. My conversations in the checkout line of Leone International Foods in Durham, North Carolina, gave me moral direction for this writing. Heartbroken Sierra Leoneans were cashing their paychecks to send as much of their earnings as they could to help loved ones caught in the chaos and horror of their country's brutal war. The courage of these individuals making their way in a new land without knowing when or how the lethal conflict would end or who would care never left me. Hardworking men and women included me in candid and dignified discussions. Their grief was palpable. The issues of war are too heavy a burden to carry alone or in silence.

I wrote the first chapter toward the war's end on a rainy Tuesday when my mother-in-law was babysitting our daughter, Lillian. I recognized that I had an elder in my own family who helped care for my child at a time when so many Sierra Leonean children were separated from or had lost theirs. Thank you, Janet Campbell, Martha Lefebvre, Anne Mandeville-Long, and all of my children's early caregivers.

Thank you also to my Peace Corps friends: Peter Andersen, Callie Black, Steve Cameron, Jim Chitty, Betsy Hobkirk, Eileen Nolan, Ray Wirth, Nina Lorch, Stella Kirkendale, Lisa Walker, Chris Thomas, Kevin Flood, Cindy Nofziger, Lila Koroma, and to the memory of Elva Heinz, who also made possible my friendship with Sarah Gborie and her son, David, my hero in humor and humility. My interactions with all of these friends spanning decades helped me process our collective experience of pre-war Sierra Leone and the subsequent trauma of the people we'd come to love as much as our own families. I am profoundly grateful to Lori Rubin for our years of intersecting paths in Kono District, Columbia Teachers College, and again in New Hampshire, and for being a mirror and the true sister I needed.

A community of writers in New Hampshire helped to refine my ideas and memories as the book progressed and as I balanced work and family. Thank you, Mimi Bull, Tina Rapp, Stephanie Minteer, Julie Cyr, Wendy Bienvenue, Deborah Murphy, Deborah Boudreau, Susan Murata, and Wendy Keith, and to the memory of Sara Miller, whose year at Fourah Bay College in the 1960s gave me another lens. Thank you to Kate Gleason, Edie Powell, Laura Cotterman, Janet Brown, Marion Roach Smith, Jill Smolowe, and John Knight for the valuable time you gave and for believing this story would find a home.

Thank you to my friends who offered insightful feedback, both in New Hampshire and beyond, including Jenna Berg, Melanie Brooks, Sally Edwards, Cindy Wright, Eleni Patarkki, Marjorie and Lily Hobbs, Rachel Simon, Theresa Betancourt, Mary McCutcheon, Diana Place, Cindy Bachman, Rosemary James, Carol Bonow, Ryan Taheri, Jackie Flanigan, Suzanne Haff, and Patricia Klindienst. Thank you also to generous Ginny Brooks, with whom I shared a classroom and parallel pregnancy, and for accompanying me through this book's long gestation. Thank you to Lisa Freeman, our beloved child whisperer who left us too early but in whose memory came the introduction to Sy Montgomery, whisperer of all creatures, who has continued on the journey we started, mentoring me with her experience and warmth on our forest walks, our shared sense of "our Lisa" accompanying us through every season since. To Howard Mansfield, thank you for dropping everything on a fall day to review the path toward this book's publication. To the Kamara family who is also part of my family. Thank you Alusine, Koko, and Kenjo, who left us too early but whose memory we keep close. Your believing these recollections would be worthy enough for Sierra Leoneans because they are based on love made all the difference.

I thank my friends at Right Sharing of World Resources and the Village Medical Project of Sierra Leone. To Reuben Koroma of the Sierra Leone Refugee Allstars for carrying the melody during the tortuous Ebola years. To all of them for their willingness to try to hold the world's problems in their hands. To the Gullah Society and Penn Center for their work that binds families across the sea. Thank you Jackie Stillwell, Sallian Sankoh, Wes Strickland, Professor Aiah Gbakima, Emory Campbell and Victoria Smalls. All of their inspiring work propelled the narration of this story. I am indebted to my colleagues at Creating Friendships for Peace. Our engagement around the world inspires me to keep asking the hard questions that might encourage people in conflict to find common ground. Thank you, Linda Ziglar.

I owe singular gratitude to my dear and patient friend Braima Moiwai, who, more than anyone, made these stories a reality. Our four decades of shared memories provided story detail and writing guardrails when I needed them most.

Thank you to Joseph Opala for tirelessly offering the profound scholarship of Sierra Leone's history, culture, and language that infuses these pages and for believing this book could matter. Thank you to Anne Dubuisson. I am indebted to her expertise and brilliant guidance. Anne's warm and generous spirit propelled me to explore and hone the essence of this story.

A heartfelt thank you to Martha Minow for her commitment to understanding the seismic consequences of political violence around the world. Her deep and principled oversight centered the moral underpinnings of this story. The serendipity of our meeting and her trust in me made this publication possible. Thank you to the University of Michigan Press directors, staff, and board, including Elizabeth Demers, Haley Winkle, Delilah McCrea, Madison Alums, Marcia LaBrenz, Danielle Coty-Fattal, and John Raymond, for their hard work. To my gracious reviewers, Professors Yinka Akinsulure-Smith, PhD and Fodei Batty, PhD.

I thank my beloved parents for showing me tikkun olam and nurturing my capacity to hold each of their memories as an eternal blessing. I miss them every day. To my brothers, Jeff and Andy, who hold those memories with me. To my cousins, Debbie Leaman, Ellen Cederbaum, and Amy Cederbaum, for their careful, loving reading of this story.

My gratitude to the Sonda family and Ma Sando and her children, Ella, Sahr Kondeh, Finda, Mohammed, Kadiatu, and Bondu, is boundless. Their struggle, endurance, and joy rooted in optimism are my north star. To the people of Gorama chiefdom, thank you for your sublime kindness. Thank you for welcoming a stranger like me into your community. Thank you for allowing this story and holding it with me as something as durable as a footpath in Sierra Leone. To the memory of Dr. Sarah E. Moten, my Peace Corps Director (1986-1988), whose tireless and inspiring work gave me a map.

Above all, are my children: Lillian, William and Lucas. I am eternally grateful for their fresh eyes and the tens of thousands of precious moments they have kept me in the present tense. Their love and interrogation stretch every part of me in the best ways. Thank you, Lilly, for accompanying me on the return to old friends and for your boundless capacity for thinking, learning, and loving. Thank you William for your purposefulness and the fortitude you bring to dedicating your life to serving others. Thank you Lucas for showing me new ways of seeing. To James Campbell: my partner and best friend, listener extra-ordinaire, thank you for buckling in for the long haul—trusting me, my voice, this story. Without him, none of this would have come about.

And finally, thank you reader, wherever you may be from, for choosing to read this book.

# Author's Note

My use of the Krio language in this book relied on the Peace Corps language instruction I received, the vocabulary in use upcountry in the mid- to late 1980s; in some cases, it has been updated to adapt to today's current vernacular and usage. I recognize that alternative spellings and pronunciations for Krio rely on other authoritative guidelines. I intend to reflect only the language as I heard and spoke it daily in Tokpombu. My spellings are subjective in large part too because Krio, Sierra Leone's lingua franca, is not a written language and is thus open to interpretation.

As necessary, the telling in this memoir also relied on the compilation of journal notes, common historical records, and my recollections. In some instances, I have altered individuals' identities by changing their names or creating composite portraits. The goal has always been to ensure the broadest range of respect for this community and its members' right to privacy.

*If you go, you hurt.*
*If you hurt, you feel.*
*If you feel, you'll be connected forever.*

CHAPTER 1

# Witchbird

Whatever white people do not know about Negroes reveals, precisely and inexorably, what they do not know about themselves.

—JAMES BALDWIN

It was September 1984—the rainy season—when I arrived in Freetown, Sierra Leone. Three months later, after a village-based training program, the Peace Corps placed me in Tokpombu, a community in Kono District in the Eastern Province. The road to Tokpombu was a slippery impasse, though still occasionally trafficked because petrol shortages had not yet become an issue. In those first weeks in the village, I collected rainwater for drinking by placing my buckets beneath a tin gutter extending off my roof. When they were full, I shared the falling water with the village children waiting their turn to take a shower under the downspout in the rain.

Even when the rains were heavy, I was hot and often thirsty. I didn't like the taste of the iodine tablets in my water. The mosaic of infected mosquito bites on my legs had healed but left faint gray marks where open sores once festered. Run belleh (diarrhea) plagued me and, worst of all, there was no more kerosene to buy, and my lamp was empty.

At night, the men of the village knocked on my door carrying plastic containers brimming with palm wine, through which I had to sift out maggots and red ants. The men said nothing except that they were "gladi" I was here. We sat in the dark and silence, growing accustomed to one another. The sounds of the night were an escalating spiral of mosquitoes, crickets, and frogs. And later, inside my house, a complete silence was interrupted only by an occasional distant owl, but not much else. At one point I noticed how we we'd all turned our chairs toward the window so that we could view the rising half-moon.

One late afternoon while sitting inside my parlor, its corrugated zinc roof locking the heat in like a stove, I heard the thrum of panicked feet, then the high-pitched cries of children stampeding toward the iron railing of my front porch, startling half a dozen goats dozing in the shade of my verandah.

A group of children in blue school uniforms pounded the metal door, making the iron bars on the windows rattle against the glass. "Sia, Besty!" Sia is what all firstborn daughters were called; everyone said it fit me because I was the first "white woman" to belong to this village. Villagers often inverted the t and s in my name.

I ran to open the door. The children's voices were clear and demanding, but I couldn't thread together the jumbled phrases in Krio, the country's lingua franca, a mix of English, Portuguese, and African dialects. Looking out over their shaven and tightly braided heads, I saw another crowd of children in my yard, also in school uniforms, their dusty bare feet navigating around piles of seed rice set out to dry on straw mats and the Marimekko bedsheets I had brought from home, decorated with bright pink, purple, and orange flowers with black inkblot centers.

When I opened the door wider, a Toyota pickup with the slogan "No Condition Is Permanent" on its side and a makeshift cabin secured to the truck bed rushed past. The children briefly turned their attention away from me—distracted by the once-a-day overflowing passengers and cargo. Specks of red clay whirled into the air.

The goats scoured the ground in search of orange peels that passengers had tossed over the sides of the truck. As I watched them and the settling dust, I remembered Tamba Lahai, the town chief, first observing me split open an orange to eat the pulp after sucking its juice. Laughing, he teased, "Goat go summons yu!" I was confused until a nearby child explained, "Nar dem part yu dey eat." *They will take you to court for eating their portion!*

Sia Angela, the teenage daughter of my landlord KT Sonda by his second wife, Gbesay, stepped forward. She was clasping the outstretched wings of a baby owl. It looked frightened.

"Sia, we found dis witchbird foh yu." Proudly, Angela held out the stiff offering.

My eyes fixed on the vine noose placed around the owl's twig-like feet. Calmly, I asked in rudimentary Krio, "Wetin appin?" *What happened?*

Angela explained that a tree had fallen across the road and destroyed its home. She wanted me to take care of the baby witchbird and make it my pet.

The bird, now stirring, looked so timid and slight. More children began to congregate and joined in, dancing and clapping. "Sia Besty go mend di bird!" *Sia Besty will take care of the bird.*

"I can't," I interrupted, as the yellow eyes of the owl stared up at me as if it already knew its fate was in my hands. "I don't know how to raise a baby owl."

"Dis bird no get Mama!," Angela persisted. "E go die." *It will die.*

I shook my head.

Then, the last attempt. "E fine lek diamond." *It's beautiful and precious like a diamond.* But this creature wasn't anything like a cold, lifeless stone. It was soft, nearly cuddly, sentient, and very much alive.

Another boy, who looked about the same age as Angela, made a less presumptuous suggestion. "Yu go snap we?" *Will you take a picture of us?*

I went inside and reached for my 35mm camera, cradled in a locally made basket I had hung from the ceiling in my "parlor" to store valuables. I had quickly learned not to leave any of my belongings on my bed, on the bench by the wall, and especially not by an open window where any child's hand could slip comfortably through the iron bars. Even with vigilance, I had lost pens, markers, crayons, a few pictures from home, and my sunglasses.

When I came back out, the bird was still gaping. Camera in hand, I pushed the zoom button. The children seemed entranced by the sight and noise of the camera lens opening and telescoping. "Yaaaaaaaaay!," they whooped.

Peering at Angela through the lens, her big toothy smile beside the brown-speckled bird with its humanlike eyes, I clicked, and the film advanced. The children cheered again at the shhhshshh sound. The idea of preserving an image on film thrilled them, even though it was unlikely they'd ever get to see the developed photographs.

I suggested they find a bowl of water for the bird and release it back into the forest. When the children ignored me, I gathered my sheets from the ground and carried them inside to fold. It was a relief to be out of their view. I had little or no privacy—in those first months, it seemed someone was always peering through my window, knocking at my door. I scooped up a cup of water to drink from a bucket I stored in an empty room everyone called my indoor kitchen.

I walked into my house's parlor, the largest room, with two west-facing windows that looked out on the street and one that faced south toward the newly constructed mud-brick church. The children's long shadows on the barren yard were dancing, whirling—unmoored and frenzied, and moving fast. A few sticks I'd set aside in my yard for cooking had made their way into their lively hands. Angela let the vine around the owl's leg extend as far as she could, then let go and backed away. More children began circling the bird, which didn't stir. I saw the shadows bring their sticks down.

"Finda, Sahr Kondeh, Angela, Bintu!," I called out. "Lef am!" *Leave it alone!* The children didn't hear me. Or they ignored me, except for Finda, who glanced up and then ran off.

Seconds later, I heard shrieks of nervous laughter. The circle broke up, and several boys were on the ground howling with amusement. A group of girls disappeared behind my house. They occasionally poked their heads around the corner to see what might happen next.

I walked outside. In the gutter of the road lay the bird, bloodied and lifeless, its eyes open. The soft feathers of its head had fallen forward, and its serrated wings drooped. I gently tipped it over with my foot, afraid to touch it. A path of driver ants had already appeared from nowhere, marching toward the bloodstained red clay.

Feeling queasy, I grabbed a "tropenzpan," a metal bowl farmers used for measuring what was once "threepence" worth of seed rice during English colonial rule. Gently, I scooped up the baby owl and put it on top of the compost pile bordering the outdoor kitchens behind our houses. I found comfort in knowing its lifeless body could rest in the makeshift grave, that it would be undisturbed in this steamy cushion of decomposing vegetation.

That's where Ma Sando found me.

She told me that to see a motherless witchbird in the daylight was a bad omen. She said a baby bird without a mother was destined to die. She elaborated that everyone was obliged to maintain the boundary between the bush and its dangerous inhabitants. Her tone implied it was the law.

She handed me a fresh pineapple and extended her arm for the blood-stained pan. "Gimme, en I go wash," she offered.

When I thanked her, she looked away and replied, "Yusehf tenki," *Thanks to you too.*

I walked back inside and set the pineapple on my bench. I folded my laundry and tucked the crisp sheets around my mattress. Then, I lay down on my bed and sobbed. I had come to Sierra Leone seeking not just a job after college, but a different way of living. And, yet, in this new and wholly unfamiliar environment, I had no habits of mind with which to take in what I saw and heard and felt. This was not the comfort of suburban of Connecticut, not the Jewish summer camps, not the semester abroad in London, not the kibbutz where I spent that following summer, and not even the liberal arts campus that told us to sample the world with new eyes. I thought I had led with my heart. Now, the motherless bird I had refused to take care of was dead.

The back door swung open. A parade of chickens marched through, pecking at rice that had fallen on the floor earlier in the day. Finda followed.

"Besty," she said, noticing my tearstained face. "No cry, ya."

I felt foolish, a girl her age, about seven, telling me not to cry.

"Dis witchbird no get een Mama," she said, echoing her mother's explanation, that the bird didn't have a mother. "E suppose foh die." *It is going to die.*

"No, Finda," I said and wiped my eyes. I don't see it that way. To me, the children's act had been a strange mix of mercy killing, brutality, and innocence.

"Nar true, Besty." *It's true.* She stomped her foot. "A witchbird can cause harm. It kills chickens, the same as a hawk or snake." She insisted it was dangerous to see an owl in town. It could mean someone was about to die.

Finda averted her eyes, a sign of respect toward adults, but then fixed them on the corner of the daybed. Changing the subject, she blurted out, "Yu go gimme dis bedsheet? E fine." *It's pretty.*

I told her that my mother had given it to me. In my Peace Corps training, I learned that if someone begged you for something you wanted to keep, to tell them it was a gift from your mother. The truth was, they had been on my childhood bed for as long as I could remember. So, in a way, they were a gift, though I'd never quite thought of it that way before.

The door opened again, and Finda's brother, Sahr Kondeh, entered. He hollered to his sister with authority that Mama needed her to help cook rice. Finda abruptly stood and dashed out, her head held high. "I dey cam, Mama!" *I'm coming Mama!*, she said sweetly, without hesitation.

I was never, not one day, so compliant with my own mother. Nor did I have to be. The command of girlhoods like mine had been to figure out how to leave our mothers and yet not leave them behind.

I curled myself into a ball, the ambient noise of the dinner hour comforting me: feet and pestles thumping, mothers calling out the names of their children in rhythmic, melodic Kono, the tribal language people spoke among themselves but not to me. I thought of the witchbird again. I found its feather on my sleeve.

## CHAPTER 2

# Folds

As the drum beats, so the dance goes.

—SIERRA LEONE PROVERB

My final undergraduate semester was steeped in a rebuke of manifest destiny, the Scramble for Africa, and American exceptionalism. The liberal progressive ideas expressed in my Imperial Colonial Rise and the Third World course were a natural extension of my father's only conviction: that our broken world needed reform and fresh ideas. He spoke convincingly that because scores are always unsettled between disparate groups, the world would always be unsettled, with festering grievances lying in wait.

Led by a professor standing on the stage of an auditorium before a hundred predominantly white and upper-level students, we were introduced to the dangers of cultural determinism (that we are "all nurture") and its biological counter, scientific racism and the eugenics movement of mid-nineteenth century America and Europe. He showed us how Europe had divided multiethnic regions of the African continent into arbitrary nations, how science faked and twisted data to serve the aims of racial superiority. He disparaged the work of well-known social scientists and writers like Margaret Mead, her mentor Franz Boaz, and Isak Dinesen, pointing to how their theories and stories reinforced narratives of colonizers and neo-colonizers, of Black African inferiority and Western development. The exception, he told us, was Albert Memmi because, as a Jew, a European, and an African, he understood the story of being a half-breed of colonization; Memmi embarked on a search to understand everyone because he felt he belonged to no one.

The impact of this litany was exhilarating and overwhelming. The idea of seeing ourselves as half-breeds of colonial empire-building, belonging to no one, meant there were new possibilities. The class pulled back the curtain on an arrangement of the world I had never before considered. I began to understand that every place is somewhere profound—there is no backwater, no dark continent—even if empire-makers opportunistically and cruelly would advance a world that believed otherwise.

By April, the professor had immersed us in all the ways that we, in America, in pursuit of happiness and material gain, had made objects of one another to answer for our existential abyss. I wasn't quite sure what this meant but, by the time I graduated, I had internalized that each of us was profoundly responsible for America's moral entanglements beyond its borders. It was incumbent on us to acknowledge our connection to a shattered world and to harness our privilege to attempt to improve it.

While my parents expected my intellectual curiosity to be kindled by my private liberal education, their suburban values came up against their Jewish history when I told them that I had applied and been accepted to the Peace Corps. My grandparents' assimilation, as with many American Jews, began as part of a targeted inferior group in Eastern Europe and fused with the superior group in America in a single generation. But this aspiration for freedom from religious persecution did not fully recapitulate how any of us might grapple with our absorption into the supremacy of whiteness in America. I saw my mother's apprehensions as overly anxious for my safety on a continent none of us knew and based on America's racial prejudices. I was their youngest and only daughter. My two brothers were on their way to becoming a lawyer and a doctor.

My father, on the other hand, enthusiastically took me to the local library to research where I had been assigned. And yet, in our small town, the only volume we could find on Sierra Leone, then a country of 3.6 million citizens, was one lone encyclopedic entry referencing how the Sierra Leone region had been called "White Man's Grave" by 18th century Europeans who met an early demise while living in the country because they had little immunity to the region's perilous tropical diseases.

My parents' opposite reactions reflected two different habits of mind.

My mother cried as I packed. She understood the dangers of being a young innocent women alone in the world. My father wrote me a card applauding my adventurous spirit. He told me to try to stay for as long as I'd committed to staying. He told me the work embodied the Jewish tradition of tikkun olam (repairing the world).

"We are neither limited nor limitless," I recalled my professor sloganeering at the end of that spring. He had admonished us to steer clear of extremes, including the contentious ethnically charged nature-nurture conflict. "It's the wrong question!," he told us. Only people who lived on and worked the land possessed knowledge worthy of consideration. When I told him I'd been posted to work as an "agricultural extension agent" in West Africa, he responded, "Examine the state of your mind to examine the state. See others so you can truly see yourself in everyone."

———

Weeks later, from a cement stoop connecting the back of my house to hers, Ma Sando stretched her long neck toward a darkening sky. "Night wan cam. We uman (women) en *pikindehm* (children) suppose foh go inside now."

Soon, the only lights in the village were those that emerged from tiny crevices in the walls of mud homes. Then the sounds would begin—not just the distant noises of a bird or an animal, but the echoes from a secret place in the forest around us, a place that women were not allowed to go: men's chants, not in any language, but in a chorus of ancient glottal notes, a pitch that sounded involuntary, as if pulled out by the gravitational force of the moon. Poro, the men's secret society, had begun its annual month-long rite of passage for boys between the ages of twelve and fifteen entering manhood.

My new friend turned down her lantern wick to a dim glow. "Good night, ya," she said with a smile, her hands beneath the bulge of a baby she had told me would have my first name, Bondu Besty, if was a girl. "Bondu" is the Kono name given to all fifth-born daughters. I had been in Tokpombu less than a summer, yet my name, like this stoop we shared every day of my being here, would tie me to this village forever.

I grabbed my lantern too and said goodnight, looking up at the moon just as I had for the last six nights when I retreated to my house, and the

Poro drums came alive. As I entered the house, I was suddenly frozen just inside the metal door, my heart racing. I had been growing accustomed to walking about the village at night with my lantern, visiting families on their front porches or beside their outdoor kitchens watching fires smolder. Afterward, I would read or just let my mind wander until I fell into a deep sleep, especially on the nights when I took the antimalarial prophylactic chloroquine, and my dreams were amplified. The unfamiliarity of this country made it relatively easy to accept and trust most of the village conventions—from the proper time of day to wash clothes, fetch water, or bathe at the stream, and when to lock myself inside my house and avoid looking out the window. Ma Sando had suggested that I keep an empty milk tin beside my bed in case I had to urinate in the middle of the night.

Still, I wondered how the women and children were able to sleep through the jarring and earsplitting refrains of the men's secret world, one from which they were so absolutely excluded. They weren't even allowed to peek out of their windows for fear of reprisal.

With my lantern held out in front of me, I stepped into the musty air of my parlor. It looked stark and lonely with its sagging daybed in one corner and a wobbly bench along the wall. I breathed in the dank air, my lips dry, my sweat a sudden sheath over the whole of my sleep-deprived body. What was this anxiety? A sign that I didn't belong, shouldn't be here; that someone would harm me? There had been no evidence of either.

Sounds from a new direction, different from the chants, began in the east: at first, just the steady echoes of a drum, then an escalating moan that spiraled into the night. I curled into the far corner of my bedroom, the way a child will hide from a monster. I had volunteered to be on the margin of a cultural past I didn't know and the bewilderment that accompanied it was unleashing an unfamiliar corner of my mind. I had expected to feel ungrounded and homesick at times, but I hadn't expected the sudden whole-body shifts that lifted everything I knew about how to live from its casing. Isn't that what being afraid of the dark is about? Not so much the literal darkness but the imaginings we fill it with.

In the daylight, none of this fazed me. When the morning sun poured in through the window, I would emerge from the canopy of my mosquito netting to look out at the sun-kissed yellow and pink house in the large compound where my landlord, KT Sonda, lived with his four wives and nearly thirty children. Sometimes I saw a pale moon in the sky too. I felt secure in my growing connection in these tropical surroundings. KT and I had the only cinderblock houses in this rainforest village of thirty mud homes. Even though we had no electricity or running water, the bathroom was an outhouse, and the propane stove had no propane to fuel it, my bungalow was a palace compared to the rest of the village. Sometimes, this difference exasperated me and then made me sad.

But with morning a long way off, I lay down, anxiety rising from my belly to my throat. Why had I put myself in a place like this, where the women and children were required to go inside while phantasmagoric sounds infused the night? Ma Sando reassured me that this "noisy season," with its ceremonies, would last only a few weeks.

———

"It's been going on for centuries," our local trainers had told us, redirecting our concerns with their warmth and reassurance. During that three-month agricultural training, twenty-seven of us had sat for hours on long wooden benches under a thatched roof and "practiced" eating local food, speaking local languages, and learning to grow rice using "Green Revolution inland valley swamp-farming techniques." On those nights, I stayed up late with a handful of other volunteers drinking Star Beer, the national brand, and communing with two of our Sierra Leonean trainers, who spelled out the cracks in their country's one-party system of democracy while we spelled out the cracks in ours. We told them stories of Vietnam, of the civil rights movement, how protesters were lied to and tear-gassed, and how conspiracies spread about the murder of Martin Luther King, Malcolm X, President Kennedy, and his brother Robert.

"Ehhh! Dis e too sad. So, yusehf get all-kind complication inside una politic lek we yone." *So, you have political obstacles the way we do?*, Sidike, our cultural trainer, said pensively.

"Of course," we confirmed, hoping to attenuate the differences between us.

"Hmmmm. To God. Mortal man business no easy," he added. "Allside." *Everywhere.*

———

I lit a green mosquito coil on the floor beside my bed, watching its embers fall away and trying to make my mind as relaxed as the smoke rising from the coil while the noises outside continued. I fingered the slim scar on my thumb where I'd cut myself opening the Swiss Army knife that my cousin Peter had given me at my going-away party, and then the other scar where I had sliced myself a second time with its scissor feature while cutting the plastic tag off a new pair of flip-flops. I pulled my bedsheets over my head to block out the noise, the weight of my own distrust of myself growing heavier than the apology I imagined I might speak the following day: "I'm very sorry. You've been so kind, so I hope I haven't inconvenienced all of you too much, but I can't stay here in Tokpombu."

Three volunteers had dropped out after training. The Peace Corps had a phrase for this, "early termination," or ET. One had been medically evacuated because she was bitten by a monkey. Two others had admitted this was all too much for them: the parasites, the ever-proximal intrusions of inquisitive children, the swamp farming knee-deep in mud. These physical obstacles mattered, but I also had a growing sense that the line connecting the reasons to be here and what "here" actually entailed was not a line but a series of dots on a scatter plot. I could stay and make connections with the people, learn about their history and traditions and how they were governed, but I also had a vague but sure sense that there was something about our job here that eclipsed all of us. The question was, did I care?

I considered how easy it would be to take my clothes off the bamboo pole suspended from the ceiling in a nook behind my bed and bunch them back into my duffle. In less than five minutes, I could pack, zip, and strap the lumpy mess onto my Honda motorbike. I could start the engine and drive out without another worry—not about cockroaches the size of my thumb, or being bitten by a monkey, or no one being able to find me if I tripped on a stump in the forest or catching a dreaded disease from any one of a number of tropical worms and microbial life lurking beneath my feet.

Then, there was this: Lassa fever, a recently discovered zoonotic illness for which humans had hardly any immunity. Fifty years of frenzied searching for lucrative diamonds had penetrated the once remote virgin forest where previously unknown species of rats now met with human activity. Traces of their urine and fecal deposits in rice fields and haylofts were proving deadly. Arguably, population growth and slash and burn forest farming practices were also at play, but nothing could compare to the destruction mining wrought on wildlife habitats.

It seemed like only yesterday when Sidike had rushed toward me after I'd passed my final motorcycle test in Gbendembu, the village-based training site; proving I could patch a flat tire and replace the engine oil and a spark plug meant that I was free to drive anywhere in Sierra Leone. "So, you will be the woman driving her motorbike to Kono to become a farmer! My God, you hit the jackpot, lady!" Holding his sides, he sputtered, "I hope you remember your poor trainers and bring us some of your diamonds!" He was referring to the Kono District's vast supply of alluvial diamond deposits that floated to the surface of streambeds running through the fertile inland valleys where rice was cultivated.

Even then, his comment struck me as incongruous with everything we'd been immersed in so far—Sierra Leone's culture, language, and agricultural practices. I was beginning to understand that the aspiration of the young generation was for diamonds, not for farming. The village's young men, like every young member of the community, had dreams about getting rich in the nearby diamond mines, the way we all have dreams about striking it rich.

He'd slung an arm around me, laughing and patting my soaked back. We'd sat together on a rotted log for a long time, where, in my blanched state, I held my knees to my chest, occasionally stomping my feet to redirect those tiny red fire ants that were always approaching.

After a pause he added. "You really gonna have diamonds under your feet, you know that?"

This was the dream of the village's young men who, three months from now, after the rice was harvested, would hurry away to take up temporary residence in far-off shantytowns to work in the diamond mines. This, too, was backbreaking work and involved pickaxes, shovels, sieves, and siphons, the tools they used to dig their way through the earth's strata—red clay, gravel, sand, and stones—until a wedding or a funeral or the next planting season called them all back to the fields. This exodus was its own seasonal preoccupation. The possibility was enough: a single gem could change a family's fortune.

All of this was, as yet, incomprehensible to me. I didn't want to see myself as only belonging to my history or even my culture. But as I learned to live, work, speak, and eat in profoundly unfamiliar ways, life in this village created a new vulnerability in me. Here I was, in someone else's history and culture—in a rainforest village of 400 rice farmers along a one-lane, rock-ribbed road connecting diamond buyers with diamond diggers. Before coming to this country, I had never even seen a rice plant. The thrumming through my walls, the percussive thumping and wild gyrations of the men's sounds continued. I pressed my damp face into my pillow. I had just turned twenty-two, and if I was honest, this discomfort was loneliness, a separateness that accompanied the entitlements of a protected suburban childhood. I didn't want to leave Sierra Leone. But I didn't know how to be here either.

In the morning, the sounds of men were replaced by the busy cadences of women and children working and laughing: the quiet scrape of short brooms as they cleared out the debris from the previous day—a mishmash of peels, stems, and leaves—and whatever the goats and chickens may have deposited. Over these rhythms, I heard the infectiously happy calls of weaver birds, broken now and then by the anguished notes of toddlers waiting for their mothers or older siblings. It was never long before a gentle hand, breast, or song intervened.

Though my mood was shaped by a kind of dazed fatigue, and an overarching truth harbored within me that I couldn't yet name from the night before, I climbed out of bed in earnest. I collected my soap, towel, and bucket of water to carry to the roofless shower hut outside. It stood next to my twenty-five-foot-deep pit latrine, which was a stable and durable mud structure—both Peace Corps requirements for hosting volunteers, similar to the requirement that I be provided a house with a cement floor.

With the sun blazing and its heat beginning to bear down on my back through the lush foliage of oil palm, papaya, banana, and plantains, I finished my bucket bath, dressed, and headed back toward my house. As I gazed across the boundary of my yard and onto an empty red-dirt road and the front yard of my neighbors, I considered how nestled we were, eggs in a carton. Beside the main artery through which had passed the early casualties of the diamond mines and Lassa fever, my house was the first in a row of six that lined up on either side. Mine was made of cement and my neighbors of mud bricks; they lived five or more to a room: I was one in four rooms. But I shared with them the tropical mirage of the early morning, golden light reflecting lush hues of green. Ma Sando called out to me from her kitchen.

Holding onto her lapa, the tie-dyed cloth wrapped around her waist, she bent over a wood stove and took the lid off an iron pot. She nudged a small, three-legged stool in my direction with her foot and asked, "Ow di morning?" Sunlight revealed faint silver in the strands of hair peeking out from her head tie.

Noting the size of my friend's belly, I asked if the baby was due soon and where, and how, and when she would give birth. She chuckled, "Nar God no mor sabi." *Only God knows.*

When I sat down beside her, she told me I looked tired. I said I found sleeping difficult when the men made weird sounds all night. With grand gestures, she explained how man business wasn't the same as woman business. She dipped a wooden spoon into a pot of rice and said plainly, "We all get differen-differen power."

"But man get mor," I ventured.

"Besty, no! We uman dem get we yone power." *We women have our own power,* she insisted, placing a grain of rice on the ball of her hand to test its consistency, and then asking me to fetch the oil.

I turned around and spotted the old rusty engine oil container and handed it to her.

"Dis palm oil go mek di jollof rice sweet." *Palm oil makes jollof rice taste delicious.*

Avoiding contentious conversation, Ma Sando shifted to a new ordering.

"Raymond bin lek jollof rice tumous" (too much), she continued, poking light fun at my predecessor for his appetite. Ray was the first white man to ever live in Tokpombu or anywhere near it. I was the second volunteer and the first white woman. In the vernacular here, white wasn't always referring to our color but our national identity—American.

"Yu lek Peace Corps tumous," I said, poking light fun back at her. In Krio, tumous implies not just a lot, but excessive.

Ma Sando smiled. "We inside Sierra Leone lek stranger di way we lek rice." She said that both were their staples.

Rice here was as daily as apples and applesauce in the maternal kitchen of my ancestors, but it was rarely on the list of foods in my mother's kitchen. I hadn't been raised with any connection to America's rice story. I did not know that for over a century, rice cultivated in the coastal Carolinas and Georgia was in high demand in European markets, or that Queen Rice (Carolina Gold) was the predecessor to King Cotton in what was the most lucrative early American industry starting in colonial times until Emancipation. And that it was built with African expertise and the horror of chattel slavery.

Before arriving, I thought all rice came from Asia, that Uncle Ben's and Carolina were mere name brands, not clues to cruel and cunning history. It was my mother's signal then, the gesture of her blown-out cheeks to indicate "starchy foods that make you fat," that had branded me most. My mother hung a decorative apron in our kitchen that read, "You can never be too rich or too thin." Yet this product bound my country of origin to the country where I now served as surely and invisibly as the diamond engagement ring my mother used to hide beneath her palm when riding the commuter train from Connecticut through Harlem to Manhattan.

Ma Sando folded her banana-leaf potholders to pull the dish from the fire and said, "Eh Besty! Tenki. Tenki!," *Thank you!*, and let out a deep exhale.

All around me, people were always thanking each other. Simple things elicited thanks, like filling a bucket of water, toting a basket, or even carrying a machete back from the farm. I felt I was the one who needed to be saying thank you for so much hospitality. Yet the things I found remarkable were ordinary parts of daily life here, like the fact that Ma Sando's daughter, Ella, washed my clothes every afternoon, or that her son, Sahr Kondeh, brought me more than the average amount of water anyone else used in a day. Before I was strong enough to tote the water myself, I received two full buckets in the morning and two full buckets in the evening. That took four trips to the water source a quarter mile away, a total of two miles a day—just for me.

My friend scooped rice onto my plate and then poured the remaining rice onto a ceramic tray for her children, sprinkling some additional salt, which was brown and stored in a glass jar. She did this for herself, too, though her own portion was the "krawo," rice she scraped from the bottom of her cast-iron cook pot—the name for the crust that provides additional iron in the diet. "Kono people dem dey eat plenti salt!" *Konos eat a lot of salt!*, she said, sticking her fingers into it, drawing her mouth to a pucker.

"I like salt too," I told her, wanting to sound agreeable.

I hadn't yet learned then how the Kono tribe migrated here in search of salt. My landlord later told me that the Kono were the ones who stayed behind. "While others left, we were the ones who waited," he said, full of pride. "Kono means wait for us here, *Ma Kono*."

"Waiting for what?," I asked, thinking he would say diamonds.

"Nar salt," he had said instead. *Salt.*

Ma Sando called for Ella, her oldest, who called Kadiatu, Sahr Kondeh, and Finda, the youngest. They crowded around us, squatting over their morning meal. Within minutes, the plate, tray, and pot were empty, and everyone told me they were belful (belly full). I thanked Ma Sando for preparing the food and returned to my house, opening both the back and front doors to encourage a cross breeze. A chicken strolled through, searching for crumbs as they always did around mealtime.

"Besty . . ." I heard children's voices call my name. Half a dozen sets of eyes peeked through the window. "Leh we sweep foh yu?" *Can we sweep for you now?*, one of them said. I knew they were all hoping I would give them money for the chore, as I sometimes did. But on that day, I asked them if they wanted to draw pictures with me instead.

Before long, the children were lying on their bellies on my floor like spokes of a wheel, the colored pencils I'd brought from home strewn among them. I thought of the game of Pick-Up-Sticks, where everything begins in a tangle, and then slowly you learn which sticks are leaning on the others. When the children were done, I held up their artwork and read aloud the titles they'd included on the top of the papers: *Fish, Rice, Cutlass, House, Man*, and *Wife*. They'd signed their names at the bottom corner: Sahr Senusi, Mohammed Conteh, Bintu Koroma, Sia Sonda, Moses Sonda.

"I like these drawings tumous!," I said.

"En dis one?," a small voice asked. From behind her back, Finda slowly relinquished her picture, a drawing labeled *Fruit Bat*. It looked like a Chihuahua puppy with wings. "Bat dey eat mortal man een soul," *A bat can will eat a human's soul*, she said.

"How do you know?," I asked, looking into her engaging brown eyes.

"All man sabi dis," *Everyone knows this*, she said, looking away from me.

I told her I didn't believe bats could do that—eat someone's soul. But I still shivered at the idea. Without warning, the back door creaked open in the wind, making all of us jump. I heard Ella calling the younger children home. "Cam quick. E wan rain." *It will rain soon.*

"E wan rain," I repeated to myself, as if the rain, like the night, made its own decisions.

# CHAPTER 3

# Chief's Decision

No race can prosper until it learns there is as much dignity in tilling a field as in writing a poem.

—BOOKER T. WASHINGTON

February marked my seventh month of living in Sierra Leone and the fourth in Tokpombu. The emerald green fields of rice that had sprung up from waterlogged swamp beds were now cracked mudflats matted with a jumble of decomposing stalks desirable only to a few opportunistic weaver birds searching for remaining seeds. As the year progressed from rainy season to dry, I recognized that I too had progressed and somehow crossed a Rubicon, with Sierra Leone's mythological deity Mami Wata—half-woman, half-fish protector of bodies of water—leading the way. It was hard to remember that only a short time ago I knew nothing about this country that had now taken me by the hand.

Sitting on my verandah one Saturday morning when the sun was near "tee-kun-tee" (in the middle of its head), the man I'd been working with every day since I'd arrived joined me. Typically, Sahr Joe and I discussed which farmers we would meet and what work we would be doing with them for the day. But on this morning, the focus of our accumulated conversations took on new meaning that was hard to pin down. What had caused that shift was serendipity—something about the light that morning or hearing the bird calls take turns with the thumping pestles or seeing Finda and Sahr Kondeh run across the street licking the oil from the bottom of their rice bowls. Or maybe all of those things.

I had an inkling for the first time of what I couldn't fully absorb before: farmers here didn't choose to grow rice for their daily consumption just because they were habituated to the taste or the feeling of its bulk in their bodies at night, or even to how it made possible the settling of their children into a contented sleep or made enough nutrition for a mother to be able to nurse. Rice felt deeper than even those deep things. It was a collective history of doing and being that seemed, in every sense, greater than its parts—blurring lines between language and culture that annually renewed its vow to the future. Somehow, comprehending this complexity—the layers of ambiguity and paradox that would necessarily emerge from something this big and whole—felt like the incentive I needed to keep going.

As the temperature rose, hovering in the high 90s, Sahr Joe, a characteristically pensive man, blurted, "Dis early dry season e warm pas before!" *This dry season is warmer than last year's.* He was concerned that if the heat kept up, the streams that flowed through the inland valley swamps would become intensely dry by April and inhospitable to second plantings of rice, dry season vegetable beds, or even the fishponds we were promoting. He proposed that the only possible redemption for cracked skin and a dry streambed was a bubbled-up diamond, which rarely, but not never, could catch a farmer's eye in the sun's glint. Then he laughed at his own exaggeration. "Instead of using our creativity to improve ourselves, we farmers in Kono are building fences in rivers." At first, I didn't understand what he meant. But then he used the term "resource curse" to emphasize the human tendency to engage with ideas that will never amount to anything.

"We have a word for this too," I said. "Quixotic."

Sahr Joe was a bony yet muscular farmer in his early forties who'd been assigned to Tokpombu by the Ministry of Agriculture. He was one rank below me with the title "agro-technician." The distinction that brought him from his home along the border with Guinea, fifty miles away, was a midlevel extension training certificate at N'Jala, one of the country's more prestigious public universities. As my counterpart, Sahr Joe, like everyone here, had been a traditional farmer ever since he'd learned to hold a short hoe or cutlass. Sitting together like this each morning, deciding what, if any, swamp rice-related work we'd be doing later that day or the following, provided me an anchor.

Sahr Joe and I both understood that I was given this higher rank despite my inferior knowledge of agriculture. He didn't mind that I had to complete the reports for the Ministry of Agriculture either. Still, the inherent insult of misplaced authority burrowed into me. Beneath the surface, I found it hard to contend with my unwarranted privilege while understanding that Sahr Joe cherished his position, if not the unfair ranking and its associated pay, which was nearly always months behind.

I wondered how he'd been picked to be an agro-tech in a village that hosted a Peace Corps volunteer and how he dealt with the fact that it elevated his status in the community. As initially complicated as it may have been for Sahr Joe to be a tech to Raymond (Ray), my Peace Corps predecessor, I knew it was even more complicated for him to be a tech to me, a woman in a man's role. And yet I never felt he wasn't in my corner, ready to convince others to accept the unearned power I'd been handed. When it came down to it, I didn't feel his conflict as much as my own self-consciousness.

I regularly told Sahr Joe, "Yu sabi pas me." *You have more knowledge and understanding than I do.*

"All nar foh try." *Everything is trying,* he'd reply, adding that I was providing new knowing on top of the old.

We were each committed to doing our best to work as full partners in a complicated and unfair hierarchal world.

Per the Ministry of Agriculture's objectives, we had been tasked to entice farmers away from upland rice farming. This widely practiced agricultural tradition involves slash and burn farming methods known to play a role in accelerating climate change by eliminating the forest canopy and removing the thin layer of forest topsoil. In its place, we were promoting new opportunities for year-round swamp rice farming, an alternative using scientifically developed short duration rice varieties that seemed a clear trade-off at the time.

Swamp rice was nothing new here. Rice from the second harvest had long been a family's insurance policy to help bridge shortfalls from the more nutrient-dense upland rice. But supplying farmers with Green Revolution resources provided by the ministry—imported Chinese shovels, new genetically modified Asian seed varieties, fertilizers, and fast-growing, disease and drought resistant strains that could, when nursed and trans-

planted, ensure two swamp rice harvests instead of one in a single growing season—was unprecedented. Further, helping farmers design and build
durable irrigation structures in their swamps could also guarantee year-
round agricultural production. We were certain then that we were fully
participating in the grassroots ideal of providing farmers with long over-
due agricultural advancements that could support both their country's
aspirations to feed themselves and compete in a global economy.

When I first met Sahr Joe, he was overcome with pride for the success
that he and Ray had achieved with their demonstration farm, the roadside
patch of land that Chief Lahai had designated for them in 1982 when he
instituted a ban on upland farming. Harvests had increased during the previous two years, and farmers could now visualize these improved methods
for themselves. As word spread that year-round swamp rice farming was
a convincing alternative to traditional practices, farmers extended their
loans to expand the distribution of seeds to the next season's farmers.

I felt a kind of dignity to be learning about this plant and the people
who cultivated it. Often, the two felt inseparable. When a few of the village women gathered at Ma Sando's swamp and taught me how to hold a
penknife between my thumb and index finger to remove the golden arches
of seeds from their stalks and how to securely tie the last strand to the
bundle for carrying back to the village, I felt buoyed by their regard for my
efforts. They showed me how to stomp barefoot on piles of rice to separate
the seeds from the stalk, spread them out to further dry on mats in the
sun, and take a daily portion to winnow and then pound in our hollowed-
out mortar and pestles to break the shell from the inside pearl. At these
times in the village, someone would hum a tune or break into a song and
the others would join, or they would pick up a rhythm to the pounding and
the others would follow. The rich and unmistakable aroma of the broken
canda (rice skin) filled the air, as smoke from the iron pots did by nightfall
when "new clean rice" boiled, and my mood continued to brighten.

It felt like knowing the life cycle of a traditional rice plant was embedded in the collective mind of this community and necessary for everyone's
well-being. It went beyond marking time with a calendar because it was
imbued with the spirit of things that benefitted from ALL our attention. It
was not like building a fence in a river, as Sahr Joe had said.

The previous night, at around dinner time, the town crier had gone door to door announcing that the village chief, Lamin Lahai, had capitulated to the pressure to lift the ban on slash and burn upland forest farming. This was a reversal of a law enacted when Sahr Joe and Raymond had begun their work.

Sahr Joe didn't object to the decision as I had expected. "We in Sierra Leone lek we African supermarket," *Sierra Leoneans like our African supermarket*, he said, referring to the way a variety of seeds are mixed into a threepence pan and then broadcast along a charred crease of a hill or mountain. "Nar dis we sabi pas all," *This is what we know best*, he said, showing his appreciation for the old ways.

Between November and January, I had visited the scenic uplands with farmers who belonged to neighboring villages, where there hadn't been a ban. There, the harvests had revealed an ample supply of rice, corn, eggplant, yams and potatoes, okra, tomatoes, and peppers. And the rice tasted better too. Its higher bran content made it heartier, more nutritious and filling—the difference between brown and white rice, although this variety cooked up red. There was always a breeze, a view, and the feeling of community where thatch-roofed barns stood hundreds of feet from one another. Working in swamps, farmers were separated from one another amid the tangle of thick, dense vegetation. But even in the upland, farmers had openly admitted that rarely, if ever, were the yields sufficient without swamp rice to supplement their diet. "Nar we yone history," *This is our history*, Sahr Joe said. "Our oral tradition ensures this. It is understandable."

Then why was he so agreeable to forgoing the swamp rice that he had worked so hard to introduce? It seemed to me then, before the so-called Blood Diamond War, that such a vast storehouse of cultural knowledge was immutable. There were also new incentives for planting shade-grown cocoa, coffee, and palm oil, but it seemed that this would only supplement, rather than erase, the customs of the past. Until the ban was lifted, I was certain everyone in this community agreed that growing enough rice using more long-term sustainable farming practices was a path forward—that it meant forever. Even though upland rice was more nutritious and flavorful, it would never adequately feed a nation the way swamp rice could when propped up by new varieties, planting techniques, and the water control structures. Yet beneath the conviviality and charm of this village, fault lines were widening, creating distance between the past and the future. Sahr Joe and I recognized that we were caught in the middle of that tremor.

From the beginning, my counterpart had cautioned me that while many farmers still expressed interest in these new approaches, the novelty of improved seeds, shovels, and even fertilizer seemed to be waning. Perhaps they had understood all along that upland rice cultivation was intrinsic to who they were as farmers, to their history and survival. He explained that some farmers had become distracted by other concerns—their labor shortages, sickness in the family, and the increasing market value of their cash crops. Diamonds too. Perhaps the shock was that he hadn't been consulted on the matter.

I asked Sahr Joe if he thought the chief had a change of heart because I was a woman. Men still mostly brushed, plowed, made fences, and stored and repaired farmhouses. Women were the seed broadcasters, transplanters, and weeders. They also managed a large share of the harvest: threshing, winnowing, and storage, and, of course, cooking. Occasionally they plowed too. It was a lot of work for everyone and suitably divided, whether in the uplands or in the swamps. Still, it was the convention to believe that the required double-digging and puddling of the heavy waterlogged clay of the swamp, and building water-control structures with thick, saturated clumps of mud, required the heavy lifting and agility of men and not women, who often worked with their babies tied to their backs or "bin get belleh" (were pregnant).

"That is not the reason!," he laughed, stretching his legs out and locking his hands behind his head.

I looked down at my lap where Ray's yellow notebook rested, a journal that I considered my bible. The pages described in careful detail a list of over fifty rice farmers he and Sahr Joe had worked with, what their concerns had been, the shovels, hoes, watering cans, and seed varieties they'd distributed. Only three of the farmers were women. Ma Sando was one of them. "Then is it because they miss Ray?"

Sahr Joe smiled, "Oh Raymond Wirth, nar bin tronga man." *Raymond was strong!* "We hardworking brodda (brother) dey inside America now—far, far away." Sensing my discomfort, he took my sweaty hand and said, "Before tumous tem dey pas, yusehf go make progress lek we yone Mista Raymond. Small small. We all." *Before long, you will make progress the way Mr. Raymond did, a little at a time. Together.*

In no rush for the train of goodwill toward Ray to pass, I did not say anything more. For now, I felt grateful just to be looking out onto the road and sharing this scenery with Sahr Joe, who was always one step ahead of me, pointing out the subtle changes that accompanied the changing seasons. I noted, too, the subtle change in our own ease and familiarity with one another.

When the harvest was complete, the routine morning exodus of farmers from the village slowed. Farmers began to catch their breath, visit their friends and neighbors, and reconnect to feelings of abundance rather than scarcity. Many were engaged in a spring cleaning of sorts, repairing the frayed floor and ceiling mats, patching rusty holes in their metal roofs, or replacing worn thatch on their barn roofs. They pulled out their nets and fishing baskets or banded together to harvest the shade-grown cocoa, coffee, and palm oil that supplemented their income. Some were finally enjoying time to socialize, offering up as much food to their neighbors or to me as they felt like cooking.

This was the first time since I'd arrived that I felt the collective exhale of this community. While there was always work for us to do, there was more assurance in the air now because families knew they had enough of their staple food. Despite all manner of agricultural changes here, rice maintained its centrality in the lives of Sierra Leoneans—not corn, not cassava, not millet, and not couscous, which characterize the starches that accompany the sauces of other regions of Africa. If farmers here ate a whole chicken, an ear of corn, and a plate full of potatoes or yams but had not consumed rice, they would tell you with straight faces that they had not eaten yet. "Rice is life," they said.

When Sahr Joe suggested it was time for us to visit the palm wine bar, I didn't resist. He already knew I didn't like palm wine, so he must have had an idea about something. On our way, he told me he wanted to check in at the house where he lived with his wife, Sia, and their two-year-old son,

Raymond. Sia had plans to go fishing later that afternoon, and he wondered whether he might be needed to look after "small-Ray." His house was a mud-walled room he rented beside Chief Lahai's in Old Town.

We met the chief sitting on the verandah in his hammock. I felt the agitation rising in me once again about his lifting of the ban. While Sahr Joe went inside, I greeted Lamin Lahai with a handshake and held his wrist with my free hand as is customary with any chief, showing respect for the weight he carries.

"You are aware that farmers in Tokpombu will be resuming traditional farming this year?"

"I am," I said, looking away respectfully. "But why did the village request help from the ministry, have a Peace Corps assigned here, if you weren't committed to what we came to do?" I didn't want to insult him; I genuinely wanted him to give me a clear answer.

The chief only smiled at me, and he called Sahr Joe from his room to help translate what he had to say from Kono to Krio. He sat up straight, planting his feet on the ground.

"After the first dry season rain, when the ground has been soaked enough, the termites will come out to mate. The flight of these bugs reminds us to return to our farms for the new season and begin to clear the underbrush with our newly sharpened cutlasses. The work is tedious. But it is *all* that we must do. After the second dry season rain, more termites will come out. These are the ones that signal to farmers that we must return to the forest to remove the trees blocking the sunlight. The training for this dangerous labor takes years to learn, and for this it commands everyone's respect. After all, when fire is set to those fields, we don't want that same fire to reach our little town."

Chief Lahai's explanation chastened me. I turned to my counterpart to be sure I understood, and he gasped. It was not the way we inhale back home but the way some farmers here will draw in a sudden, even loud, quick breath to show they are fully attending and understand.

He continued. "We have an agreement with all creatures who live here—and those termites are telling us what to do, Sia Tokpombu." His eyes softened. "Many of us are illiterate farmers. We don't rely on paper or pens here to plan our lives. We have agreements with every living thing around us, and never have we missed an appointment. We all want to survive!"

Walking toward the palm wine bar, I told Sahr Joe how the chief's words reminded me of King Solomon's story, the one where he offers to cut a baby in half to share it between two fraught "mothers," but in reality to determine its true mother—of course the birth mother would prefer another woman to raise her baby rather than see it dead. I tried to explain the analogy: that sometimes drastic measures offer clarity by revealing who we are and where we come from—things we base our character on—the whole rather than its parts.

Joe looked at me in a pitying way. As if he already knew, I spent too much time trying too hard to understand too many things. He said simply, "Knowledge no get worry. Leh we dey drink now."

# CHAPTER 4

# Do You Want a Box?

We feel and experience ourselves to be eternal.
—BARUCH SPINOZA

Less than a hundred yards from my house, the palm wine bar sat at the boundary between the two parts of the village, Old Town and New Town. When Sahr Joe invited me there, the usual long ribbon of children inevitably left their mother's kitchen fires to follow us, stopping short at the bar's entrance where they congregated beneath a tall cotton tree. The children began singing the same songs as when they gathered at my front porch railing.

"Jesus loves me, this I know . . ." It was the only Christian song I ever heard the children sing—and they sang it regularly. "Because the Bible tells me so."

My whereabouts had become a hobby for my new little friends—the toddler girls in dresses and a few leaning close to each other or getting picked up by an older sibling. The same went for the toddler boys, whose too-small T-shirts didn't entirely cover their dusty, uncircumcised penises. Boys are not circumcised until it's time to come of age—to join the Poro society.

Some of the older ones wore faded T-shirts with US team logos, all bought at "the junks"—flea markets that sold donated clothes. Many children had infected cuts or gashes on their legs or arms, everyday bumps and bruises that would have healed quickly with soap and running warm water, Neosporin, and Band-Aids. There was no clinic for twelve miles in either direction. I submitted to the conditions here the way everyone did.

The bar's entrance was an assemblage of brightly colored vertical plastic strips. When I parted the curtain, I was met with the smell of dirt floor, sweet wine, and cheap aftershave. My eyes landed on KT, my landlord, who smiled and then stuck his head out to remind the children that the palm wine bar was off-limits.

The bar itself was snug, and its palm-frond roofing did little to muffle the sounds of any critters burrowing in the thatch above. The conversation was noisy, too. When the palm wine tapper, the village "Limba man," greeted me, I noticed his shorts were splattered with tree sap and shards of palm tree bark, suggesting he'd only just climbed down from a thirty-foot tree somewhere. A man with a thick, well-defined upper body, he was first in a row of ten men (recent Poro graduates) and a handful of farmers, including KT. They all stooped to greet Sahr Joe and me from where they were huddled on curved benches along the circular bamboo periphery, and when they sat back down, they made space for us to sit beside the bar's entrance.

I felt my landlord's eyes land on me. KT cleared his throat and began reciting a formal greeting, which I'd come to expect from an elder at village meetings, though not here at the palm wine bar.

"Sia Tokpombu dohn lef een Mammy en een Daddy foh dey live wit we." *Sia Tokpombu has left everything in her world to live here among us.* "E dey learn Krio en e dey eat we food." *She is learning our culture through our language and food.* The words were kind and elevated my resolve to get along with him, to see beyond this man whose seemingly outsized influence in the village sometimes torqued my sense of fairness. Whenever KT spoke, his words, according to the other farmers I'd met in the village, carried the weight of an elephant. He was a retired high school teacher and a former accountant for a joint United Nations and government program, the IADP (Integrated Agricultural Development Project).

"This where my Christian brothers congregate," he said, his eyes now scanning the cramped room. "This is how we discuss everything—from the rice harvest to who got lucky and found a diamond, to the political conundrums we are having, even the scarcity of fish in our rivers—so we welcome you, Sia Tokpombu."

I told him that in America, we call this "from soup to nuts." The phrase drew grins.

The tapper rinsed a white plastic cup in a calabash of water and tipped a five-gallon plastic jug stamped with a faded sticker that read "WFP," which stood for UN World Food Programme and meant that it was once filled with peanut oil, part of a now defunct national school meal program. It reminded me of an earlier conversation I had had with Sahr Joe and Raymond during the first days of our transition. We'd gone round and round as to whether the American food aid to Sierra Leone that arrived according to Public Law 480, a law first enacted in the 1950s (when Sierra Leone was still ruled by the British), had in the long run hurt local farmers because it disincentivized farmer productivity by suppressing the local market value of rice. "There are people who abuse this opportunity to make money all sides," Joe said. "Your American farmers grow with machines that produce big harvests and send this aid to us at the time we are harvesting our own rice by hand. It arrives too late and drives our prices down."

I watched the palm wine pour out foamy, like beer from a keg but the color of milk.

The tapper then poured a second cup. "This is my greeting to Sahr Joe and Besty for how you are helping us with our swamp work," he said eagerly.

"Yes. We all welcome you here," echoed KT. He raised his cup, talking over the quiet voice of the tapper: "We get the beeest from God to Man," referring to how the fermented beverage tapped directly from the palm's top.

The farmers, including the new Poro initiates, held their plastic cups in the air and then took a few glugs of wine to toast me. It wouldn't be long before they left the village, some returning to school and many to the mines. If you were a young man born in Kono, you spent your nights dreaming about finding something shiny.

I thanked the tapper, lifted the wine to my lips, and blew the foam with its floating ants and tiny maggots (ones that had escaped the tapper's sieve) to the earthen floor, the way I'd seen others do.

With his cultural obligation now fulfilled, my landlord spilled the dregs of his cup and leaned forward, offering words for the Poro graduates. "All of you," he said, his eyes narrowing on them, pointing his finger. "You have all become men. Is that not why you are invited here to drink with your elders today?" He paused and rubbed his hands and reverted from English to Krio, "But I know all you boys want to do is show off—looking for those tiny pieces of stone. But those diamond tidbits won't nourish your aging parents."

"Think about it," he said, then briskly stood, saying he couldn't stay because he had to deal with family matters.

We sat quietly and reflectively. We knew that most of KT's wealth had come from diamonds. Eventually Sahr Joe recited a proverb, "Watasai stone no fraid ren." *KT is a river stone that is not afraid of rain.*

The usual playfulness I'd come to expect in conversation resumed, no doubt aided by the frothy drink in our cups. Sahr Binah, the local primary school teacher, was sitting across from me. He brought up yesterday's fracas when Mohammed, the taxi driver whose daily back and forth trips from one end of the diamond district to the other had landed him in a ditch and nearly killed one of the free-roaming village goats. "He flew through town with bald tires!"

"Lajeelah."

"E bin foh kill we beef!" His carelessness could have cost us our livelihood. (All edible animals are called beef.)

Sahr Joe put in, "Mohammed e dry-yai" *dry-eyed* (shameless).

"A gallon of petrol is not easy to find now, so he's spending all of his money filling his tank instead of making car repairs."

"Yes, he overloads his vehicle to make a better profit."

I remembered the moment, too. I heard the blaring horn, screeching brakes, hysterical chickens, and bleating goats, followed by Mohammed's "Jesus-Allah," an expletive that respectfully acknowledges both religions practiced in this village. KT had spread his arms out among the gathering crowd like a Moses leading his people. I watched him restore harmony in the village rather than fuel aggression. Without assigning blame and within only minutes, he diffused the intensity between the two aggrieved parties: Mohammed, the driver who had insisted that villagers should be tying their goats, and Pa Sorie, the goat owner who had seen practically everything from the verandah where he sat most days teaching Arabic to young boys with slates and chalk.

Binah now thanked me for providing my patch kit. "Those passengers would have languished there all day because Mohammed had only a jack and a pump to repair his tire!" He sucked his teeth.

"He is an irresponsible driver. But nar trouble go mek monkey cham peppeh." *Trouble will make a monkey eat pepper.* (Problems will make you do anything.) Sahr Joe threw up his hands and held the floor with the final word: "Let's just agree that Mohammed overloaded his vehicle, plain and simple."

It became clear that this was a long-standing community tension that had more to do with the buildup of previous resentments rather than the actual incident. There were no police on hand for traffic violations, no one to issue citations and tickets. Looking at Mohammed's car, I knew it would never pass inspection back home. There were zero treads on any of the four tires. "Tell me, Sia Tokpombu, do you overload your vehicles in America?," Binah asked.

I told him only what I understood at that time—that in America, there were police with flashing red and blue lights and loud sirens who would pull you over for violating the law and that having too many passengers in the front or back seat could be seen as a violation.

"So yu gubbament dey protect yu?" *So, your government protects you?*

"E dey try." *It tries.* I answered the question wanting to acknowledge the limitations of our legal system, how complex it is to implement punishment with repair for the harm caused.

Sahr Joe elaborated by telling us how Ray had had told him there was "boku crime" in America that was punished but that punishment was often unfair.

Binah looked incredulous. He crossed his arms repeatedly. "Ehhhh God, nar sorry heart we dey pray foh." *We pray for those who have no power.*

I heard it as a plea.

I took slow sips of wine and got lost in thought about America. For the farmers here, my country didn't feel like a real place. And how could anyone living in Tokpombu possibly imagine it? In 1985, America was still an idea, a golden land, a mirage in the distance that had no exact form and couldn't be reached.

A man sitting between three Poro teenagers introduced himself as Aiah. He announced that Bockerie, a man who had left the village over a decade ago, had found a big-big diamond the other day!

"Ehhhh?," someone said. "Ow much e get?"

"I no sure."

The Limba tapper said that Kono men don't know the value of their labor. But at least they will be able "foh buy small eat" (to be able to purchase provisions at the market).

The men laughed, and all took another slug.

Musa, one of the teens, recited the four C's, how a diamond gets its value: "carat, color, clarity, and cut."

"By August dis year, wine go be we eat," continued the tapper. *By August, when last year's harvest is depleted, there will only be wine to sustain us.* This comment made everyone laugh.

"By God's grace, we no go get dat problem dis year!," Sahr Joe replied. "By the grace of God, with Peace Corps' help, our harvest will be better this year."

I looked down into my more than half-empty cup, thinking this wine was sweet. The tapper leaned forward to refill my cup and then poured the last drops for himself. He set the jug on its side in front of him and announced it was empty. As he stepped out through the plastic strips to refill it and when he parted the curtain door, the smell of fried sweet potatoes fanned through the air. I looked up to see Ma Sando at the entry, momentarily resting the entire tray where the tapper had been seated.

"Yu go buy?," she asked the group, peering her head inside. "Twenty bob each."

A few men slipped coins into her free hand and stooped to pour hot pepper sauce over the thick fried slices. When Ma Sando stood, I saw the undulations of her growing belly, the nine-month-old baby kicking where she'd tied her lappa. It was moving to witness the transformation taking place in my friend's body. She turned to me and said, "Dis pikin gladi." *This child is happy.*

Knowing that Ma Sando's baby would share my name, the men began asking Sahr Joe how his toddler, "small-Ray," was doing, adding that the child would have to begin holding a cutlass and going to church the way Mr. Raymond did, which generated more laughter and goodwill toward Ray's efforts in this community.

Then Pa Bindi very suddenly and unexpectedly asked me when I would raise the money for the church roof that Raymond had helped to build. He was referring to the mud-brick A-frame United Methodist Church (UMC) building between our houses. Ray had built this church with funds from his hometown Catholic church in New Hampshire. Since my arrival here, it was assumed that I would continue the work Ray had begun: growing rice and developing swamps, making vegetable gardens, and helping the village replace a thatched roof on the village church with a more durable metal one. Until now, I'd ignored the last expectation.

Binah also joined in the request. "Yes, Raymond liked to attend church with us and he raised money from America so we could build a church."

I stiffened. Every Sunday, I heard, "Sia Besty, yu go meet we inside we church today?" And every week for the last ten that I'd been in Tokpombu, I'd politely declined. Since when were Peace Corps sent here to build churches?

Binah continued. "We brodda bin sabi een Bible bettah-bettah won—chapter and verse—to God." *Our brother mastered his Bible stories.*

I thought about Ray and wondered if this was true. He had hardly told me anything about this church. With the refills of wine continuing to loosen my inhibitions, I blurted out words I knew I would later regret and scrutinize.

"Peace Corps volunteers *aren't* missionaries! We Peace Corps no get nutting foh do wit religion—at all." The room quieted. I continued stumbling over my Krio. "If you wanted someone to build you a church, then you should have asked your government for a missionary and not a Peace Corps volunteer."

I held my sides, waiting for a response. The whole bar stayed silent.

Finally, we heard a *plink, plink, plink.* A sudden and unexpected rain shower sent water dripping through the palm leaf roof into a metal bucket in the middle of the bar. My face felt hot. I wanted to begin the conversation all over.

Pa Bindi looked at me kindly, not the least bit riled. "We all work foh God," he said. More plink plunk plinking into the bucket.

"Yes-o," Ma Sando said. "All ting nar God." *Everything is God.*

The men in the circle smiled at me. No one pushed back. I took another sip of wine and felt myself relax.

"I no sabi Christian church boku." I said finally. *I don't know much about Christianity.*

"Eh?," Musa asked. "Yu nohto Christian?" *You are not Christian?* "No."

"Oh, yu nar Muslim way een dey drink?" *Then you are Muslim who drinks?*

On Sundays here, I watched the followers of Mohammed, who lived in the row of houses across the road from mine, cheerfully assemble in the United Methodist church to sit beside their Christian companions. The Christians said that they also enjoyed invitations to Ramadan meals with their Muslim brothers and sisters.

Pa Bindi leaned into me. Holding up two of his fingers, he said, "The only difference between a Christian man and a Muslim man is the number of times they like to pray each day and how they prefer to wash and bury their dead. Muslim men," he continued, "dem go ber (bury) dem body inside dirty lek so." He gestured a six-inch gap between the imagined dead body and the imagined dirt. "And dem wrap di body inside fine-fine cotton. But Christian man, e de ber inside box." He mimed placing a body into a long rectangle coffin.

Amara agreed. "All mortal men get only one holy book, pray to one God, and pay respect to we neighbor dem."

Aiah turned to me and asked, "Will they bury you in a box or wrap you in cloth?"

I explained that I didn't follow Jesus or Mohammed and then paused for a minute. "But in my religion also we bury our dead fas-fas (very fast) in a box, in fine cotton." Then I completed the thought with "I don't go to a church or a mosque because I am . . . Jewish."

"You are *Jews*?," squealed Pa Bindi. (He pronounced it "juice.")

My chest thumped. I didn't know if the men knew what Jewish was or even why I needed to tell them this.

Ma Sando frowned. "Besty, yu nohto *Jews*. Kai nar *Jews*."

"Udat nar Kai?," I asked. *Who is Kai?*

"Di albino boy inside yonda (yonder) village."

Everyone in the bar started laughing.

Just then, Joe Samuel, a tall, gray-haired man in a trench coat, ducked through the door. The first time I met Joe Samuel, he'd been crossing the road to visit KT. When I was introduced, I recognized his name from the yellow notebook where Ray described him as a retired and distinguished government worker, World War II veteran, and master farmer from Tembeda, a village three miles away off a bush road. KT had told me that Joe Samuel had fought on the side of the British in Burma and that he considered being enlisted the best education of his life, making him a self-described "worldly man instead of a village boy."

When the men became silent again, I asked Joe Samuel to explain to them that I was Jewish and not "Jews" like Kai.

His gray eyebrows creased together. Then to everyone, he said thoughtfully, "Sia Besty is saying that she is a 'Jewman' from the tribe of Abraham, not 'Jews' like Kai. She is a Jewman like Jesus was."

Sahr Binah's eyes lit up. "Oh, di same lek Albert Einstein, the scientist."

Tamba quickly recited, "E = mc2," invoking his high school physics class at the Jaima Secondary School twelve miles north, where KT had retired from teaching math. Everyone in the bar, including the tapper, repeated the word, "Jewman."

Joe Samuel suggested that missionaries were the first people to use the word "Jews." The same word was being applied to two distinct marginalized groups.

I pushed back, "Jew-*uman* (woman)."

"Okay, Jew-uman." The men repeated this new word. I silently considered the hardship of being a woman with albinism here.

"We in Kono are all Christians and Muslims within the very same families," Joe Samuel said. "No one should live for nothing. We remember everyone. Ancestors first, then Jesus or Mohammed. Every mortal man has the right to choose for himself which religion they want to follow. Fambul tik dey bend but no dey brok." *A family tree bends but doesn't break.*

Sahr Joe added, "When we bless our ancestors, we recite all their names and even have a name for those we remember even though we no longer know their names: Nde-ble-sia."

I repeated the word, in part because it felt like permission to remember.

Once during a game of double solitaire, I asked my grandmother what her maiden name, Cederbaum, meant.

"When my father Max arrived at the port, they asked him his name. He picked Cederbaum."

"He wasn't already a Cederbaum?"

"No. He had to pick. Last names for most Jews aren't like last names for people with coats of arms. There isn't any honor with your name, only a way to track what you owe. It's how they got you to pay taxes." Then she added, "You do your own honor, Betsy."

"Ceder is for the cedar trees in the old country. Baum is for the bombs in the war."

For a long time, I believed my grandmother's answer. Yet Baum is the German word for tree, and the difference between a bomb and a tree is a distinction this woman with a sharp eye for details didn't bother with in this case.

"Maybe they weren't Cederbaums," she continued, her tone unconcerned. "But the people in line in front of them were, so they took their name. They didn't speak English, so there were a lot of mistakes."

My mother's family kept their name, Warsh. But my mother always said she didn't like it because children at school would tease her, "Go *warsh* your clothes."

"How did Grandpa get the name Small?," I asked, referring to her husband, who died the year before I was born.

"Who knows!" My grandmother said this a lot—"Who knows! Maybe he was Smolinky or Smolansky, or Smoliwicz. Or Klein, German for small. It's unknowable." She drew a card and continued, "At the turn of the century, a lot of Jews in America changed their names."

I still didn't understand why someone would change their name.

"Did it ever feel like a secret or a lie, Grandma?"

"Yes. Something like that."

When Sahr Joe finished speaking, I shared with the men how Jews also had a way of remembering their dead. I described my grandmother's ritual yahrzeit, how we sometimes lit a candle to remember her. There was comfort in sharing our rituals, and I now understood something I hadn't thought much of before—what we lose when we don't know our ancestors—the good deeds of their lives disappearing with their names. When we change a name, we lose the memory of the person.

Noblesi resurrects memory.

———

Sahr Joe, a very pregnant Ma Sando, and I walked down the road between the two rows of houses, Christians on one side of the street and Muslims on the other—respectfully and without disagreement. If there were any fault lines here, they didn't come from religion but from the split between Old Town and New Town, a crack that KT maintained had widened after the country's independence from Britain. Many Kono farmers felt betrayed when the government joined with the former British authority to create the National Diamond Mining Company, the NDMC.

"Of course, I remember all of this," KT said. "After independence, the ones who moved to the mainline were newcomers, like my own family. We were the ones who profited most from palm oil and planted coffee and cocoa because we took advantage of the old British programs encouraging us to cultivate our lands with cash crops." He spread his arms out in that Moses way again. "Every generation brings something to Tokpombu worth remembering."

KT took a step toward me. "Modernization *is* coming," he said. He meant change. I assumed this involved building schools, clinics, and paving roads that would help farmers get their produce to market. Perhaps, in a broader sense, he was referring to the country's conflicted politics— that his government, the one-party democratic system ruled by a man of questionable trust—was going to evolve past this current hardship and uncertainty.

When we arrived at the patio between my house and Ma Sando's, I noted that KT's house was so large and imposing compared to all the others.

The people in Old Town were less likely to send their children to school, to leave the village for the mines. Aside from salt, they had hardly any foreign goods, no metal spoons, or bowls. They wore shoes less often, languished on their porches more than in New Town, and new ideas about the world didn't flit from one house to another as they did along the mainline. The hills surrounding Old Town were an untouchable world of virgin forest, a place held sacred and apart as it provided its own kind of shelter with a canopy of ancient walnut, breadfruit, and cotton hardwood trees arching over the village like an ancient protector.

New Town evoked New Testament (or what the New Testament had always seemed to me), so it was not surprising that the church was located there. It seemed to bend toward the new Africa—the Africa restless for Western materials and technology, the Africa that wanted to send its children to primary and secondary schools based on foreign models and built with foreign aid. This was the Africa that had taught its children English but also proudly encouraged Krio. The self-determined Pan Africa that could choose to mine and trade its diamonds, cut down its trees, fly its own planes, even have its own space station or anything else it desired. This Pan Africa engaged the broader world on its own terms. Such terms were yet to be determined.

## CHAPTER 5

# Good, Better, Best

What we have learned from one another becomes our own reflection.
—RALPH WALDO EMERSON

After sharing my dinner, rice with cassava leaf stew, I watched Finda and Sahr Kondeh run out of my house to join the other children as they gathered around Mama Sia to listen to a story. Mama Sia was not just a matriarch, a woman who appeared to be officially in charge of her large family, including her three co-wives, but somehow, the future of this community. She felt like both a line and an anchor in a world of change. There was always something strong, cohesive, and flexible in every one of Mama Sia's interactions.

As I settled in for the story, I found the tonal quality of vowels and consonants floating along octaves of sound reassuring—as if I were part of it all—though I couldn't understand what she was saying and still knew practically nothing about the long history of where I was living.

I knew that I was not just being hosted by this community. They were shaping me, as I had come to shape them, though before this moment I wouldn't have called it that. I would have said I was there to help farmers grow rice and to find new understanding. Of course, it had to be both of those things.

This coexistence was the genius of the Peace Corps if we were up to the mission. Whether or not I was here to fill slots meant to stave off the threat of communism, now waning in the eighties, or simply expressing a humanitarian impulse by helping another country better meet its nutritional needs, it was undeniable that by growing and eating rice together we were learning to hold onto each other in ways that would have some kind of significance for many years to come.

As the night settled down, a sliver of moon appeared in the sky above us. I watched the children fold themselves into one another—an arm slung over a shoulder, a head resting on a lap. Everyone here was always conscious of the moon's phases and tonight's would reveal a more bottomless and starlit sky. Sia Sam, teacher Binah's wife, had made the rounds through town with new batches of kerosene to sell earlier in the day.

The passing down of oral tradition through the description of a moral tale can seem little more than entertainment to pass the time—a lesser substitute for unlucky children who don't have books, television, films, or phones. But on this clear night, I saw it for the powerful phenomenon that it was. Mama Sia's stories were not just a vehicle for educating the next generation; they were how a way of life was conveyed to every child in the village. The tradition of storytelling by the elders and the cultural scripts implied therein, the fables and folktales, riddles and proverbs, histories and legends all reached back through family lines. They embodied and transmitted an adaptable moral code and functional roadmap for how to live in the world. It made you close to the ancestors and, therefore, close to God.

Before everyone went inside, Sahr Kondeh looked up and pointed to a glimmering light moving across the night sky. "Raymond bin tehl me nar America dey mek star." *Raymond told me that America makes stars.* He said, distinguishing between the real stars and a satellite. With Sahr's intimate knowledge of the constellations above, a satellite was as easy to spot as a plane. I asked him to tell me what Mama Sia's story had been about.

"Greed," he said and then recounted the tale of a greedy spider who robbed and begged at the door of so many villages that finally everyone decided to play a trick on him and teach him a lesson.

"Seven different villages cleverly advertised that they were all going to have a celebration," he said. "The spider, hearing this, wanted to steal as much food as he could from each celebration, so he enlisted his seven children's help. He tied seven long ropes around his middle, one for each child, and instructed each one to tug on the other end of the rope when the party started. But when the parties all began simultaneously, each child gave him a tug, causing so much pain his middle began to shrivel. And now, because of that day, all spiders have tiny middles just as their greedy father did."

I asked Sahr what he thought of the story.

"*That's why spiders have tiny middles.*" At twelve, he still retained a concrete view of the world.

"Mama Sia was smart to tell you that story," I said. "How did she learn stories?"

"I no know. Sometime, een gran-mama bin tehl am." *Maybe her forebears passed the story down.*

I could tell from his answer that the scope of his oral history, the elders' tradition of storytelling in his village, was something Sahr didn't see because it had always been there.

But then he said, "Foh greedy no fine."

"At all," I said, thinking how we celebrate greed in America.

A sudden deep voice echoed behind us and said, "E no fine at all." When I turned around, I saw Finda and Bondu Betsy's father, Tamba Charles, approaching. He set his cup of palm wine on the stoop and looked at me, "Oh ya, we get boku spidah inside we swit Salone." *We have many spiders inside our beautiful Sierra Leone.* "Salone" is used as an affectionate shorthand for Sierra Leone.

Tamba called Sahr Kondeh close to him, reaching into his pocket to offer him a coin. I knew he was rewarding Sahr for rehearsing Mama Sia's story with me. Sahr looked pleased and sat taller when he rejoined the children.

"My grandparents told me about many things over and over so when they died, I would remember." Tamba said. "Any shared telling of a story, any memory of an elder should be rewarded." With his tone tightening, he explained by saying, "Kapu sense, no kapu word." *Seize upon the sense, not the word.* Memorizing without understanding is dangerous.

"Dangerous?"

"Book sense e important. But nar one grain." *Book knowledge is critical, but reading takes place alone.*

Tamba Charles then challenged me to set aside my books, letters, and pen for a month. He suggested that both knowledge and wisdom were the result of listening closely and remembering. "Especially the mistakes of others," he said. "Body go dohn, bone dey lef." If in the end, we are only our bones, so why wouldn't any of us tell our stories?

Tamba's remark made me aware how much family history—including my own family's—gets lost before it's passed down. Stories, millions of them that were meant to be told to the next generation but got buried instead.

———

The following morning, Mr. Aiah Musa, the headmaster, performed his weekly ritual of stopping by my house to request that I spend the day with him at the local school. He realized what I had so far rejected: everyone saw that I was a more suitable fit here for the task of teaching their children English, the primary reason parents sent them to school. Most of the children already spoke two or three languages—Krio, Kono, and Mende. Some even spoke Mandingo and Temne. English, the official language, is what you learned in school. I surprised Mr. Musa by saying yes, that I was already dressed and ready to join him. With most of the sweet potato and cassava already planted in the swamp beds, the dry season rush was over and I knew I could afford the time.

Together Mr. Musa and walked from my house to the Tikonkor Primary School, one mile south in the direction of Kangama, the chiefdom headquarters. It was a particularly breezy day with leaves tossing overhead and the early morning sun showering speckles onto the dirt road. We passed a few women toting large baskets of freshly washed clothes and pails of water. They smiled approvingly, "Sia Tokpombu dey go skool wit Mr. Musa today! We gladi!"

Musa, a thin, medium-sized man, like most men here, stood out for the way he wore his sideburns Beatles-long and a pair of 1970s tortoise-rimmed Aviator glasses. Sweat soaked through the underarms of his polyester leisure suit and made his Brut cologne smell even more pungent. Along the way, he assailed me with questions about life in America: buildings that scraped the sky, highways as wide as a rainbow, tunnels that carried people inside rivers. I was taken aback when he suggested that Americans were so full of plentitude that they could kill every village chicken to have a platter full of wings. "Raymond told me about all this stuffs," he said, conjuring a manufactured Disney America. "Frozen supermarkets, houses stacked above the clouds in New York, Chicago, Miami." The way he slowly recited the name of each city gave me the sense that he took delight in saying the words out loud, as if it somehow made him closer to all possibilities. "Passengers going from one city to the next inside those airplanes, packed like small fish in a can in the sky. Lajeelah."

As we neared the school, our quiet footsteps merged with village chatter. Tikonkor Primary School was flanked on one side by an orchard of well-established guava trees, with a backdrop of hardwoods and lush canopies where dark gray bark was harvested for chewing sticks (the local equivalent of toothbrushes). Across the road sat a few cement homes with families milling around, women and children going about their chores.

One woman sat on her front porch railing, plaiting another woman's hair. A few people reflexively called out, "Morning-o" and "Sia Tokpombu has finally come to greet our schoolchildren."

Mr. Musa and I called back, "Enchenna!" And then, "Good morning."

"Ow yu sleep?," an older man asked, echoed by a young woman.

"I sleep well," I told them.

"We tehl God tenki," they answered together, smiling. I loved these conversations, the daily acknowledgment, the caring, and the repetition of phrases that made deeper connections than the generic American "How are you?," which only returns a singular response: "Fine."

I felt happy visiting the school my little friends attended each day and where their parents had quietly wished for me to be because I was an English-speaking woman. Typically, we agriculture volunteers distinguished ourselves from the volunteers teaching in the schools, believing our work fell outside the bounds of cultural imperialism because growing food was an uncontestable necessity. I felt proud of my association with agriculture. To teach English was to transfer a language and culture—*the American way*, as I saw it then.

On the other hand, speaking and reading English was the only pathway for a student to attend higher education in their country and, if they were extremely lucky, to become eligible for university abroad where they could come into contact with the world's systems.

I still wanted to believe that growing rice in swamps by building water control systems could irrigate the future of this community and bring together the fruits of both worlds. But of course, my optimism was problematic too. The difficulty was that the Green Revolution rice farming methods alone, without consideration for the socioeconomic circumstances of the country's traditional farmers, were insufficient, even if we volunteers did our jobs well. There were other issues besides the diamond mines. Roads and vehicles were unreliable for bringing goods to market and the arrival of subsidized American rice coming in as food aid at harvest time did not help. In the planning and implementation of agricultural assistance programs such as ours, rice farmers, who knew more than anyone about the application of new technology, were never consulted. They could have provided donor nations a fuller account and made their aid much more effective.

A granny sat on a bench in front of a rickety square table across the school road. I was sure she was the oldest woman I'd ever seen here, maybe more aged than the old chief, her skin mottled like a newborn's. She wore a pink and white lace scarf around her head, the same colors as the inside of the guavas she was selling on her table. At her bidding, Mr. Musa scooped up a handful of them and placed them in my backpack. "Tenki, tenki," I said and reached into my pocket for a few coins.

But she screwed up her face, refusing my offer. "Nar somba (gift)," she said in a barely audible voice. She craned her neck sideways to spit out her tali, powdered tobacco she kept under her tongue, then motioned for me to take a bite from one of the guavas.

I wiped off the guava with my blouse and took a bite, "Mmmm, e swit-o (so sweet)," I said, luxuriating in its mild pear-like flavor and the soft grainy flesh.

Then she stood suddenly and wagged her finger at Mr. Musa, speaking Kono words that sounded animated and forceful. The men and women on the porch stopped talking to each other and watched. While she spoke, he slid his glasses onto his forehead and pulled a handkerchief from his chest pocket to wipe his face. "Yes, Ma. Yes, Ma," he said over and over. Finally, he pointed to his watch to signal that he and I should be heading toward the school.

The guava granny sat back down, looking pleased, nodding and muttering to herself.

Without comprehending what had been said, it was impossible not to sense how Mr. Musa's authority had been undone by the old woman, so quickly had his composure deteriorated from knowledgeable and curious headmaster to compliant schoolboy—in a matter of seconds.

Once we were out of earshot, I asked Mr. Musa what had happened.

"The old woman is insisting I pay a debt. She tells me I am only teaching these children to become thieves." He bent his head. "She doesn't understand the constraints of this kind of employment, or what it means for the children to receive book learning," he said.

Soon we stood at the large blue and white painted placard that read "Tikonkor Primary School/UMC," behind which a small, whitewashed building was set back from the road. The schools here were mostly established by churches, which suggested that they were two inseparable and interwoven entities because, without the church, the school would never have existed. Both reflected complementary Western knowledge systems—if you buy the needle, you also buy the thread. This school was producing children who might attempt to read the Bible or help translate the Bible into Kono.

With renewed composure, Mr. Musa waved his arms when he saw the teachers gathered among a yard full of students. Despite the stifling heat of the day, all three men were dressed neatly in starched and creased pants and long-sleeved T-shirts tucked in with cinched belts. A group of nearly forty blue-uniformed children began assembling by the door. Some of the boys' heads were newly shaven, and every girl wore her hair in neat braids.

Mr. Musa stood tall when he told me, "We all live inside these decrepit mud homes, but we still take time to look our best in what we are wearing." He added that some of the children walked from villages as many as five miles away. His comment recalled the stark contrasts of my Peace Corps training group. How we had arrived fresh-faced with our own neat and stylish haircuts that had grown long and stringy, how our clean sneakers were now dirty and torn, and all our cottons—shirts, jeans, and dresses—were faded and frayed within months from washing on rocks by the stream. We agriculture volunteers had all laughed at ourselves for how relaxed we had become since arriving, but our trainers, Sierra Leonean college graduates, had taken exception to this laughter. "Even the English dressed up for us— in coats and ties!"

It was a fair point. Why would I not dress here the way I would for a job in America or, if not the specific job, because mine was working in swamps, for my life after the job, presenting myself with care when meeting with friends and community members.

Excitement showed in the children's faces as we approached. I recognized some of my neighbors from Tokpombu and some from other tiny villages I had visited in the chiefdom. They were the same kids who ran toward me on my motorbike rides, calling my name or shouting "Pummoi" (the Mende word for stranger across the ocean or "white man") or "Piscops" (the accent, without the r's articulated), police.

Their teachers began organizing the students according to grade levels and height, straightening their small frames as needed. Then all the students began singing the national anthem, a song instituted when Sierra Leone declared itself an independent nation in 1961. In clear, strong voices, fixed with soldier-straight arms at their sides, every child bellowed "High We Exalt Thee, Realm of the Free" to the same melody as the British "God Save the Queen," as well as "My Country Tis of Thee," the song I'd sung in grade school, hand over heart. This tune tied Sierra Leone's history to two superpowers.

As I waved my thanks to the students, Mr. Musa led me onto the verandah, introducing me in a now-familiar way. "How many of you remember Mr. Raymond, our agriculture expert? Raise your hands."

All hands went up. So did my eyebrows.

"Leh we tehl good morning to we uman Peace Corps way e dohn replace we brodda Raymond, Sia Tokpombu."

"Good Morning, Sia Tokpombu," the students said in thunderous unison before turning quiet.

In his most official tone yet, Mr. Musa turned to introduce me to his staff: Binah, who most days I saw in passing on the way to the waterside, the farm, the barrie, the palm wine bar; Mr. Alpha, a tall man with an imposing but gentle presence and a veteran teacher; and Mr. Morsay, a short, thin man who seemed to be the most junior of the three.

Mr. Alpha beat the end of a thick pointing stick against a metal tire rim that served as a school bell, and the kids filed inside.

"I hope you will understand how we make do in our little classroom," Mr. Musa said as he called the children according to grade into the single room with its screenless windows wide open. I looked around at the dented ceiling, chipped paint, cracked cement floors, and rotting shutters on the windows. The headmaster picked up a double D battery and described how his students were skilled at blackening the chalkboard with the dark powdery contents of leaky, worn-out batteries they brought from home and mixed with water to make a paint that absorbed the white chalk.

I told Musa that I was sure the goop was poisonous, but he only laughed off my concern.

We stood at the front as the children crammed onto eight long benches and settled at their tiny desks. Mr. Musa and Alpha monitored them closely. I couldn't help noticing that it was nothing like the near semicircle arrangement of children clustered attentively around Mama Sia last evening.

"We no get plenti," Mr. Musa said, "but yu go see. These children are so eager to learn what we must teach them. Parents here want their children to speak English and to read and write. It is a source of pride for children to interpret letters for their parents."

I recalled Tamba Charles's suggestion last night that I do the opposite: to set down my books, my writing pad, and my pen to see what I might retain.

Right away, Alpha, still holding the stick, motioned for Morsay to take over while he gave me his assessment of what I was now seeing firsthand. "We have too many problems in our little school. The district council that constructed our schoolhouse all but dissolved several years back. We no longer receive designations from the UMC mission and not from the government either." He pointed out that the children's uniforms cost twice as much as their school fees. He blamed the Ministry of Education, which had promised them labor and funding but delivered nothing. "At the end of the day, there is no one looking out for what we teach these children." He swayed from side to side, "We don't own this school. You want to know the truth? Dis skool dey own all of we." *This school owns us!.*

The teachers were showing up and bringing their integrity and improvisation to the job. And yet the covenant between them and their government was elusive. The law only works when everyone holds it up, and the government wasn't keeping up its share of the bargain, neither for the rights of the children nor for the teachers who were filling in gaps for all their futures.

I followed Alpha's eyes as they moved to water stains that had dripped from the top of the wall to the termite-damaged window frame. "And we only see our salaries once every three or four months, sometimes six. Can you just imagine that in your country?" It was a statement more than a question. Alpha described how he supplemented his income, how each of the four teachers still had to attend to their rice farms to support themselves and their families. "I also operate the small provisions shop across this street," he said, confirming how hard it was to make ends meet.

The children waited patiently for the conversation with their teachers to wind down. I made a funny face at a few of them, and I saw them biting the inside of their cheeks to keep from laughing.

"Do you have schools like this, with so few amenities in America?," Mr. Musa asked.

I shrugged. At this point in my life, I didn't yet have firsthand experience (as a teacher, a counselor, or a parent) stumbling over the divots of America's public schools. I hadn't yet assimilated that there were generations of segregated classrooms where those on one side of the divide were offered opportunity and tax breaks, and those on the other were provided asbestos and lead. I did not yet grasp the painful reality that form follows funding and funding follows leaders who publicize the story-—the loudest, not the best and the brightest. I wondered whether this unpalatable view of aspects of America's un-exceptionalism would be credible here.

Mr. Musa pulled out a chair for me and I sat down next to the teacher's desk, which wasn't much bigger or sturdier than any market woman's table. It was nothing like the old-fashioned kind in my elementary school, those bathtub-sized desks that were heavier than they needed to be—-exuding authority with their walnut stain, teacher's log, and bowl full of stickers or M&M's and stacks of workbooks to be graded. The only thing on his desk was a small clock.

The headmaster lifted his hands like a choir director and called on the children to recite the words written in cursive on the blackboard: "Good. Better. Best. We shall never rest until good is better, better best." The children repeated this phrase in choral response with rhythm and confidence, reminding me of how fluidly children become cultural receptacles.

Was what was "best" for me as an American student in a small Connecticut town the same best for these Sierra Leonean children in Kono

District? And what is best when the majority of humanity—women and children—are left out of educational systems?

To the children still staring up at us, Musa announced, "You may sit down now. Let us welcome our visitor. She has come from America to live with us and work with our families."

The students immediately placed their elbows on their tiny desks and leaned forward from their benches to listen to what I might say. I was uncomfortable with the heat, the dust, and the toxic blackboard, but also the pretense of my "top-down" expertise. Alpha, still carrying the stick, paced the periphery like a security guard. The students averted their eyes when he looked at them, a sign of respect.

Mr. Musa clasped his hands together. "Before we begin on our main lesson, does anyone have questions for our visitor today?"

No one spoke up.

"Well, then, can anyone tell me what Peace Corps is doing for our us?" He waited a long minute, agitated. In the awkward silence I felt lost.

"Dem dey help we," *They try to help us,* Finda finally spoke up. I loved hearing the bold sound of her voice. Finda had given me more practice speaking Krio and Kono than anyone, since her mother sent her to check on me every day after she came home from school.

"Yes. They help us a lot," Musa said in Krio, clapping and looking relieved that the children had provided an answer. I was relieved too. "How does Besty help us?" He looked at Finda and then her brother, Sahr Kondeh, and repeated the question in Krio. "Nohto di same Mamy born you?" *Don't you come from the same mother?*

We all waited again for them to answer. Seeing such a complicated question posed to these young children was painful when I wasn't sure I could answer it myself.

Both children looked at the floor. "We no know," Finda finally said. Sahr Kondeh, who had been so full of spirit and confidence the previous evening, now put his hands over his forehead to cover his eyes. Even his fingers were curled inward.

Musa turned away. "Anyone else? Angela?"

For a moment, it seemed the room held only the self-conscious, drawn-in breaths of the classmates and of me.

"She goes to our farms and teaches us, like how Mr. Raymond did," Angela finally said.

"Exactly so!," Mr. Musa exclaimed. And what does she *learn* us?" (learn and teach are used interchangeably here).

More silence. I tapped Mr. Musa on the shoulder, wanting to relieve the students whose thin frames seemed curled in their uncertainty. He nodded for me to take the floor.

"I'm here to help your families grow more rice and vegetable gardens in their swamps," I offered, "yes, like Mr. Raymond did with all of you." Mr. Musa signaled to Alpha who translated into both Krio and into Kono for the younger children who still didn't speak English or Krio. "Your government in Sierra Leone and my government in America made an agreement for almost two hundred volunteers to live and work in your country. Some teach at schools, some do agriculture work, some build fishponds, some even help dig latrines and wells in villages."

My spirits rose as the students became animated with interest. I explained that by digging dirt mounds and ditches inside the swamp, we could direct the water from the stream to drier land so that every rice plant could get enough water to grow tall and strong. I paused nervously, then added, "Like all of you." I told the children that I would continue to plant rice in the school swamp with them the way Raymond had.

I looked out at the sea of children and thought about how Ray said he'd never resolved with the teachers whether they had supplemented their incomes by keeping the school's harvest for themselves or whether they shared them with the students' families so lunch could be provided. None of these children could possibly comprehend a childhood like mine where we all grabbed snacks from refrigerators stocked with cans of soda and drawers filled with Nabisco cookies, bags of Wise potato chips, and individually wrapped Hostess Ring Dings cakes any time we felt like having a snack. They would never know a brand-new elementary school with color everywhere—on the walls, on the desks, on the big stage where we performed our plays in costumes with sets painted by volunteer mothers, kids' art glued to bulletin boards, books shelved everywhere.

These children had no books, no workbooks, no reading material with stories about children who resembled them, nothing to inspire or carry them beyond what they'd always known. And yet there was Mama Sia, one wife among four to a man who built a pink house in the forest for his thirty children, a traditional woman in whose breath the moral imagination of this village could be assured and sustained in one of the stories she told.

Next to me, I noticed the time on the clock at the teacher's desk. It read 5:30 p.m. I looked at the watch on Mr. Musa's wrist. It also had the wrong time. It now read 11:46 p.m. I tapped his watch so he could fix it.

When I did, he just grinned and said quietly, "Nar furniture." The watch is only for decoration. "Nar foh bluff." *It's for bluffing.*

Many men wore watches long after the battery had died. Just like they proudly displayed their radios and cassette players that no longer played. "Furniture" as status items to show off. Even if someone couldn't yet afford to replace the batteries or repair broken parts, they hoped one day they would.

Mr. Musa announced to classes 3–6 that it was time for general cleaning and instructed the kids to grab the machetes they brought from home and to begin clearing the schoolyard of the stubborn vines that were always threatening to overrun it. He raised his wrist with the broken watch on it and put the index finger of his other hand to his lips for the students to remain quiet while they exited the building.

Moments later, the younger children traded places with the older students. Binah spent what felt like the next half hour reciting the alphabet with strict adherence to the relentless call and response. Every child was closely monitored and inspected as if kindling a future required complete obedience, even as the teachers themselves were appalled by the greed and rigidity of their country's leaders.

The total concentration was broken only when Morsay, Musa, Binah, and Alpha signaled each other and simultaneously said "Skool don-don." *The school day is over.*

The children exited the classroom with their sweaty faces and now soiled uniforms. I thought of the time it would take them to get them cleaned and pressed for the next day after they finished doing the chores their parents expected them to do. They were both students and groundskeepers.

With the schoolroom now vacant, I turned to Mr. Musa. "It must be hard to teach without any books."

"Well, of course," he said, "but all of life is improvising." He motioned me closer to his desk with a smile and slid open its drawer. He pulled out a thin grade-school primer, its cover emblazoned with a water-color illustration of two freckled and rosy-cheeked children skipping rope in front of a school with a British flag waving above it.

He handed me a dated and well-worn book and I opened it, reading: "See John. See Mary. John is going to school. Mary is going to school."

"We copy lessons from this to the blackboard," he said proudly, "and have the children copy them. In this way, they learn handwriting, English, and basic maths."

It was incomprehensible that he would be able to accomplish a job of this magnitude with so few resources, but what was the yardstick, after all? Everyone in the chiefdom regarded these men highly. "Dem dey try," *They are trying*, their parents said.

When Mr. Musa saw that Finda was waiting for me on the school verandah, he remarked, "Maybe this titi (girl) will one day become a teacher."

I thanked the headmaster for my visit to the school and offered to return to help them teach English. I also knew how this community believed I could do something to improve the conditions of their classroom like I'd been asked to do for the church. Fundraising. Speaking English and fundraising. The agricultural expertise farmers were seeking was my ability to harvest money.

Outside, Finda jumped and skipped alongside me. Kai, a tall boy Sahr Kondeh considered his best friend, ran toward the guava lady, gave her a big hug, and took a seat on the stool beside her. He called out, "We get swit guava. Guava. Guava." I was suddenly reminded of the guavas in my backpack that the granny had given me and took a few more out for the children.

Just then, Mr. Musa gently pushed past me. He took a two leone note from his trousers pocket and extended his hand toward the granny. One note was now worth seven leones to the dollar, up from 1.3 leones when I had first arrived.

She squinted her glassy eyes to read the amount of the bill. "Uhaaah!" she screamed with a wide smile, grabbing Mr. Musa's hands. "Engway. Engway ka. Engway kaka. Kaka. Kaka." She was thanking him and calling out in approval for everyone to hear. This payment, a mere thirty-five cents, vindicated them both.

The guava lady called out to me in Kono words that I didn't understand, waving her gnarly hands, summoning me toward her.

Sahr Kondeh told me she wanted to know if we have guavas inside America.

"No, we no get," I told her. "We have pears." It was the closest thing I could think of to a guava, with its speckled green skin.

"I no know pears," she said and pinched a piece of tobacco under her gum. Then she shooed the children away and leaned in close again. "One day, the students will want more to eat than they can pay for."

As the children and I walked home, I knew my understanding of what I'd witnessed was far from complete. But I sensed something settling in, and I was beginning to have enough familiarity with life here to believe I could trust this understanding. For good to be better, for goodness itself to prevail, I now saw that the farmers of this village and I would have to restrain from pulling on the rope of our expectations at the same time until we could hardly breathe.

# CHAPTER 6

# Swimming Lessons

Kiddushin 29a: *A father is obligated to do the following for his son: to circumcise him, to redeem him if he is a first born, to teach him Torah, to find him a wife, and to teach him a trade. Others say: teaching him how to swim as well.*

The unexpected attention of Ella, Ma Sando's eldest daughter, bursting through the front door with a load of laundry I'd left outside to dry overnight and my six-week-old kitten hidden in the basket brightened my spirits for a minute—until she scolded me for letting my cat wander along the path to the waterside. "There are boys in the village who will eat this cat," she said as she set down the basket and handed him over to me.

"Which boys?"

"The hungry, angry ones with nothing better to do," she yelled back as she walked out.

Soon after, KT's gruff voice burst through the open window in my bedroom. "Ella bin fetch yu cat?" he said and then, "Yu dey lef foh patrol today?" Patrol was a term used by the colonial masters and he sounded accusatory.

Of course, KT already knew the answer—that I had planned a visit to the National Diamond Mining Compound, the NDMC. Concealing my annoyance at his pretense (KT was always aware of my plans), I stuck my head close to the iron bars on the window, "Morningo, KT. How is your family today?

"Duya (Please), I wan leh we talk now-now." KT's voice was low and commanding, and his impatient glance was impossible to miss.

I felt tempted to disengage from our subtle power play and walk away without giving him an answer. And yet, as my landlord and official host of my stay, I understood that his knowing my whereabouts was protection and guidance, just as my being here gave him a measure of prestige. Though I felt independent, I had to accept our intertwining and notice how we might grow our mutual respect within the terms of this unlikely arrangement.

"Ay dey cam just now," I said, now waving through the window as if I were in a rush, but then slowly pouring the treated water into a flask, leaving some for my new cat in a bowl by the door. I took my time walking toward KT with my backpack stuffed with what I'd already decided to take for the trip ahead: a wallet, bathing suit and towel, shampoo, and a change of clothes.

KT was sitting beneath the canopy of unripe green fruit hanging from the branches of a large mango tree. Everyone called it *"KT's tree."* His smile reminded me of how complicated the terms of my living here were. He held up a piece of paper and recited his list for his family: caustic soda (for homemade soap), a notebook, tomato paste and fresh fish for wife Gbesay, whose turn it was to cook that day.

"You will fetch these things at Bumpe Junction today," he told me, referring to a littered shantytown for illicit miners on the edge of diamond fields. With "pan body" shops along an intersection, it was also the last place where you could stock merchandise before the jacked-up prices of Koidu, the diamond capital six miles farther down the road.

It stuck me that our lists were the same. Everybody here had pretty much the same list.

KT sipped his Nescafe and motioned for me to sit beside him in a reclining chair slighter lower to the ground. He was comfortably seated in a "chief's" chair—two pieces of carved and stained ebony wood that fit together at perpendicular angles. The tray table between us was a tree stump. He reached into his shirt pocket to grab the usual small wad of leones to cover the cost of the items he was asking me to buy. "So, you have decided to spend your day at the National Diamond Mining Company?," he said, his voice again deepening and hinting disapproval.

He had a troubled look on his face and as he placed his hands over his head, I saw that his demeanor expressed a level of concern that went beyond his usual assertion of dominance. "To teach children to swim is the sole purpose of your going?," he asked.

I described the plan to give swimming lessons to some of the miners' children. Inside the company premises was a restaurant bar with a swimming pool. Called the Yengema Club, it was a storied place frequented mainly by British expatriate families who worked for the company. It was also a hub for foreign businessmen who had dealings in Kono: sometimes Belgians or Israelis, Syrians, and Lebanese.

KT placed his hands over his head again, a repose that told me he disapproved.

"Wetin mek ah dey go . . . , " *The reason I am going*, I repeated, calculating that KT always preferred I speak English, the official language in which he was fluent, rather than Krio, "is because Sierra Leonean children whose parents work for the NDMC don't have regular access to the pool the way the expat children do."

KT crossed his legs and began to rock. I saw that there was no way to win at this moment.

"You will find, Sia Tokpombu, that those diamond company children are not like the children here in the village. Their parents are laborers for the English miners, so they are being torn too quickly from village life, their roots—coming of age without a proper community to support them."

His comment made me defensive. "I'm assisting Stella, the Peace Corps volunteer posted in Jaima. She's arranged weekly swimming lessons and lot of children have already signed up," I said.

He set his notebook down and began pulling on his clean-shaven chin. KT had already met Stella, whom he regarded as a free-spirited American. "So, you want to go the extra mile for your Peace Corps ideas more than for the ideas we farmers have in Tokpombu?"

I heard his question as the objection it was. Of course, I knew there was merit in his counsel.

KT disapproved of any hint of hedonism he'd seen in volunteers—meeting up on weekends, drinking, having sex. He also understood that many volunteers valued the opportunity of living in his country for the freedom and privilege it gave them. But he wanted more from all of us and particularly from me. By pushing back on my outing to the NDMC he was suggesting that going there for any reason demanded more thoughtful consideration on my part. His message was clear: the nuanced world of cultural exchange had to go beyond friendship and goodwill if there was to be real understanding. There was work to be done.

"Those Kono children don't even go to the river to fish and now you are going to teach them how to swim!" He laughed for so long his belly heaved.

Learning to swim was more than a requirement of my childhood; it was a parental obligation with moral dimensions, the edge of a pool a metaphor for getting to safety at the border of anywhere. All my Jewish friends, plus their siblings and mine, took swimming lessons at the Jewish Community Center. But KT was noting a different tradition and obligation—one that had been negotiated with layers of meaning. In his world, if a child knew how to swim, they might leave the shore and be carried off by a crocodile. Mamy Wata, whose spirit protected children at the waterside, would always admonish them for going to any river alone where they might drown or be carried away. Knowing how to swim could cause *more*, not less, risk.

"Why shouldn't they learn?," I asked.

KT rubbed his temples with his knuckles. With a softening voice he said again, "This trend is not sustainable. These pool children will grow up angry. Some of the grown ones already are. It's predictable."

My feelings about this patriarch was tempered at this moment. His care for his people, their traditions, and their history constantly challenged me.

Over the growing noise of his family members going about their daily activities, KT set his glasses on his knees and wiped his eyes repeatedly. Last month almost every household had someone fending off pink eye and I'd been relieved that I hadn't caught it. As a child, we weren't allowed to swim until it cleared up. Suddenly he leaned forward and put his elbows on both knees. "What kind of opportunities will lie ahead for these children when they are under the thumb of the mining operations? The mines will drown them. But their parents don't know this because they themselves are already drowning!"

KT's disgust pointed to the harsh crosscurrents of geopolitics and its laws affecting his people—the global allure to exploit natural resources for profit, regardless of whose rights were either taken away or violated in the process. He picked his notebook off the ground and began drawing a Venn diagram. The first circle represented "Lebanese diamond dealers," immigrants who, fleeing the Ottoman Empire, mostly arrived in Sierra Leone in the late 1890s, making them the largest nonindigenous group in the country, but not yet its citizens. Over time, they ascended the ranks as a merchant class that would deal with the country's supplies of gold and diamonds—both legally and illegally.

He drew a second circle called "Strangers" (presumably, I fit into this category).

Finally, he added a third circle for "We Yone" (Our Own). "One day, there will be no more diamonds in the ground," he said. "Or there will be more somewhere else. What then?" He pointed to the small overlapping area at the intersection of all three groups. "What will the Lebanese man do for my country then? They have been here a long time, not to help Sierra Leoneans, but to help grow their business contacts in Beirut." He was referring to the cash support this community offered Hezbollah through the sale of diamonds from the region. I understood how this sketch was really a Venn diagram of KT's life—the one he'd first followed in pursuit of money and power but then rejected and so dropped out.

"And does your family who came to America from Russia send money to help businessmen in Moscow?"

"Of course not," he answered for me over the sudden loud voices of his family on the verandah. His third wife, Kumba, then delivered a small tray with two heaping plates of rice and a bowl of okra stew and moved the table in front of me, TV dinner style.

As I scooped a small dollop of stew onto a mound of the "small" rice too big for me to finish, KT said a short prayer before taking his spoon and scooping it onto his plate of rice. "We give thanks for life, isn't that correct, Besty Small-small." He then continued speaking his mind. "All of this excavation and destruction of farmland! It is spreading. It will always spread somewhere. What kind of citizens will we be in this kind of Sierra Leone then?" He held his palms flat and empty.

"KT, who here, with any means, hasn't benefited from this industry?," I challenged. "Haven't you benefited, built your house, with diamond money?"

"You, Sia Tokpombu, have liver to ask me this," he scoffed.

"Yes, I *am* asking."

Nine months in this village had filled me with new courage. KT surprised me by offering a carefully considered answer.

"If the diamond industry did what it professed to do, bring security and safety to my people, we would all be benefiting and I would not object. But it is not. We Sierra Leoneans are relying on the markets in London, Antwerp, Geneva, and even inside your New York to change our fortunes!"

He went on to suggest that Sierra Leone's politicians were answering the call to another actor, not the citizen farmers begging for justice and a legal framework around commercial interests in their relatively new country, but leaders who refused to plug the gaping hole that carried the country's wealth away. Initially, postcolonial countries like Sierra Leone did receive some relief from their country's poverty by having a global platform through which the modern economy fueled its supply and demand. But it came at a higher cost, bringing wealth and power to those who already had it.

If I took KT at his word, which I did, it meant that I had to realize not just the extent to which the imposition of a foreign system by the British and others had long distorted the leadership of Sierra Leone, but how their leaders stole from this imposition at an unprecedented rate. The complicated interweaving of the world's vast international economic system and the political order required to maintain its existence beyond an empty shell were taking a toll.

I thought of the trips I'd made and the photos I took while spellbound by the dazzling spectacle of midtown jewelry shops and then uptown to Fifth Avenue, where Tiffany's stands beside Godiva, the chocolate store.

"We are at the mercy of global demands for what is rightfully ours. My people will never believe that this diamond has no worth." With his coffee now on its way to his lips, KT said, "How our drums beat, we shall dance." Then, "Go enjoy teaching the children to swim, Sia Tokpombu. Come find me when you return and tell me about your experiences."

I rolled my motorbike from my kitchen, where I stowed it at night, and into my front yard, topping off the petrol with an extra container I kept under lock and key in the room where I stored tools and seed rice. I drove out of the village wearing my bright yellow Peace Corps-issued motorbike helmet. All I could think about was jumping into a cold chlorinated swimming pool.

I slowed down at a checkpoint with a long wooden barricade and five policemen waved me on with bright smiles.

"Greetings, Sia Tokpombu."

A little girl, maybe eight or nine, was milling around and asked me, "Yu go buy fish foh me?" The officers scoffed.

"Not today, but maybe next time," I said.

Stella was waiting outside her home with her local boyfriend, George—a high school math teacher (as KT had once been), whose charm made it easy to be their sidekick for the day. She gave me a warm greeting and then signaled for George to hop onto the back of her motorbike, and we headed out with me following close behind. He dropped two Heinemann African Writers Series books into a bag he straddled across his chest like a sash: Chinua Achebe's *Things Fall Apart* and *No Longer At Ease*.

We traveled together for nine long miles on a heavily cratered dirt road toward Yengema, the diamond center of Kono District. The vegetation changed gradually from forest to savannah. Large palms, cotton, redwood, and mahogany trees were replaced with thick mats of seven-foot-tall elephant grasses, with rice fields becoming increasingly scarce. In my rearview mirror, the whirling red cloud from my motorbike tires became thinner, too, its long, dusty shape beginning to slow down and fall. George pointed to a dirt road I would come to know well, and as we turned off, it widened out and came to an end at a chain link fence. We wobbled to a stop there, in a large gravel parking lot.

We had arrived at the unmarked accessway of the National Diamond Mining Company, a land mass amounting to just less than ten square miles, a completely different topography from the canopied rainforest where I lived. We parked our motorbikes and walked toward a manicured lawn appointed with well-watered country club shrubs. A tidy gravel path led us to an imposing, whitewashed brick building with substantial mahogany doors.

Suddenly, we all became aware of a distant rattle growing louder. As all three of us looked up, a helicopter flew overhead, dragging its shadow over the sloping metal roof.

"Look how they've sent a chopper," George said. "They must have found a big-big diamond."

"Where do the smaller sized diamonds go?," I asked.

George pointed his finger. "Over yonda! Next to dat gray dump truck." I squinted until I saw a truck moving in the distance. "That truck will carry the dirt and stones they've excavated to a separation house," he explained, "where it will be sorted out from the diamonds. One hundred mortal men won't be able to do what these big machines can do for us here!" George seemed impressed by the machinery, yet he had a disgusted edge to his voice, like KT or the two men who had invited me to meet the old chief from Gandehun. It was the contradictory edge I was coming to expect.

There was an undeniably impressive aspect to all this mechanization in so unmechanized a country. "Do they find diamonds in every load?," I asked.

"Oh yea, my sista. My people aren't crazed for this stuff for nothing. The second largest diamond ever found on the planet earth, the Star of Sierra Leone, they found it just five miles from where our feet are planted now!"

It could have sounded like bragging but I knew it was something more significant. This alluvial diamond, discovered under the auspices of a state-sponsored mining and exploration company (Diminico), illuminated the larger tension taking place here. On the one hand, there was a magnetic draw to the Star of Sierra Leone Diamond, a simple mineral made of carbon, that surpassed even the four C's criteria to D-level criteria, indicating that it was chemically pure and structurally flawless and was worth millions of dollars, a shocking thing back then. It also shined a light on the contradiction people in the older generation felt—that what was alluring was also a profound obscenity.

I squinted under the bright sun as George guided us past the fence, two gasoline pumps, a golf course on our right, and in the distance, an airstrip. I had been told my job with the Ministry of Agriculture was to increase swamp rice production. Yet the Peace Corps had placed me in a part of the country where the destruction of farmland was systematically taking place at an unstoppable rate. It was not simply that I was running up against tradition or even the men who feigned interest in seeds or fertilizers to access cheap, easily breakable Chinese-made shovels for diamond digging. It was my growing awareness that the entire region was at the mercy of a global machinery capable of encroaching on arable farmland and causing irreparable destruction that would affect generations.

George offered his thoughts before I could. "Sierra Leone's one-hundred-year contract with DeBeers will end soon, but what does this mean? It doesn't mean shit." He paused to tie his shoelace and then continued, "The Sierra Leone diamond is still colonized. We yoné diamonds will always be controlled by those who buy them, not those who dig them!"

George's assessment was troubling in unexpected ways. Not simply because I came from a country where diamonds have been slipped breathlessly onto the fingers of fiancés for generations, but because I knew of the long history of diamonds in my own cultural past. Diamonds were long considered portable security for Jews—you could hide them and bribe with them, sew them into the hem of dresses or your pants if you had to, just to survive. My mother had created lore and mystique around the large diamond she kept locked in a safe. It was one that she had inherited from a relative of her father's who'd fled Poland. A woman who kept up with the fashions of the times, she knew which jewelry was meant for which occasion. She and my grandmothers had always invited me into their walk-in closets to see their designer clothes and jewels—to touch them, to tell me how they could be mine or how my daughters might have them one day.

KT had said a mouthful when he'd warned that the biggest toll of this industry wasn't environmental but instead the vacuum it left between generations.

George began to describe how many of his students had dropped out to work in the mines. He said they were abandoning the responsibility of helping their parents farm.

"When it rains here, my people are looking down on the ground, searching for something shiny to grab," he said. "People in Kono think they will get rich if they find a shiny rock. They are not educated to know the real worth this diamond has on the other side of the world. They just dig and dig to get what the foreign man tells them it's worth."

I listened, the intensity of his mood hollowing my spirit. Stella put her arms around George. I held my sides. "We are fools to think those same politicians who play in this game will deliver us justice because it's a game they benefit so greatly from."

"We have so many high school dropouts now," he continued. "They will spend the next five years looking for diamonds and then, they won't find anything! Or if they find a bauble, they'll spend the money fast. Nuttin go lef." *There will be nothing left!* He smiled sadly. "And by the time they decide to go back to school, they will be older than their teachers." George lit a Marlboro and drew on it long and hard. "To hell with this, man. Fuck these mudda fuckin diamonds!"

George, Stella, and I took a few more heavy steps toward the door. We could see our reflections in the windowpanes, with our helmets under the crook of our arms. In many ways, we were orbiting a world that resembled the one where I'd spent most of my life. Maybe, too, it was the same one and I hadn't traveled so far after all.

A guard dressed in brown camouflage and heavy black lace-up boots stood by the door and abruptly motioned for us to come inside. After we explained that we were there to teach swimming lessons to the employees' children, we followed him to a corner in the lobby. He asked George for his country identification. George dropped his head quietly and pulled out a weathered piece of paper. The guard asked George to give his name.

"Braima Moiwai." He used his family name. "George" was a nickname his schoolmates had given him to invoke George Foreman, the boxer.

"Mende man?," the guard asked, referring to George's ethnic group, one that geographically and culturally overlaps with Kono.

"Yes, sir. I teach at the Jaima Nimikoro Secondary School."

"Pass now." The guard handed George his ID with a satisfied look and told us we could pass to the inside.

I saw the muscle clench in George's jaw as he told us he thought it was crazy that the National Diamond Mining Compound asked for identification from nationals but not white women. It was painful for me to watch how George's bravado had turned to submission.

We walked into a substantial bar with wooden beams across its slightly vaulted ceiling and joined a seated mix of Lebanese diamond dealers, chiefs, ministers, and a few mining managers from England. They turned their heads toward us with a bored look, then went back to watching *One Flew Over the Cuckoo's Nest* on a VCR mounted above a small refrigerator.

From the way George had talked outside, I thought it would be like a Bond movie where the bad guys were obvious and aggressive. But here the various people seemed mild-mannered, regular Joes with well-paid work supporting their fledgling bank accounts and depressed economies back home. These men, too, were dancing to the beat of a drum.

When George ordered the national brand, Star beer, the waiter, a man in a white-collared shirt and black pants said, "Di factory no dey mek." *The factory isn't making any.* George ordered a Coke instead. Meanwhile, I became distracted by the waiter's nametag, made with the same Dynamo sticker gun my mother used to label the dry goods in our pantry when I was growing up. My mother ordered hers via a 1-800 number flashing on the screen of an infomercial during the *Dinah Shore Show*.

George lit a cigarette but then left it in the pinched lip of an ashtray, its ash slowly consuming itself. He told us he'd wait for us here until the lessons were done.

———

I followed Stella into a women's locker room where we raced to change into our suits, then hurried through a set of glass doors to a patio populated by tables with holes for umbrellas but no umbrellas. A chain link fence surrounded an almost Olympic-sized swimming pool. A crowd of elementary and middle school-aged boys in shorts was milling around on the concrete. I counted twelve, more than expected. A few of them roughhoused on the edge of the pool, playing a game of "Dare" to see who would jump into the water first. Several of the younger ones just stared into the water, complacent in their waiting and watching the boys brave enough to put their heads underwater in the shallow end.

"No girls?," I asked Stella.

"Guess not today."

"Do we have a plan?"

"Not really. We can improvise. Like we always do."

Stella called the group into a huddle along the fence, explaining how she and I would combine water safety and beginner swimming every week for the next two months.

The boys lowered their gaze nervously when she spoke. I took in the smell of chlorine and watched a young redheaded girl I hadn't noticed before making her way toward the diving board until her mother told her she didn't want her daughter swimming in the pool just then. While Stella reviewed the club rules, the boys appeared uncomfortable. When I heard the Yengema Club employee begin to speak directly behind me, I realized then that he was the source of the tension.

"You children," he said, "are very fortunate for what these volunteers are doing for you. But let me assure you, if we are going to succeed at this unusual arrangement, you must comply with our Yengema Club rules. After class, this is not your pool, so duya, scatta (disperse)—return to your barracks." He snapped his fingers and almost spat when he said, "Duya, scatta." *Please leave.*

Stella seemed unfazed. "My friend Betsy and I have been looking forward to this. We hope you all enjoy a sense of safety and well-being in the water."

The boys knocked into each other in playful ways and even accidentally, and then apologetically, into me until they were all standing waist-deep in the pool. Stella and I divided them into two groups. My half consisted of the reluctant beginners, who winced when they put their faces in the water. We stayed at the shallow end. I taught them how to move their arms like "chickens," "airplanes," and "soldiers," the way I'd been taught to swim. The children were amused and laughed. One boy swallowed a mouthful of water, spit it out, and then kept spitting because the surprising taste of the chlorine was so repugnant to him.

The redheaded girl and her mother were engaged in a sunscreen battle over how much to glob on. The girl's younger sister loudly slurped her bottle of Fanta, while her mother hushed her to be more "ladylike."

After class, the boys "scatta'd," as they'd been told. The club's possible manager (I didn't know for sure who he was) followed close behind to ensure they left the premises. Stella and I headed back toward the locker room, passing a dining room now decked with white linens and china place settings in preparation for the dinner hour ahead.

I stopped in the women's room, where a large wall mirror reflected the new definition of my muscles from all the carrying of water buckets, pounding food with a pestle, and working a shovel and hoe. Back home, full-length mirrors were as standard as windows, reliable assurance that one was put together "just right."

"Jeesh," Stella said. "Nohto bettay man dat." *He isn't a good man.*

"Pretty much," I agreed.

After showering, we rejoined George at the bar where he introduced me to a woman named Marieya, a Russian nurse who'd married a man whose father was a Freetown-born Sierra Leonean, a Krio, and whose mother, a Kono, was born and raised in Yengema. (Krios are the descendants of people who were enslaved but then repatriated to Sierra Leone after being granted their freedom.) A lot of Krio families sent their sons to study at universities in Moscow, and it wasn't uncommon for them to come back with Russian wives.

During our friendly exchange, I learned that Marieya's husband, a doctor, had come home to practice medicine in the mining community. Marieya worked part-time as a nurse in the clinic when she wasn't caring for their three young children. Stella asked her if she wanted her son, Sasha, to join the class. She was thrilled. "He needs to be a better swimmer," she said.

Marieya contended she was amazed that Americans like us came to live here "in the villages" and that she wished there was something like this for young people in Russia. I told her I thought it was impressive that she was raising her family here in Kono.

She laughed through the melancholy in her voice: "I guess dees eez true, but what choice do I have now? This is where my husband works. I decided many things young and in love." I noted how mild Marieya was, despite having a jaw that looked perpetually clenched.

"How did you experience the class, Sia Tokpombu?," George offered, lightening the tone, his voice a raspy slur from the combination of cigarettes and the gin he had ordered called "Sassman."

"I'm not sure." I still wanted this to be the compelling arrangement I'd hoped for—a weekly respite from uncertain village work, the familiarity of teaching swimming lessons, free petrol from the compound pump, hot showers, a menu that offered spaghetti, and bread with margarine. "I don't like how the children are being treated," I answered. I told him it mimicked America's segregated pools.

"Not just the children, all of us Sierra Leoneans are paying the price too," George said, looking at Stella. "My brothers here are all servants and they could have been going to a mining school in England and run this thing. To hell with them all!"

When Stella imitated how the manager had spoken to the kids, her boyfriend's eyes hardly blinked. I could tell he already knew how it had gone down. Marieya, distracted by a group of wives who were gathering around a table, excused herself to join them.

George suggested we leave then. Once we were in the parking lot, a safe distance away from the club members, he revved up his diatribe, repeating every complaint I'd ever heard here in one long sentence.

"Salone dohn craze." *Sierra Leone has gone mad.* "This NDMC is not why our parents gave birth to us! Our grandparents would never want this kind of life for us." He kicked a few stones across the lot. "Dis fucking club foh go back nar England. And when I go there, ask me for pass, but not here, not in my own country! You saw how that manager is silencing those children. How can that man be instructing them when he is silencing them?" He sucked his teeth and then, for what seemed a long while, lifted his head toward the late afternoon's faint pale moon as if searching for something, somewhere, to redeem this experience.

It hit me then that this place was the collective tracheotomy of the nation, the site of the incision. No wonder George was trying to knock himself out with gin and cigarettes.

--------

On the morning of the fifth week of class, a lorry driver brought me a note from Stella telling me that she had a bad case of runny belly and wouldn't make it to class that day. She told me to stop at George's house to collect the notes and wished me well.

So, I drove alone and took a different route through the illicit mining fields. At one point, I downshifted my motorbike to a putter and looked out over a cratered landscape through which a wide, well-graded road twisted forward, slag heaps of sand flanking it almost as far as the eye could see. The lush green mountains I was used to seeing were gone, or so far in the distance they seemed like a mirage or an oasis in this manmade desert. Hordes of men carrying shovels, pickaxes, and sifters were searching for alluvial diamonds. As I watched them labor between the mounds, I couldn't help thinking of how America was built, all the generations of Africans who had helped to build our country too, the backbreaking hours of erecting halls of power that never held any intention of including them, of uplifting them in the experiment to create a more decent, dignified, and secure society. Here, the men weren't even building up; they were digging down, unearthing, making places where even a seed couldn't grow.

George wasn't the only one here with antimining sentiments. Ma Sando often said, "If nohto yu ber, nohto yu foh dig-dig." *If you didn't bury it, you shouldn't be the one to be digging it up.* And yet voices like hers went unheard.

A few miners in the distance waved as I drove past. I smiled and honked my horn. Turning onto the final stretch of road, I saw the usual children who lived in shantytowns—tin-walled huts with rusty tin roofs—so delighted by the sound of an approaching motorbike, they gathered by the road's edge to see who was coming and to call out. The national corporation here was its own separate world, accountable only to itself and its foreign stakeholders. If there was a movement toward building a better future for Sierra Leone, the National Diamond Mining Company was the hammer beating that vision down.

I parked my motorbike in the lot. Inside, I ran into Marieya, her son Sasha holding his hand with a new haircut that looked severely shorn. As I was explaining why Stella hadn't joined me, Marieya put her hands into the pockets of her skirt and looked up at me.

"Deez wives here have, um, new concernz."

"New concerns?"

"The vee-ruz, HIV/AIDS . . ." Her face was stricken with shame as she explained how the expatriate families who were members of the club were no longer welcoming the laborers' children at the pool. The global fear of this epidemic spreading across parts of Africa (and, also back home) had raised the alarm for safety inside the compound.

"Yes, zay are quite afraid."

It didn't matter that by now scientists knew that the disease was not transmissible in a chlorinated pool. Our swimming class had just been cancelled. KT and George had been right. In this compound these children called home, they would never be treated as equals.

I refilled my tank with the free petrol one last time and drove back to Tokpombu the long way, gazing out at the lush, mountainous horizon. I doubted I would ever see the boys at the Yengema Club again, and I wondered, too, what reason they'd be given for why we'd stopped holding classes. How many of these injustices would fill the circles in KT's Venn diagram until the tiny circles exploded?

# CHAPTER 7

# Bawbee(s)

When black people are talked about, the focus tends to be on black men;
and when women are talked about, the focus tends to be on white women.

—BELL HOOKS

Our five-day staging—the initial Peace Corps orientation—had taken
place at a hotel in Philadelphia, where our recently returned Peace Corps
trainers prepared us for the journey ahead. The most memorable part was
this anonymous Peace Corps saying: "If you go to Asia, you will come back
more spiritual. If you go to Latin America, you will come back a revolutionary. But if you go to Africa, you will come back laughing."

Kai, a Jaima Secondary School student who'd returned home for the
weekend, showed up behind my house one Saturday morning. I was on my
way to the compost heap carrying a rusty piece of metal I used for a dustpan. We made small talk for a while before he reached into a bag he was
carrying and pulled out a sealed envelope addressed *"Madam Besty Small."*

This letter would be one more in an accumulating stack that I'd
received from farmers making all kinds of requests: from paying school
fees to bringing bird whistles from America. Still, I opened the letter with
as much curiosity as Kai seemed to have.

*Madam Besty,*

*I do not know whether any love interests occupy you currently because I
am writing this letter to tell you that I want you to consider me to be your*

*primary suitor. If you are willing and able, this affection would please me,
and I would return it in kind favor.*

*Faithfully yours in the name of Jesus Christ, the Lord, and Savior.*

*With Love Absolut,
Desmond*

"Udat nar Desmond?" *Who is Desmond?,* I asked.

Kai became animated as he told me his "brodda" had seen me passing
on my motorbike. (The word brother in Sierra Leone is loosely appropri-
ated.) I folded the note and stuffed it into my pocket while Kai followed
me and the empty dustpan back to my house. At the verandah, Kai didn't
budge. He leaned back on the railing and cupped his hands into his chin.
"Wetin dey inside di letter?," he asked me. "Yu get boyfriend?"

"I no get." I picked up the short-handled broom I'd left on the steps and
shook it at the far end of the verandah.

"You go consider?"

Again, I waited, "I noh sure."

Kai sucked his teeth and crossed his arms. "Eh, Sia Gorama. Yu business tronga." *You are difficult to deal with.*

I didn't respond and Kai didn't leave either.

"Yu no wan man?," he said.

"It's not that."

"Oh, so nar get-get no want, want-want no get bizness," he shrugged,
then laughed. *You want what the opposite of what you have.*

I shrugged and laughed too, but not as comfortably as he did.

_____

Late in the afternoon, I found my way far along a bush road toward Tamba's
farm. He was an illicit diamond miner who had a run-out-of-luck story
and returned home with a wife and new baby to feed. He asked me to help
him create a few rice plots with drainage ditches in his father's swamp, and
I was happy for the work.

Sahr Joe and Tamba spotted me on the trail above and called out, "Sia
Tokpombu! Sia Tokpombu!"

From a distance, I could see how most of the saplings had been cleared away. The underbrush, too, had been removed according to our plan. The late afternoon sun gilded the two men's silhouettes as they bent rhythmically from the waist, swinging their short hoes as they aerated clumps of the newly exposed, loamy soil with fluid movements, making this difficult labor appear graceful. Behind them, long shadows began covering the surrounding hills. These densely forested mounds with patches of old growth were grooved with jagged rock boulders. Winding footpaths, centuries old, were overgrown with cocoa, coffee, and oil palm, and sometimes a pineapple patch or a grove of oranges, grapefruits, or breadfruit.

"Ente-o," I said, descending the path toward the men, a playful way of saying "Good afternoon-o" in Kono.

The men responded with the highest compliment I could earn here. "Eh, Sia Besty," Sahr Joe said, "yu nar Kono uman now." *You are a Kono woman now.*

"Yes-o," Tamba confirmed and then laughed.

I laughed too and gestured the way a Kono woman would, bending at the waist and clapping my hands. This motion made Tamba and Sahr Joe laugh louder, the sound echoing softly in the valley.

Removing my flip-flops, I slipped my feet into the shin-high dirt where my friends had plowed, squishing the mud between my toes so the clumps dissolved into the water, making a more nutritious soup than would otherwise be available for these young, water-loving rice plants.

"Yu dey pohto photo di swamp dirty." *You are plowing the swamp,* Tamba said.

The men chortled again, seeming amused at the sight of an American woman doing labor that traditionally belonged to men.

My own laughter had less ease. I had become preoccupied with the things that lived inside the mud that might cause me harm. For the last year, my Peace-Corps-issue, hip-high waders—mandatory protective footwear in the swamps against such dangers as the life-threatening liver fluke, schistosomiasis—sat in the corner of my bedroom. At this point in my stay, I preferred rejecting any visible and blatant barrier between me and these farmers whose respect I had been trying to earn.

"Leh we all *pohto-pohto* (plow) di dirty now," the men offered. They dropped their hoes on the periphery of the field and began jumping on the plowed part, flattening and leveling the mud so it was no longer cratered but was a smooth opalescent shade of bluish brown.

"Yu dey try foh work lek man, Sia Tokpombu," Tamba said.

I corrected him. "I am working like how the books taught me to work." I was referring to the agriculture manuals provided by all Peace Corps agriculture extension agents. I had read and reread over 200 illustrated pages detailing how to improve rice yields: how to nurse and transplant seeds, how to build irrigation structures, how to reduce the incidence of pests and bacterial and viral diseases—all of which required more effort than the traditional swamp methods of brushing, light plowing, and broadcasting seeds.

"Eh, Betsy," Tamba quipped, "when you're somewhere where they walk on three sticks, you should walk on three sticks."

I told him we have a similar expression: "When in Rome, do as the Romans do."

But there was a contradiction we were all ignoring. The inland valley swamp work that I'd been assigned primarily involved the men's side of the division of labor, not the women's side.

Women were only recruited when there were shortages of men, owing to the allure of the diamond mines. Men still mostly brushed (cleared the undergrowth), did the digging (with shovels), made fences, and thatched roof barns. Women were the seed broadcasters, transplanters, and weeders. They also managed a large share of the harvesting, threshing, winnowing, and storage. Occasionally they plowed too. It was always a lot of daily work for everyone and consistently divided. But according to the culture, puddling the dirt and building three-foot-high dirt walls, as we were preparing to do on this day, with hoes and shovels, required the heavy lifting by men—not women, many of whom were pregnant, nursing an infant, or carrying a baby on their back.

Still, the three-month training on sustainability I'd been given made sense. By encouraging rice cultivation in swamps during the rainy season and raised-vegetable beds in those same swamps during the dry, farmers would see their yields grow beyond anything they'd ever expected from their upland farms.

Tamba, Sahr Joe, and I continued stomping until my discomfort dissolved like the mud. But a few seconds later, my foot struck a mass, and I squealed, thinking it might be a turtle or snake.

Tamba handed me his hoe in a flash, and reflexively, I struck the mass, which turned out to be only a mud-covered stone. The men burst out with more laughter from deep in their gullets, telling me that turtles and snakes would never put themselves in our way like that. Everyone understood that everything had a role here. Except me, I thought.

"I gladi foh dis day," Sahr Joe said, then politely stepped aside to relieve himself, walking yards up the trail. Sahr Joe was one of only a handful of men who understood the public health link between the urine of infected humans in the water and snail larvae that caused schistosomiasis, second only to malaria as the most devastating parasitic disease.

Tamba moved closer to help me puddle. As we worked in tandem, I felt love for living inside the rainforest and growing food on this land. I felt myself opening to the unfolding friendships with the farmers of this community and to their land. The work and these relationships had steadied me. This way of living—off and with the land—was nurturing an essence in me I hadn't known existed. I was learning to be more empathetic, more tolerant of what I couldn't understand, and stand up for myself in new ways. As hard as living here sometimes felt, I was still willing—and that mattered to me.

Then, abruptly, this feeling changed.

"Yu bawbee fine," Tamba suddenly said.

My breasts? I stepped back. "What did you say?"

"Yu bawbee. Dem fine so." (very much).

I glared suspiciously at each man.

The women here routinely left their breasts uncovered while they nursed their children or other wives' children and worked at their farms. I learned to see how they were life-giving sources of maternal bonding and sustenance for a child who would hopefully survive.

Tamba lifted his arm playfully, his eyes bright, his chest heaving. A slight wind seemed to come from beneath us, and the beads of sweat around his face and neck began to drip. Tamba raised an arm and gestured forward.

I continued puddling the mud, ignoring him as the swamp and sky reeled before me. He was married. His wife was a kumbra (nursing mother).

"My bawbees are not . . . They are thighs!," I bumbled. I was referring to the fact that, here, thighs were the sensual part of the body that women covered, and not their breasts. I also knew that Tamba knew that where I came from, women always covered them. I continued to feign composure.

Tamba insisted, "Yu bawbee fine-o." This time, he added an inflection to his voice and stepped closer, so his intention was now clear and undeniable. He elaborated, "Yu nar fine titi" (girl). And then, "Yu nar fine uman. I lek yu." *You are a fine girl. You are a fine woman. I like you.*

"I like you too." Anxiety welled in my chest.

I didn't know where this overture would lead. I understood being Raymond's successor had been confusing and disappointing for the men here. Many farmers in the chiefdom had been eager to work with the new Peace Corps—synonymous with the only American they'd ever known, Raymond, the white man, the American, the Westerner, the rich man, their friend, and their brother. My being here was unlike the earlier arrangement. I had been assigned to the part of the labor that belonged to the men, not the women.

There was no getting around the fact either that for months now, I'd been submitting to playing the part they'd given me—agreeing to be the stranger, and this was a land that, above all, welcomed strangers.

Suddenly, we heard farmers who were heading back to town calling down from the trail, "Eh, Sia Besty. Tenki foh di work!"

I waved back, thinking I was about to be relieved from the discomfort, but they all disappeared into the vegetation. I felt Tamba's eyes still considering me. I kept puddling.

Then he nudged my foot with his and lifted his arm, saying, "Yu go gree foh leh ah touch dem?"

I stepped away. Tamba kept smiling and he stepped toward me, his flirty eyes steady on me and then unblinking.

I stood tall and gave him a level look, pretending I wasn't shaken. "No!," I said, removing all doubt. The pupa inside me, cocooned by Sierra Leonean hospitality toward strangers, was now hanging upside down and by a thread. Or was it?

From the first day I arrived, parents here sent their children to do chores for me, village women regularly cooked for me without my asking, as they did for their husbands. They often brought me extra dishes to taste even after I'd eaten and even when their own supplies were running low—the same as they did for any Big Man. Most evenings, men brought me palm wine, sat with me for a bit, and asked me questions about my family, home, and life in America. "Di same moon yu dey look," they always said, as if asking for confirmation, an acknowledgment that we lived worlds apart.

And there was this benefit above all others: I came here because I could.

I had been enjoying the power bestowed upon the Peace Corps and other Americans and Europeans in Sierra Leone and for me here in Tokpombu. Yet, below the surface, it was consistently complicated and confusing. Tamba's question only touched on how it was always a field sown of emotion and complexity.

I kept working, squishing my feet into a new corner of the mud until I'd regained my composure. Then I calmly thanked Tamba and said, "I get fine man." *I already have a good boyfriend.* "I'm not here for any more of that."

"*Really?*," he said, and then, after a pause, "OK." He tilted his head and smiled. And that was where it ended. He accepted my answer. He didn't seem insulted. It all trickled past us like swamp water.

I puddled some more, pleased by the small area we'd prepared for nursing rice. Sahr Joe suddenly called out from behind a large granite rock above us and motioned for us to join him. I recognized he was holding a gallon jug of wine.

Tamba slid his hand into mine in the friendliest of ways, the way most men here hold hands with other men, but not women. "Leh we drink now. Dis work today e dohn dohn." I looked at the sky, noticing the late afternoon hues of pink. We rinsed our feet in the stream running through the middle of the swamp. I put my flip-flops back on and followed my friend's lead along the field's yet unplowed and less watery parts.

Sahr Joe's wife and small-Ray, along with a few other women, called down to us, letting us know they were headed for Tokpombu with dinner, the loads they would cook balanced on their heads. Their husbands would have the chance to bathe at home with water the women boiled to warm their bucket baths.

Tamba and I entered the farm hut where Joe handed us our cups, segments from a nearby bamboo tree he'd just cut. These made the perfect vessels for our drinks. The three of us talked again about rice and the future harvest. Tamba remarked that Peace Corps agriculture was a good thing for this country—"even their agriculture women."

I wondered if, in the end, I was bound to be less of the agricultural expert that Peace Corps intended and more of a feminist export. We take our bodies with us.

Tamba and Sahr Joe laughed uproariously. "You know, Sia Besty, Kono women have labored with us from the beginning. Our problem is that we are suffering." Tamba offered that if a man wanted to eat well, he'd do well to treat a woman correctly. "I don't want any women's bad-bad juju," he said.

———

Later, back in the village, I returned from the waterside with Ma Sando's daughter, Finda. She helped me remove my bucket from the top of my head and set it down in the corner of my kitchen. She watched me pour a capful of Dettol, a disinfectant, into the water. She told me she didn't like the smell, that it made her nose tingle, and grabbed the bucket to lead me outside to where my shower-house was though my shower was a bucket bath.

I told her I didn't like the smell much either but that it killed the germs and bacteria that can make a person sick.

"You go eat wit we way yu don finish foh was?" *Will you eat with us after you've bathed?*, Finda asked. Her boundless energy was contagious. I followed her out the back door, squinted into the last of the sun's glare, relieved that nightfall had begun to bring its coolness. The scent of things rancid, of leaves freshly pounded in their mortars, of dried spices burning off their peppered steam in cast iron pots was a table setting for our appetites.

Ma Sando, and KT's co-wives, Gbesay and Fengai, greeted me cheerfully as they dished rice from their pots, adjusting the lappas they had tied around their waists, which allowed them to move about their kitchen fires more freely. Each woman casually exposed her breasts the way one rolls up one's sleeves or puts on an apron.

I observed in these kitchens how the division of labor was so rigidly maintained yet performed with serious intention. Cooking—a woman's chore—was both work and joy and nothing about it was fifty-fifty. They assumed total control of their kitchens and seemed then to prefer it that way.

"Besty, cam leh we eat rice," Ma Sando said. She called Finda to join us.

As she scooped the cassava leaf sauce on top of the large bowl of rice, I walked closer to her and whispered, "Today, Tamba bin ask foh touch me bawbee." I looked down at my breasts and pointed.

Ma Sando called the three women over, and she asked me to tell them what I had just told her. They joined her in a collective giggle, slapped their knees, and whooped. "Eh Tamba. Dat man nar true character!"

"E get liva!" (nerve) Fengai said above all the others. "We bawbee nar nuttin," she added. "Look, we yone" (ours), she said, lifting hers up the way you hold a up a fine filet.

"Yu see ow we pikin dehm all dey suck?," Ma Sando echoed.

The women burst into laughter so hard they couldn't contain it. They told me that after I had a baby and became a "kumbra" (nursing mother), my breasts wouldn't be the way they were now—firm and upright. "E bin wan foh play-play wit you." *He wanted to joke with you.*

Then they complimented my breasts the way Tamba had.

"He must have thought you were lonely," Fengai said.

The truth was, I sometimes was a little lonely. But with my women friends, I could more easily laugh.

# CHAPTER 8

# Beauty Season

If you don't look right, you're not going to be loved. So, I always wanted to try to look right. I think when you're poor you cut yourself, and when you're rich you have plastic surgery.

—JANE FONDA

In my parlor on the day of the big Bondo dance, Ma Sando's daughter, Ella, told me that my hair was a problem. "E too slippul (slippery)," she said. Ready to give up, she slapped the wooden pick through the air as if swatting a fly.

It didn't matter to me whether my braids were as clean and tight as those worn by Mamy Yoko, the famous nineteenth-century paramount chief whose power and influence in the  Bondo society had helped her expand her chiefdom. Ella, of course, wanted to get it "just right." For me, whenever it came to beauty standards, the recollection of my nose job while still a tender teenager kicked up dust.

I pointed to the enamel cup and a pair of scissors balanced on my chair's wide arm and suggested that water might help it stick. "You can trim my bangs, too, if you want."

To Ella and the other girls, who had turned my parlor into an improv beauty shop, it was essential that my wavy slippul hair turn out okay and "fine like one big diamond." And since they were preparing for me to join them on a night that would mark the most important and sacred event of their lives, one that would link them to the collective supernatural power owned by women, I took them seriously.

At sunset, these pubescent girls, along with a dozen or more from the village, would begin their initiation into the Bondo secret society, the female equivalent of the men's Poro. It was now time for the celebratory ritual that readied them to cross the threshold from childhood to womanhood. The girls would be separated from the community, spending the next two or possibly three months in the "Sacred Forest."

Ella expected me to sit still and scolded me when I didn't. "Yu dey benben en ton." *You are twisting and turning.*

"But e no easy foh sidohn so." *But it's not so easy to sit like this for hours.* The girls scoffed at me and told me I needed to learn patience. As a nonmember of the Bondo, I could not ask questions, and they didn't offer any information. Maybe the girls who were about to join didn't know much about it either.

The preparations, though, were a different story.

The girls had been public about getting their hair ready all along. A bolt of Chinese fabric mysteriously appeared and was making the rounds from family to family, and there was excitement in deciding on new styles of clothes for the village tailor to sew. Like last year, cooking had also become a shared activity among families. Now that the harvest was over, there was enough for everyone to eat.

All over Tokpombu—Old Town and New Town—women set their yields out to dry on large mats in the sun: rice, beans, cayenne, okra, cocoa, and coffee. The previous week, Ma Sando and Sia Sam asked whether I was going on patrol so that I might bring them two bags of Maggi. With the shortage of local fish, women used the foil-wrapped bouillon to flavor their food. They often asked me to get them handfuls of cubes at a time but asking for two large bags of cubes was unprecedented. A few days earlier, Mama Sia, KT's first wife, had also asked me to purchase a large plastic container from the market in Koidu to store additional palm oil. Usually, she kept her palm oil in reusable powdered milk tins, the way everyone did. I made a special trip for this purpose. I even tried to give the items as gifts, but they insisted on paying me. They told me how they had been saving up for this occasion and that spending their money on Bondo was good luck. Rice too had been plentiful in the upland this year, and after the coffee trees had been pruned, they sprouted surprising and fragrant November blooms in large quantities, a bumper crop bringing unexpected wealth to New Town.

Ella told me I was fidgeting again. "Yu no wan foh look fine?"

"Yes, ah dey wan," *Yes, I want,* I agreed, summoning Two-Stroke, the stray kitten presented to me a few months back by the policemen in Jaima. (His name commemorated the leaky can of Two-Stroke engine oil I'd purchased for my motorbike that had coated him while he rode home inside my backpack.)

"Whatever you cut will grow back, so it's not a problem if you make a mistake," I assured Ella. "It's not like a bunion or a nose," I added.

It's also not like what was about to happen to the girls.

"It will be a big-big problem if your hair isn't right," Ella countered. "Yu no wan foh wowo." *You don't want to look ugly.*

I laughed when she said this, remembering that when Bondu Betsy was born, her mother told me not to say she was "fine" but that she was "wowo." *Say she is ugly so that she'll become fine.* It reminded me of how my grandmother would spit into her hand after someone complimented us, protecting us from the evil eye.

Two-Stroke tried to find a comfortable spot on my lap and stretched himself in a way I wished I could. Ella continued to insist that it was essential for me to look "fine tumous" for tonight's dance. I told Ella that some of the women asked me to take pictures tonight when they plaited the initiates' hair before leading them into the bush. "I go learn yu ow foh snap." *I will show you how to use the camera.*

Ella squealed and clapped her hands.

This feeling of being included was altogether different from the intimidation I'd felt during the men's Poro initiation when I first arrived—the obedience required while the phantasmagoric sounds bounced off the walls of my cement bungalow in the dark of night. Even though I'd grown comfortable with most village ways, I remained privately unnerved by what I couldn't speak of, what would be done to these girls during their extended stay in the bush—the ritual clitorectomy. In preparing for life in the remote villages of Sierra Leone, volunteers were warned not to interfere with traditional circumcision practices, whether for boys or girls. It wasn't our place to understand it or to judge it. We were to regard these rituals as long-honored customs, possibly predating Judaism, Christianity, Islam, and Western civilization, some of our trainers said.

Living in a society that had accepted the beauty of every young woman, going about my day with no real mirrors and without full-page product ads in glossy magazines telling me, "I'm worth it," or asking "Does she or doesn't she?," was as reviving as it was novel. To be cut off from an economy that planted seeds of female insecurity and further fertilized them with its impossible standards of beauty was liberating. Still, I felt intensely conflicted by what was happening to these girls. Being beautiful, coming of age through Bondo, considered the most precious time in a girl's life, was a rite of passage that left me heavy with emotion I couldn't speak. I looked down at the cement floor.

Unexpectedly, out of the corner of my eye, I felt Finda's gaze settle on me. She took a step toward me and lifted her arm until her hand reached the tip of my nose. With her characteristic feistiness, she asked, "Udat mek yu nos?" *Who made your nose?* I felt my eyebrows arch. I blushed, uncomfortable with her observation.

She nodded and pushed the tip of her nose sideways, which resembled how mine bent slightly, "Yu feba Lebanese uman, but you no get nose way Lebanese uman get." *You resemble a Lebanese woman but you don't have their same nose.*

How could this child tell the natural from the fake? I felt an old shame rise within me. My own rite of passage, the nose job that my parents and grandmothers insisted would make a "big difference," never stopped feeling like an unsettled matter between us. Back then, when I finally complied, I couldn't have told you how I felt about my beauty. I only knew that it had been undermined because my nose didn't match the movie stars, the images in the stacks of magazines, or even most of my friends.

I told Finda that when I was young, I broke my nose in a sporting event and my mother took me to the doctor to fix it. It was the same explanation I offered anyone who asked if something had cut me and pointed to the scar along my big toe where I'd had a bunion removed at fifteen: "Me mama bin carry n go nar doctor foh mend am." *My mother took me to a doctor to fix it.*

"If you don't tell, no one will know," my mother had said. She felt this way about her age too. "A woman who tells her age will tell anything."

Now I was far from home and immersed in a society that honored its elders and seemed to be presenting a secure future to its daughters: the promise of being safely included within a cohesive group. I had come to understand that belonging and being beautiful ought to be every girl's birthright and that the intention of Bondo, by preparing the girls for their gendered lives as women, both ensured it and made it sacred.

"Yu been feel am way dem cut yu nos?" *Was it painful to have your nose cut?*, Finda asked.

"It was," I replied.

———

For my nose, my mother insisted we go to "the best of the best," a doctor whose name was Diamond, a familiar Jewish name.

"With Dr. Diamond," my mother said as we drove from southern Connecticut over the Hutchinson River Parkway, "you know what you'll get. But really, you have to be the one to decide. It's your choice."

Mine? Really? I was barely sixteen! My mother sensed my reservations. "Stop making this bigger than it is, Betsy. It's just your nose. We'll turn around and go home if you don't want one. I said it was your choice."

A part of me knew that buried in my family's intentions was the belief that they were protecting me, even hiding me, from some unforeseeable future event. "Always be prepared," they said.

Dr. Diamond was MOT (a member of the tribe) and he offered what my father called "ski-jump noses—the best kind." Samantha, the wife of advertising executive Darrin Stephens in the television series *Bewitched*, had that kind of nose. So did Mary Tyler Moore, who stood up to Lou Grant in the newsroom.

It was significant that my mother drove me into Manhattan for the appointment on a school day with a doctor's note, making it an excused absence. The elevator spilled right into a waiting room generous with the usual magazines of the decade: *Good Housekeeping*, *Family Circle*, *Woman's Day*, *Time*, and *Life* presented on a coffee table, plus a binder of *Noses Up Close*—before and after photos along with patient testimonials. Before I had the chance to look at any of them, Dr. Diamond opened the door to his office and bent his finger, signaling for only me to enter, not my mother.

There I saw more pictures of noses in frames—all "ski jumps" and suppos-edly famous patients too.

Dr. Diamond offered me a seat in an upholstered wingback chair across from his, a coffee table between us displaying a stack of 5x7 black and white pre-op photos of my own nose taken by a mall photographer that we'd mailed him the previous month. He adjusted the "cards" to face me. "What do you see?" he asked.

"People's faces," I said.

I resisted the word "ugly." But I felt it. How could I not? The family joke at our dinner table about my father had been: "When they were passing out noses, you thought they said roses, so you said you want a big red one."

"So," Dr. Diamond said, "are you here for you or your mother? Or maybe your father." It was a trick question he applied with the fine motor precision of an endodontist—drilling down into the relational roots of my teenage self. He probably had asked it hundreds, if not thousands, of times before.

Would anyone really want their nose broken with a hammer, if society, beginning with our mothers and fathers, had tendered the message, "You are beautiful just as you are"? I never did see myself as a girl who wanted to be admitted to a hospital floor reserved for teens whose parents sched-uled their Wednesday rhinoplasty appointments.

On the elevator down, I glared at my mother. I made her the one respon-sible for the audacity, for asking me to consider the confused set of choices that this day represented.

"You're still young," she said. "Maybe you need to grow up a little more, wait another year, and see how you feel then. But do it before college so that nobody will know. Or . . ."

We grilled hot dogs for supper that night, and my grandmother arrived with baked apples for dessert. With my two brothers now in college, it was now just me and my parents, and my grandmother. We discussed the day.

My grandmother said, "It's too late for me, but I would have loved a nose job!"

Did we all look at ourselves and not like what we saw!

After my high school graduation in 1980, I told my parents I wanted to get a nose job after all. In truth, it only partly felt like a choice.

They arranged for a local ENT (otolaryngologist) who had some experience in plastic surgery to perform the operation. I spent much of the
summer in a brown polyester uniform working the drive-thru window of a
Burger King, hoping that no one I knew would drive up and see my swollen,
bandaged nose. Complete healing would take three months: there were so
many nerve endings, as with all our body parts, the healing was delicate,
and the slightest pressure could scar me for life.

———————

Ella tugged on my hair and brought me out of my thoughts. The girls
encouraged her to keep going, nodding when it looked right. They waved
their hands in the air and scissored their fingers, pretending to cut.

This afternoon would be the last one where I would know them as
"girls." When they returned from Bondo, these children who had been my
constant companions, who had helped me refine my bucket-toting skills,
shown me how to pound the dirt out of my clothes on rocks in the streambed, taught me how long to cook cassava leaves so that their poison dissi-
pates, would be women. This would be a passage for me too.

When I had first arrived, Estelle and Ella often offered to wash my
clothes, and I gladly handed them over, clean or dirty, because I knew they
liked to try them on, pretending they were *American girls*. Once, I found
them at the river playing "New York Taxi," a game they'd made up after
I described American taxis in New York City. I saw Estelle sitting in the
water holding a pretend steering wheel and Ella running from the trail
and hailing the "taxi," wearing changes of my clothes each time she got
in. "Come inside now, Madam," the driver said. The girl pretending to be
me walked "fas-fas" (fast) and stooped her shoulders slightly forward the
way I'd told them New Yorkers do. When the girls saw me watching them,
they looked scared, expecting me to be angry. But I'd found their imitation
heartwarming.

I felt nervous about how life in Tokpombu might change tomorrow and
in the coming weeks—not to see these girls at the waterside, near the fire,
on the bush roads, or, most especially, in my house. I would miss them.
By joining Bondo, these girls were about to become full members of this
community, could even become wives, marrying at a very young age. They

would be folded into an experience that would put them on the other side of their lives, respected as women following the traditional farming calendar, not a school calendar.

The wet hank fell to the ground. The girls crowded around my feet to pick my hair off the cement floor and rub it between their fingertips. Bintu stood tall with her arms above her head and then let go, inches of my hair falling not as wet clumps now but as featherlike strands. The others watched them float to the floor. They seemed so youthful and full of promise, and I tasted a tear on my lip, surprised by the intensity of my emotions.

Matru noticed. "Eh, Besty. No cry, yah."

I was embarrassed and wondered what she thought I was crying about.

Estelle looked at my fallen clippings on the floor and straight away ran to my kitchen, returning with a broom. She stooped over and began sweeping, saying, "Udat go ber dis hair?"

"Bury my hair?"

"Yu no want bird foh mek nest wit yu hair, Besty."

"Why not?"

She seemed incredulous that I didn't know the reason. "E go gi yu bad-bad headache." *It will give you a nasty headache.* Years later, I met a Gullah woman in South Carolina and shared stories of my experiences with rice farming in Sierra Leone. She told me that she also buried her hair after getting it cut. "It will give you a God-awful migraine if you don't," she said.

"We get foh mek yu braids, yah," Ella said. *We still have to tie your braids.*

The girls exchanged glances. Estelle opened a cloth pouch containing a collection of tiny rubber bands and passed a few to Ella, which she slid over her thumb for future use. Bintu pulled out another bag and, after digging into it, opened her palms to display an arrangement of colored beads for the ends of my braids.

"Wait-o!" Bintu said with sudden urgency. "We get foh check foh crabloss!" She thought they needed to check for lice.

I tried to explain that my head didn't itch, so it was unlikely I had any. No one believed me.

Ella parted my hair and brought her face close to my scalp. "E no dey hold wata. E too slippul for crabloss." *It doesn't hold water. It's too slippery for lice.*

Phew.

I grew restless again, knowing it could take hours before the girls finished. Even my cat skittered away. For a second, I thought I would reach for a book. But the feeling was overtaken by the realization that I would be missing a moment where these girls were not just bringing me into their circle by doing my hair—they had placed me in the center of their circle on a day that would mean something unique in all our lives, and forever. A before and an after.

The girls continued pulling and scratching at my hair until I simply couldn't sit still any longer. "I taya," I said. *I'm tired.* I got up and stretched myself in all directions.

Ella exhaled. "Misehf taya," *I'm tired too,* she said, and offered the rubber bands and comb to Estelle, who had no trouble taking over.

"You have to sit quietly," she commanded me.

I sat back down.

Rather than dipping her hands into the water to tighten her grip on my hair, she sent the other girls to grab their mother's hair gel. They returned with a lone jar of Super Glow hair gel.

A few minutes later, Finda walked into my house carrying Two Stroke. "E wan yu," *He wants you,* she said, though I know it was she, and not Two Stroke, who wanted an excuse to join the older girls. I wasn't the only one who was going to miss their company. Finda wiggled into the chair with the other girls and watched everything intently. I wondered if she was taking notes for the time when she would prepare for Bondo. I'd be long gone by then.

Ella again took over braiding my hair. After she finished yet another braid, I stood up and ran my hands over my new hairdo. Finda suddenly jumped up with a severe expression on her face. She pulled the top sheet off my bed in the corner and motioned to the window. "Wait. We no wan man foh look inside."

"Why shouldn't men see my hairdressing?," I asked while I watched Ella help Finda tie my sheet around the top of the iron bars of my window, and then secured the bottom.

Ella smiled. "Way yu dey pan dance dis night, Besty, yu go luk fine tumous!" *When you dance tonight, Besty, you will look fine too much.* She clapped her hands and danced around the room. The other girls gestured with whoops and clapped to show their agreement. I recalled my own passage to adulthood at fifteen: a confirmation ceremony in the temple sanctuary followed by a backyard celebration beneath a white tent. This rite of passage were amended to mirror aspects of Christian confirmation ceremonies at a time when many Jews were assimilating into mainstream America's religious culture. Now, I was in the back row of another's ancient unamended ritual. There was a sense of something integral and enduring, with irrefutable evidence all around me that the vitality of this annual passage enacted and amplified female sources of power and authority while also entrenching the community's tribal and political life.

———

The sun was safely behind the house across the street from mine. Standing nearby, I observed the same girls who'd plaited my hair now lying down on yards of new, tie-dyed material on the ground in front of the porch, their faces covered in white clay. Behind them, a crowd of older women had the girls' heads on their laps while they put the finishing touches on the plaited hair. As promised, I took photos of the girls looking up at the twilight sky, looking up with seeming anticipation, while villagers playfully complimented my braids.

After sunset, the women invited me to join them as they began to dance. We sang, "Kambo yo manda, ninnyba kambo, kambo yo manda tahhhh . . . oh ya oh!" *The light is changing; the light has changed in you. You are the light!*

And then "Ella" was substituted for the word "Kambo," and the song repeated with the name of each initiate. "Ella yo man da . . ." The beads along my forehead felt slippery against my skin. They rattled as I shook my head, and the sounds blended in perfectly with the rattle of the shakere (beaded gourd), making a rhythm all around us.

I heard Mama Sia and Gbesay call my name. "Besty yo man da . . ." We danced with our feet hardly leaving the ground, swaying back and forth on the dirt road, weaving in and around the homes of Tokpombu together, Old Town and New Town, the moonlight guiding the way. I felt whole like the full moon above us, no longer stretched between oceans. The days here, with their bright lights, had showed me the edges of our lives, but the moonlight dissolved those edges. As I danced and sang at the top of my lungs with Ma Sando behind me, holding my shoulders, and my own hands on Sia Sam in front of me, I was filled by the villagers' kindness and inclusion, how this ritual transcended daily life, giving it meaning and context.

Blood. Blade.

Birth. Childhood to adulthood. Marriage. Children. Death.

The girls were led by the elder women in a weaving line out of the village for their first of many nights away from home. I offered the elder women sterile gauze, alcohol, bacitracin from my medical kit aware that the village sowei, the ritual cutter, whomever she was, might be able to prevent infection.

Over the next two months, the girls occasionally made appearances in the village. One such day, Ma Sando rushed through the back door, calling, "Sia Besty, go luk. Yu go must see." She grabbed my hand and opened my front door. A dance was taking place. At first, three rows of girls in grass skirts were dancing, covered in white clay, beads crisscrossed between their breasts. Then they arranged themselves in a circle, still dancing with high kicks and dramatic sways of their hips. A devil wearing a heavy black mask with a grass top appeared in the middle of them, which brought on an even greater frenzy of dance. Villagers drew near, seemingly transfixed. The dance lasted half an hour and ended with radiant faces, clapping, and the lightest feeling I'd yet experienced in the village as if we were all new seeds rising from the weight of our lives. When the girls and the devil retreated, we returned to our day, but the joy it put inside me felt lasting.

One afternoon, as Sahr Joe and I returned to the village from the final harvest of our demonstration swamp, he pressed his fingers to his lips to signal for me to be quiet. Filtering out the sounds of late afternoon birds, I soon heard other sounds I recognized: the girls, softly singing and laughing just ahead. In Old Town, two girls were seated on a chair beside Bintu, both wearing beautiful Chinese cotton dresses. Their lips showed bright red lipstick and their hair was newly plaited; they wore pretty, gold-colored sandals.

Joe explained that the Bondo initiates were being presented to the village as marriageable women. He stood still for a moment to behold them with the respect of a father and an elder. He told me they'd go back to the forest for a little while, but that Bondo was almost over.

The following week, Ella and all the girls were back within the fold of the community. Their eyes were bright and clear. Each girl looked rounder, more substantial than she had before Bondo. They were beautiful, every one of them. Despite what I imagined to be their terrifying, humiliating, and painful circumcisions, they radiated a contentment and a connection beyond anything I'd experienced in any of my own rites of passage.

Over the next few weeks, the pace of life settled down with a new quality. Ella and Estelle held themselves erect now. They were no longer children but young women ready to take on the responsibilities of womanhood. I could see it in how they had filled out and drew closer to their mothers, tending the fire for cooking. These girls seemed to pick up their pestles to pound the rice with new confidence, as if they knew for sure they were doing it the right way. They scolded their younger brothers and sisters with more authority than before. Their very gestures seemed to say, "This is the way things are done." They went about all their business like this, having been taught by their elders in the way of the tradition. I felt I could see in them an understanding of their power—that their survival and dignity as women were the backbones of life all around them.

Finda complained to me about her older sister. "Besty, Ella doesn't have time to spend with me again." She was barely eight then. No one had been as patient with me or as fun as this little girl. More than anyone, Finda distracted me from feeling lonely.

"Ella nar uman now." *Ella is a woman now*, I told her. "But I can still play with you Finda, because we yone no don join Bondo." . . . *because we have not joined Bondo yet*. I took Finda's hand and led her into my parlor. I asked her whether she wanted to draw or play Pick-Up-Sticks. Finda sat cross-legged beside me, tightly holding the game in her hands. Before letting go, she turned away as if someone had called to her. Instead of throwing them gently in the air to see where they might land, she smashed the wooden needles to the floor. We watched them scatter, each rolling to its own vibration.

## CHAPTER 9

# Those Who Were Not Loyal

Love beareth all things, believeth all things, hopeth all things, endureth all things.
—CORINTHIANS 13:7

I rolled my motorcycle out onto my verandah, the morning sun slanting through the window bars and across the concrete floor. I had accepted an invitation to Jagbwema, a village where one of the oldest chiefs—an esteemed master farmer—resided.

My muscles hadn't fully recovered from yesterday's work on the demonstration farm, an acre tract of land a few hundred yards past the village boundary where Ray and Sahr Joe had experimented with irrigated plots and new varieties of hybrid seeds. I'd plowed stalks of harvested rice back into the soil in the early morning, poured out bags of seed rice to dry on prepared mats in the early afternoon, and then scooped them back into the burlap bags at the day's end. My muscles ached, and I'd had a restless night's sleep.

"Eh, Sia Besty," Ma Sando called to me on her way back from fetching water. Then she peered more closely at my face. "Ow yu sleep?"

"I couldn't. There was too much wailing last night in Old Town."

She unloaded her bucket on my stoop, wiping sweat from her neck. Her eyes darkened. "Mama Bintu, dat longa (tall), dry (thin) wan. Een baby dohn die—nar stillborn."

"What!" I felt my shoulders tighten and set my motorbike on its kickstand. Only a few days ago, Bintu, a healthy young woman, had been so cheerful. She said that she wanted me to take her and her baby to America with me.

"Ow Bintu now?," I asked. *How is Bintu now?*

"We no sabi. " *We don't know.*

Ma Sando took off her headscarf to retie it, running her long fingers through the dry, loose cornrows in her hair. "Di village midwife bin try but e no hep." *The village midwife tried all night to safely deliver the baby, but it didn't help."*

We stood facing each other, our silence restrained. Ma Sando's baby, my namesake, slept bundled under pieces of cloth on the straw mattress she shared with her mother, brothers, and sisters. "We no get clinic, Sia Tokpombu." She swept the ground from side to side with one of her bare feet. Her voice was nearly hollow.

And yet it took only a moment before Ma Sando shook herself and hoisted her full bucket back up onto her head, her strong frame stretching toward the sky. In a voice as firm now as it was weak moments ago, she said, "We tehl God tenki Bintu no die."

I grabbed the handlebars of my motorbike and kicked the stand up. Through the path between the church and my house, Ma Sando's oldest daughter Ella ran toward me with something big and round in her arms. I turned the key in the ignition.

"Wait me," she called over the rev of the engine.

Ella lobbed a football-shaped bush yam into my arms. "Ah bin forget. Ma Sando wan leh yu carry n go wit dis somba foh di chief." *I almost forgot! Ma Sando wants you to take this gift to the chief.* She also cautioned me to "take time" crossing the thin webbing of the hammock bridge. She said that it stood as high as the trees and was the only way to get to Jagbwema, which bordered the outer reaches of Gorama Chiefdom, my official territory.

I drove off with a heavy heart.

---

Two men flagged me down in the middle of the road a few miles beyond the village. I recognized them right away: Mansa and Vandi, teachers from the chiefdom headquarters, Kangama, five miles away, who'd suggested this meeting. Their greeting was so effusive that meeting them felt like a reunion with old friends.

"Good morning-o, Sia Tokpombu!," Mansa called out in a jovial tone, directing me out of the middle of the narrow road as if traffic was about to approach, even though most of the traffic was pedestrian. I drove toward an unmarked spot he pointed to—tall grasses and vines along the side of the road curtaining off the forest trail. Vandi flaunted nails that were long and filed, a popular statement in the cities by men who did pen and paper work and not hard physical labor.

Mansa steered my motorbike as we moved onto the forest path leading us to Jagbwema. Where the trail became impassible, they pointed to an abandoned palm wine bar where I could leave my motorbike. I nervously followed the teachers' single file amid increasingly thick and encroaching vegetation.

Both men had dressed for the day. Their clothes were impeccably ironed and their shirts were tucked into their belted pants, which were perfectly creased. I joked with Vandi about how I might still need my motorbike helmet for the hammock bridge. Mansa reassured, "No 'fraid, Sia Besty. Dis bridge e sturdy." He offered to carry my backpack. I understood that I could not make this journey alone and that the teachers' assistance was crucial.

As we climbed deeper into the rock-ribbed forest, Mansa, who'd been walking in front of me, said, "Eh. Dis pack heavy-o. Wetin yu get inside dis bag? Mortal man? Baby?" *What do have inside this bag?*

After looking inside and zipping it back up, he handed the pack to Vandi behind me. "Yu foh take turn, Vandi. I don't want to carry Besty's baby all by myself!"

Vandi slid his arms through the straps of the pack and comically bent forward under its weight until it fell over his head. When he stood back up, he unzipped the backpack like his friend did and looked inside. "I also just want to be sure it is really a bush yam!"

With each new patch of forest, we breathed in the sweet smells of decay and rot along the trail. We passed through patches of old growth and deforested fallow land. Stretches of shade-grown cash crops: coffee, cocoa, oil palm, and sometimes, alongside the trail, bananas and plantains—giant upside-down tulips held by green, yellow, or red bundled claws dimmed the bright daylight. As we maneuvered around the snake-like roots of towering cotton trees embedded in the hard-packed forest floor, we heard birdsongs and occasional monkey screeches echo above the constant buzz and hum of insects. When we reached the bridge, stopping for a rest before crossing,

Vandi lit a filter-less cigarette. He extolled its health benefits, comparing them favorably to the imported (and largely unaffordable) Dunhill's and Marlboro's. At the same time, I tried to steer clear of the smoke. He took a long draw, gasped it out, noting that cigarette smoke drives away bugs, then complained that there were too many bugs in the forest.

He wasn't referring to ordinary insects but the ones that cause river blindness (onchocerciasis), which began as skin irritations and discoloration and was a severe problem in the chiefdom. Its late-stage symptoms were like those of glaucoma.

"What about snakes?," I asked, looking up into the palm trees above us. I never could shake the stories I'd heard about pythons that would drop down onto the shoulders of unsuspecting farmers.

"Eh, if yu 'fraid snake," Vandi said earnestly, "yu go draw dat snake near." He dropped his cigarette and ground out its ember with his foot.

Mansa stepped onto the platform of the bridge and shouted back to me, "Dis nar wonderful example of we Sierra Leonean technology."

I cautiously regarded the structure, anchored by immense tree trunks with water swirling around precipitous rocks below. Mansa danced over the narrow planks to the other side with the ease and grace of a tightrope walker. I studied the closely woven bridge that stretched more like a spider web than a hammock across the river.

"Pass now," Vandi encouraged me from behind.

"Are you sure it's strong enough?"

"Plenti strong. This bridge is made of rattan. It is how we thatch our roofs, tote our loads, keep the beef from eating our harvests!"

When I still hesitated, Vandi said, "Rattan is a very strong rope. Like an umbilical cord."

I took a deep breath and inched my way across, tightly holding onto the thin ropes on each side of the bridge, with Vandi following close behind.

He said that when the rains became heavy, there would be a lot more water flowing in the river and with the increase in water would come crocodiles.

"Now is not the time to tell me that," I said and scrambled to the platform on the other side. "How old is the bridge?"

Mansa kicked the platform with his foot as proof of the bridge's stability. "We are talking about one hundred rainy seasons."

His answer didn't appease my fear. I knew we had to cross it again on the way back.

"Is the chief expecting us?" I wanted to change the subject.

"Of course he's expecting us. He's a ninety-nine-year-old man. He is not going anywhere!"

"Oh, yes," Vandi added, his chest full of pride. "This man has lived through everything, Sia Tokpombu: colonial times, independence, Sir Milton Margai (the first prime minister) until Papa Siaka (Sierra Leone's first president)."

"Ahhh, Besty," Mansa said, his mood suddenly somber, "dis we President Stevens has been stealing and stealing from us for twenty good years."

"To God!," Vandi added, whacking at a branch with the machete he was carrying. "Nar tiefman! (thief)."

Since arriving, I'd heard many stories about President Siaka Stevens— his one-party system's mismanagement of the government coffers and how so many of his people were living lavishly, without compassion for those who were suffering, as they made deposits and withdrawals from Swiss bank accounts.

"We don disappoint-o," Mansa said, repeating the words as if it were a refrain in an overplayed song.

"If everyone is so disappointed, why do I hear farmers praise him?" I was thinking of the posters I'd seen with Stevens's face on the walls of homes, street corners, and shops—even tacked to the walls of schools and clinics. "On New Year's Day, I have heard people sing and dance, 'We tell God tenki, we no die-o. Papa Siaka, e no die-o.'" *We give thanks to God for being alive. We give thanks that Papa Siaka is still alive.*

The men looked at each other and began to laugh.

"Watin make you laugh?," I asked.

"Nar dry laugh," Mansa said. "A Sierra Leone man's laugh isn't a laugh."

Vandi clapped his hands and continued riffing, bending over until he finally rested his palms on his knees to catch his breath. He sputtered, "A Sierra Leone man's sorry is also a laugh." He meant that sometimes, being sorry was to laugh at someone, as if to say there was never enough compassion for each other in this world—laughter chasing after misery.

Vandi turned to me, the crease between his eyes deepening. "Of course, wherever you tie a cow is where it will eat," he said. "Our politicians are all cows!"

The men continued revealing hard truths about their country's decline, how it impacted them, and how they viewed their future. "Sia Tokpombu, you understand we are talking about the father of our young country."

The teachers' contradictory words were dizzying. Here they were, still feeling civic pride for their leader whom they also despised for his betrayal and perhaps also absorbing the very guilt the perpetrators refused to own.

We continued along the trail, scrambling up a steep incline that left me breathless, then downhill again, crossing over a palm-log bridge. We passed another cacao patch, but this one was infested with "black pod," a virus that consumed half of the harvest each year. The understory was growing denser and denser. The bitterness I had felt emanating from the men just a short while ago had all but faded.

Vandi addressed my earlier question. "We sing for Siaka not to die because we know he is not acting alone. The wrong people surround him. They are the ones who are steering him poorly."

"But didn't he pick them?"

"No. Those are his cronies," Vandi said. "They were not men from the oldest lines of our traditional ruling families. They were the young men from families who had sent their boys to boarding schools in the old British system—boys without loyalty who wanted to rule without opposition."

Vandi pulled a penknife from his pocket and sliced a few bananas from a low-hanging bunch. He handed the fruit to Mansa and me and said, "Before—before dem strangers bin cam foh live wit we—we bin get system, we bin get we yone democracy. Now, we get won party en two system en won foot dey mas di foot nar di odda inside won box."

I repeated the Krio words back to them in English: *"You are saying that before strangers came to live among you—you had your own kind of democratic system, but it was ignored?"*

*"Yes."*

*"And now, you have only one political party functioning within two systems, the old and the new, and they are crushing each other inside a container that can't easily hold both kinds of ideas?"*

*"Nar correct.* Sierra Leone's colonial history of indirect rule still exerts influence and it continues to break us."

Mansa described the esteemed Bo School, a secondary school established over a century ago. Its aim had been to instill cultural pride and strength in the sons and nominees of future chiefs, paramount chiefs, and local officials at the hands of the British. Mansa added, "But those handpicked students grew up in boarding schools away from their villages without close family attachments. You could say they were chosen by those who were not loyal in the first place. They didn't even know the true value of the traditions they were learning because they were not learning how to become rice farmers, only members of their own elite society. They looked down on us!" Then he said thoughtfully, "If it were not for Poro, they would be ostracized."

Vandi added, "Nar falamakita! As yu sell yusehf, nar so di world go buy you." *Those who follow the market! As you sell yourself, the world will buy you.*

"Everyone wants a good life for themselves, to whatever extent possible," Mansa said. "Our leaders want material wealth in this country—even though their elders cautioned them to beware of that. How can any of us resist this? It is inevitable. Our mortal man condition."

"But this interpretation of life is so bleak," I protested. "It has no air."

"Oh, but it does," Vandi said. "At the end of the day, we can only hope these men and their power will be our welfare system."

Mansa nodded enthusiastically. "Nar so! Nar dis we all believe—the African welfare system. If we betray them, we betray ourselves."

"So, you really think these chiefs and ministers alike will just one day decide to share the wealth with you that they've been stealing?"

"Yes-o," Vandi said and put his hands on his hips. "I read about it in a book. It is supposed to trickle down."

I assumed he was referring to then-president Ronald Reagan's economic policy of "trickle-down economics." The success of this policy seemed like an open question in both our countries—giving to the wealthy few and assuming that they will provide for those with less or without.

I shook my head again. "And all these big men who drive Mercedes? You believe these are also people who will help you?"

"Why not?," Vandi agreed. "The people inside the villages here think it is an honor to have their chiefs park their Mercedes at the palm wine bar. Their wealth is everyone's wealth. This is our tradition."

I looked forward to meeting this village chief who had earned their trust.

———

My first impression of Jagbwema was that it was more of a campsite than a hamlet. The whole clearing wasn't much larger than a baseball diamond. Beyond a thin border of tall trees lay a farm where the crops had been harvested and the residue burned in preparation for the rains. A small circle of twelve thatched roofed mud huts surrounded a court barrie.

Our arrival in the hamlet set off a chain reaction: goats bleating, hens clucking, and mangy dogs barking until an exasperated young woman who introduced herself as Kady took charge, smacking the unlucky mother goat that was nearest the smooth arrangement of rice and palm kernels drying on mats in the high noon sun.

Mansa didn't need to tell her that we'd come to see the chief. It's what anyone does when they reach a new village. We followed Kady to a hut in the middle of the circle, no bigger or smaller than the others. Inside, a thin but still very strong-looking old man glanced up from a grass mat he was weaving.

"Enti," *Good afternoon*, the chief greeted us.

I offered him my right hand to shake, held up by my left, and then held it against my heart, the customary greeting to any chief.

The old man gestured for us to sit on the nearby three-legged stools. Vandi set my backpack down in front of us. Mansa translated as the chief addressed us in Kono, though I was told he spoke at least five tribal languages, as most traditional men did.

"Welcome to our village, Sia Tokpombu," the chief said to me. Though his voice was gravelly, it gave me the reassuring sensation of my own grandmother's hand resting on my shoulders. "I heard that you had arrived," he said, struggling a little for air. "I heard that a woman was sent to replace Mister Raymond." He was silent for a moment. He asked me if my landlord KT Sonda was "holding me fine" to inquire if I were being treated well.

"Yes, he holds me fine," I replied.

The chief smiled at me. "How are you managing?"

I surprised them all by answering with the few Kono phrases I'd learned. "Ya ta ni'g mboa boa Engway. Engway ka. Engway kakaka." *I am well, thank you. Thank you so much.*

The three men's faces lit up at the sound of my voice in their mother tongue. They laughed and tapped each other's arms and their own knees.

"How is the farm work?," the chief continued. "How is life for you inside Tokpombu village?"

"I fall down and grap (stand up)." *I am adjusting,* I answered, this time in Krio.

And then, in a very chiefly way, Chief Jusu told me that everyone in Gorama knew how I'd left my own family to come live in Sierra Leone. "Your mother, your father, we tehl dem plenti plenti tenki."

I opened the backpack and held up the yam, saying, "Ma Sando bin send dis foh yu." *Ma Sando sent this for you.*

He looked happy. "Ehhh! Ma Sando! It's been a looong time. How is her new baby, Bondu Besty?"

I told him they were both well, and he answered quickly, "Ah tehl God tenki." The chief grinned, the folds around his eyes fanning out like butterfly wings.

Kady knocked at the door and presented us with a platter of oranges that had been peeled to the rind in a skillful, diagonal pattern. Mansa, Vandi, and I squeezed the sweet juice while the chief resumed his weaving and talking.

"My fore-parents, my great-great-great grandfather, founded this village." He punctuated the words he wanted to emphasize like a beat in a song or on a drum. "He was the first village chief, and I am the fourth one in this line."

He explained the local structure of governance inside Gorama, how there are many, many villages like his inside the entire chiefdom and two ruling families in bitter dispute. He said that the paramount chief was an old man like himself and that he'd ruled for over half a century. "Morigbe Forewa died during Raymond's time, but this left many questions about who was legitimately in rightful ownership of the ceremonial staff." He went on to describe how there were two ruling families in this chiefdom who were aspiring to this honor, the Forewa who ruled for "too many years," and the Kono Bundors, who had waited so patiently.

"We village chiefs are one of these many," he continued. "My father's family founded this village and another family founded Tokpombu, on my mother's line." He set his jaw tightly and, for a minute, his face looked made of stone. "But we chiefs do not act alone. Every chief inside Gorama reports the affairs of his village to the paramount chief. This paramount chief is the one who then reports to the district officer (DO), who has a direct line to our president."

Vandi demonstrated the hierarchy the chief had just explained by scratching a map into the dirt floor with a piece of stick. The chief twisted his torso around to reach for an old, rusted Ovaltine tin behind him. He pulled out a pipe and a plastic baggy, from which he pulled a tobacco leaf, breaking off pieces of it to tamp down into his pipe.

"Yes, there is only one DO for all of Kono," he said finally, confirming my thoughts through the mumble of his pipe while striking a match to the bowl. His glare intensified. "He is the eye of our president. More than any chief or any elected official inside Kono District combined." Clearing his throat, he said, "You understand how some people among us believe this district officer holds a lot of direct power."

Vandi looked at me with an eager expression as if he could suddenly summarize a complicated past in one note. "This is the legacy of rule by the British," he said, tapping the floor with one of his palms as if reciting a page out of a book in front of him.

I repeated a proverb I'd often heard KT and so many others recite: "Ow di bata dey beat, nar so di dance dey go." *How the drum beats, so the dance goes.* Is this what he meant? Was there only one drummer orchestrating the footsteps of an entire country?

The chief put his hand over his heart and sighed. He licked his dry lips and spoke again. "Yu see dis?" He bent one hand behind his back. "Dem bin don tie we hand. Lek so." *Like this.* "This is how all we chiefs (and all of our citizens) live here now. And all of this poses a serious problem for all of we inside Sierra Leone."

The chief's words were distressful to hear. The control and repression he was implying at the hands of the president reflected the same tactics that had benefited eons of emperors, sheiks, pashas, and feudal lords of the past. Trickle down here was a promise as empty as its name suggested—a drip of hope that would give rise to embitterment and usher in a new generation of discontent. Not unlike what the guava granny had forecast about P. S. Musa's students at the Tikonkor Primary School.

I looked down at the lines in the dirt and up at the lines on the chief's face. I could almost imagine a marker drawing an indelible ink line around this political landscape.

He puffed on his pipe. "Ahh, dis poor-poor country. We de struggle. Leh we try no more." *We must all keep trying.* I was beginning to understand that there had been another Sierra Leone before the one I was experiencing, before this so-called democracy that the men were carrying—an inexpressible load they held close in their hearts.

"Yes, Pa," Vandi said. "We foh try. We country bin swit-o."

"Yes-o," Mansa agreed. "We inside Sierra Leone get foh bia." *We citizens of Sierra Leone must bear up.*

At this, the chief glared at the two men. "Dis country no ebba bin swit." *At no time was this country sweet*, he said quietly but with unambiguous frustration. "A longa time ago, Englishmen came. They came and took some of us away. They snatched us like a hawk—our young ones, not the old, the ones who were strong."

The chief continued, cupping his hands together as if holding a baby bird. "After all of this, they colonized us. The English made themselves chiefs on top of us in a land that was unfamiliar to them. It was no contest." He stretched his long thin arms out straight. "You obey the ones who point their guns so, of course, we had to obey them."

"After all of that, they gave us our independence. They told us, 'All man free. All man get foh gladi.'" *Everyone should be happy.*

The teachers looked at one another and clapped in agreement. Yet the chief only scoffed at their acceptance, saying that they didn't remember what that freedom felt like, but he did. He continued speaking with labored breaths. "The strangers did not teach us about this kind of freedom, this kind of democracy. We all hoped that Siaka Stevens would be the first leader who was not in the pocket of the British, who would not be a houseboy for Britain." He held on to his hands, as if for comfort, and cried out "Ahhhh!" before exhaling.

He rubbed his hands over his face, the folds so deep they stayed where they were instead of smoothing out at his touch. "I have lived through all of these things. So, I know. Why did Bintu's baby die?" he asked softly.

I was surprised that he could have already known what happened at dawn in Tokpombu.

"Our own country is stillborn too!," he said, with a sigh. "Mansa, Vandi, tell me, have you teachers received your salaries from our fadda (father, that is, President Siaka Stevens) this year?," the chief asked.

"No," Vandi said. Mansa held up his hand and counted five months on his fingers since they had last received a paycheck.

The chief leaned forward, Vandi translating "Yes, he is the father, and our first father. For this, he deserves our respect and loyalty. But he is not a *good fadda*. And he is not leading the way a *good father* leads, inside his one-party system." He held his hands about a foot apart. "A snake will always give birth to something long, yes? Stevens and his cronies have been stealing and stealing for twenty good years. They are all dancing to the same beat that gave us these problems in the first place. We are not truly ruling ourselves, yet! Dat snake dey all abot." He repeated. *That snake is crawling about everywhere.*

There was complete silence for a few minutes.

Then he said, "We get so many tiefmen (thiefs) inside we country." He almost spit out the word "tief," a vein throbbing in his neck. He then made a hole with his thumb and index finger. "You see this?" He said it was the size of the diamond Siaka found just ten miles from here. "It was big like an egg (a promise). But he took it. He put it in his own pocket."

Kady knocked and entered again, this time carrying a tray with an acrylic yarn coverlet. She lifted it to reveal a plate of steaming heaps of red rice smothered in a fish stew. Kady stooped around our circle with a plastic tea kettle and a ceramic bowl. The men washed their hands in the thin line of water. Kady handed me a spoon. We shuffled our stools closer together while Kady moved a wobbly corner table to the middle of the circle we'd made. Then we dug into the warm greasy heap of food. The chief lobbed the biggest piece of fish over to "my side," which is the traditional way to honor a stranger who visits. Kady, also in the traditional way, left instead of joining us for our meal.

We ate in complete silence. The fish filled me quickly, so I dipped my spoon into the tray with less frequency. I waited for the others to finish, watching them suck the marrow from the small fish bones and toss them to the ground. With the tray nearly empty now, the chief stretched out his legs on his bench and rinsed his right hand in the stream from the kettle that Vandi tipped for him. His eyes looked soberly at the teachers. "These boys know the future is up to them now." He rubbed one flat palm against the other as if washing his hands of a problem he could no longer carry, and then he yawned. "What is freedom when you've lost the loyalty of your neighbors, when there is fighting among families?" Mansa stood up and motioned for me to do the same. "Leh yu rest now," he said.

The two men gently helped Chief Jusu to his feet, his bare toes clutching the earth to steady himself. He wobbled toward the door, reaching for his cane and then the doorknob. With bowed legs, he escorted us back into the bright daylight.

"If I don't see you again," the chief said, "I am so happy to have met you." He turned to the teachers, "Nar foh bia no more." *Bear up, that's all you can do.* I extended my hand to say good-bye, in the same format in which I'd greeted him. This time, when I held the chief's hand, I felt its tired pulse.

On the way back, we walked in silence until we had returned to the hammock bridge. Stopping to rest before crossing, I thanked the teachers for taking me to meet the chief.

"He has lived and seen it all," Mansa said. "And he's not afraid to tell the truth." He put his arm around my shoulder. "Our generation, we are more fed up because we expect things our parents and especially our grandparents didn't know or care about."

I stood beside these teachers listening to the flow of the water, feeling their lament, but also our connection. I thought about the strength of the river for a moment and not the hammock bridge that supported our crossing. I thought of how, over time, it had likely smoothed out this land—both the high parts and the low parts. I wondered what would happen to this country.

"Eh, Sia Tokpombu," Mansa said, looking down at the rapids below. "That chief is like an old waterside stone. E no fraid ren." *He's not afraid of rain.*

# CHAPTER 10

# Fishpond

As I cast indeed my net into their sea and meant to catch good fish;
but always did I draw up the head of some ancient God.

—FRIEDRICH NIETZSCHE

Before the sun was even a glimmer, I sat up in my bed feeling energetic and looking forward to the predictable routines of the morning. My body, ready to meet the day, was now synchronized with the hens and ducks who, when released from the straw huts where they boarded each night, exploded down the alley of kitchens, clucking and quacking at the same time that they scoured the earth for as much leftover seed as they could find before the morning brooms had cleared it away. Even my ears were delighted by reliably happy rhythms: sandaled feet scuffling across the road; the beats of the doun-doun drum announcing the start of morning chores and the call to prayer; the morning chant to Allah, which reverberated not only through the walls of my house, but somehow even in my chest. "We all gladi today!," Pa Bindi said exuberantly. Our diligence had paid off: the fish we'd placed in the fishpond we'd created were ready for harvesting. Everyone in the village had been alerted. Pa Bindi told me that this was going to be his proudest moment in a "looooong time!" As of today, he would hold status as the first man in the chiefdom to harvest from a constructed fishpond.

But our ambitions did not stop there. Today, we would drain the pond and deliver at least one or two mature fish to every family in the village, a welcome (and essential) protein source in a region where there were too few streams to meet the demand of a growing population. First, though, the adult fish would lay new eggs that would spawn a new generation of young fish while we refilled the pond.

I followed Pa Bindi beneath the canopy of KT's fruit trees—an orange and grapefruit orchard that bordered the path down to the stream, and we chatted about how quickly the four months had passed since David, a Peace Corps fisheries volunteer, accepted my invitation to teach Sahr Joe and me how to build fishponds in Gorama. The three of us had worked to master the construction for an entire week. I understood what was required by studying the bullet points outlined on a few mimeographed worksheets about the farming of tilapia, a fish native to North Africa. I also read the booklet cover to cover. It described a quality, not quantity, approach to best pond practices that emphasized "proper site selection, management and record-keeping."

We waved to our neighbors as we passed them, acknowledging their curiosity and confirming, "Yes. Today nar di day." *Today is the day.* As we approached the waterside, Pa made a noise that sounded like he was clearing his throat in a loud, deliberate manner: guttural at first, then high pitched. A voice called back, providing the "all clear"—no women were bathing.

Descending now toward the stream, we were greeted by women who had gathered with hooped nets and woven fishing baskets. I watched Sia Fengai, the leader among the women, standing in knee-high water upstream, call out to frighten the fish she'd spotted; this alerted her companions below to ready their nets and scoop up as many as they could when the fish reached them in the current. Clusters of women had been fishing from streams together like this for hundreds of years. But with fewer fish now, and the larger ones rare, farmers were enthusiastic about the possibility of building fishponds. No one had ever domesticated fish in this chiefdom. Sia Fengai called out, "Which time? When the sun stands on your shadow?" It's a phrase that means noon.

"No. We will harvest the first fishpond in Gorama just before cooking time." Pa Bindi stood with his chest puffed out like a proud father.

"Oh yahhh," she said. "We gladi too much!" All the women clapped with excitement, their eyes on Pa.

"This fish get foh swito !," he said. "Tilapia get plenty bone foh suck." (chew)." This fish will be delicious. *Fishbones are a vital calcium source here.*

Building and stocking the pond had been a collective effort. Men took turns coming to the aid of Pa Bindi, helping him build secure walls around the pond that could withstand a heavy storm so the fish wouldn't escape. The women took turns cooking food to bring to the men as they labored.

This project had begun fifty miles away at the Makali fish station, where I'd retrieved the fingerling fish (*pikinfish*) by placing them in plastic containers that I secured to the back of my motorbike. I made several stops along the two-and-a-half-hour journey to replenish the water for the fragile fish and, when I arrived in the village, again swapped out some of the original water before gently stocking the pond.

To build such a pond, it was necessary to have a stream that ran year-round through the swamp—preferably an already or partially developed swamp, like Pa Bindi's. The labor of clearing away the razor-sharp elephant grasses had been grueling, and the payoff uncertain. I hoped it would become a demo for the other farmers in the chiefdom. It was more than that for Pa Bindi. Our efforts captured something in his imagination: unlike a battery, radio, or car engine, this was something he could build with his own hands. "Fishponds are new, but they are new on top of old," he'd told me, signaling that such ponds were in keeping with the long tradition of stewardship of the land.

When we arrived, I set my metal buckets down beside the down-sloping end of the pond. I reached into my backpack and pulled out a small piece of mesh and a new bamboo pipe I'd been saving for this occasion. I unfolded the instructions David had left for me, explaining how the filter would prevent fish from escaping when we drained the pond.

"Yes, o. We don't want any fish foh lef inside dis pond," Pa said, examining the mesh, then setting it aside for a moment while he unplugged the mud from the drainage pipe. Together we figured out how to insert the mesh.

We discussed how the fish would collect in the pit we'd dug—a natural holding tank—where we would scoop them out with nets and their offspring would remain safely in the shallows, along with more eggs in the mud below. The mesh would prevent both the eggs and smaller fish from flowing out with the water. When the babies matured and reproduced, we would know that we'd created a self-sustaining biosphere.

"We'll start to refill the pond before heading back to the village with the fish," I said.

Together, we put things in place. As the water began to slowly drain, I stood on the bank feeling a deep satisfaction. So far, from the time we'd built the pond, to when I visited to the Makali Fish station to fetch the two jugs of fish for the pond, every step had progressed smoothly.

Pa Bindi pointed to a fern growing near the pond and described how this was a good plant to see by his swamp—suggesting that soil conditions were already improving since he had three developed plots and a pond. I was skeptical that we'd see such a marked change, but I couldn't know. I didn't have Pa Bindi's intimate knowledge of this land.

I told Pa Bindi I'd meet him in three hours when the pond water would be less than an inch deep; I'd explain the rest then. He cut off a walking stick for me from the underbrush with his machete and handed it to me, reminding me to step with caution as I entered the dense layers of forest. The V-shaped opening at the bottom of the stick was to restrain a snake in the off-chance I encountered one.

This was the longest solitary walk inside the forest—nearly three miles—where I would be completely alone. Before today, someone had always been in front of me or close behind and with a machete; even children carried them.

I started out with a sense of wonder stronger than any apprehension. Before long, I entered a dark thicket of bamboo trees that suddenly lit up in a silvery green with tree trunks so shiny with dew you'd think there had been a rain. The faint sound of a stream caught my attention. I recognized this spot from the time Finda and Sahr Kondeh had brought me here for the "beeest wata nar we chiefdom." Beside the spring was the stream where their mother and the other village women had gone on one of their "fishing expeditions" last year. Just like the uplands, the streams here were fished on a seasonal rotation. I remembered how later that night, when we were sitting on the back porch, Ella described how fisherwomen sometimes used leaves that released a dye into the water, tricking the fish into gathering in this dark "safe" harbor where they could be netted efficiently.

Pa Bindi had told me a story about how pumwes (white men) had distributed sacks of fertilizer for swamp farming with a warning label, "Kills Fish." One woman who knew how to read this had told all the others.

"Wetin appin?," I asked.

He explained in Krio that the fertilizer killed all the fish in the stream.

I asked what the fish tasted like. He said the taste was no different and that everyone was excited by having so many fish to cook at one time. Then he drew a stark portrait of how the fertilizer poisoned the stream and how the surface darkened. Pa Bindi said it had been a hard lesson.

But we both knew it was more than that.

As I reached Tembeda, I encountered several women with babies tied to their backs. A toddler let out a blood-curdling cry when he saw me, presumably jolted by the unfamiliarity of my light complexion, as if I were a monster, which provoked a gale of laughter. I knew they'd be talking about it for days.

Tembeda was a postcard West African village with its circular collection of six round mud huts with thatched palm-frond roofs. Goats and sheep were nestled beneath the shaded hut awnings. I called out to a group of children kicking a plastic bag filled with sand, asking them where Joe Samuel's house was. The children pointed to an A-frame kitchen where two women were occupied beside a stove. One of the women smiled through a space between her front teeth and extended her wrist for me to shake since her hands were still coated in the oil they were preparing.

"Joe Samuel dey?," I asked. Is Joe Samuel here?

"E don lef," she said. *He left.*

"Usai?" *Where?*

"To another village. We man left early."

Joe left! Even though it wasn't unusual for someone to be delayed or change plans, it still took me aback.

The older of the two women stood slowly so that I could tell her hip was in pain; the lines in her face fell heavily too. She told me her name was Mariatu. The younger woman, Fatmata, dressed in jeans, eyed me curiously.

"Yu nar Lebanese?," she blurted. "I saw a woman who looks like you near Farrah's shop in Koidu." She picked up one of the surrounding toddlers whose neck and wrists were bedecked with cowry shells.

"Me nar Peace Corps, nohto Lebanese," I said, happy to make the distinction between the diamond miners and me.

"I heard about you, but we haven't met until today." She studied me further. "You favor a person who is diluted."

"Wetin diluted?"

"Person who is mixed."

"I no mix," I said.

We both smiled. This wasn't the first-time people thought I was Lebanese—mixed. I had black hair, brown eyes, and olive skin.

She ran her hands over my nose, forehead, and cheekbones. Then she told me my forearms had hair like a Lebanese. Grabbing them, she pointed to my neck. "Yu get cut neck." ("Cut" necks, lined with horizontal creases, are considered a sign of beauty.)

I laughed and pulled the gift from my backpack, "Ma Sando bin send dis."

"Ma Sando de always somba we! (gifts us)," she said, pleased. *Ma Sando always thinks of us!*

I asked the women how far Joe Samuel's swamp was, thinking I could go there alone. But their answer discouraged me.

"E far lek Tokpombu."

My head was beginning to soak with sweat. "Do you think Joe Samuel will be back soon?"

"We no know," Mariatu said.

I wasn't sure if it made sense to wait any longer. Mariatu then scooped cooked rice from a pot on the fire and spread it onto the enamel tray. She handed me a spoon. "Leh we eat now." she said. "Yu nar we stranger." *We always show hospitality to our strangers.*

I held up my right hand, reciting the now familiar proverb. "If you are some side where they walk on three sticks . . ." Then, as was customary, I only scooped up small handfuls of the dish from the segment facing me, never crossing the imaginary line drawn by etiquette around the others' food.

Mariatu turned her head and surprised me by calling out to the children who were still kicking the sandbag and waiting for their turn to eat, "Abu, Matru, carry Sia Tokpombu nar di orange garden." She stood and disappeared behind the cement house in the village.

Abu and Matru held my hands as they led me to a grassy path on the far side off the village. We walked about 800 yards into the forest past a tall coconut tree until we reached a muddy stream where we dipped our toes, then we continued to a grove of thick orange trees loaded with ripe green fruit. Abu scrambled up the tree and beat the branches with a stick while Matru spread out a large net to catch them. We squatted in a circle, peeling and sucking oranges, the juices squirting out the sides of our mouths. Abu said every fruit or nut tree in the village belonged to a child born here. Every placenta is buried with a seedling.

With the sun standing on our shadows, we took our time on the path back to the village. I stopped to admire the arching palm fronds of the towering coconut tree, its trunk arched like a fishtail. I wondered how old it was and who had planted it. Had that child survived, led a good life, a long life?

When we arrived back at the kitchen of Joe Samuel's wives, there was still no sign of him. I'd been waiting now for what felt like almost two hours and needed to be heading back to Bindi's pond. I looked at Fatmata, who just shrugged and then scooped water from a bucket and splashed it onto her children's faces. "E dey cam." *He's coming.* "E dey pan Blackman Time today." *He's on Black man's time today.*

Our trainer Sidiki had spoken to the put-down implied by so-called Black Man's Time, noting that how we keep time can support the making of hierarchies among people in the same way skin color can.

"It has always been about more than a wisecrack about being late!," he said. "We are referring to how the BBC announced Greenwich Mean Time 'at the top of the hour.'" In former days, Sierra Leoneans learned the hours, but not the minutes. "We actually adjusted our own time to these hourly newscasts." In America, time was money. Teachers held you accountable by telling you that you could never keep a job if you weren't on time: bosses fired people who showed up late, missed deadlines. Here, it seemed the only lateness that mattered was the harvest.

When it was time to depart, I tore a piece of paper out of a notepad I kept in the front zipper of my backpack and wrote, *Dear Joe Samuel, I'm sorry we were not able to meet today. I enjoyed my time in Tembeda with your family. Thank you for the hospitality. Sia Tokpombu.*

I thanked the co-wives, Mariatu and Fatmata, and we hugged goodbye like old friends, promising to see one another again soon.

With a steady, hurried pace, I headed back down the trail. A sudden thump called my attention to a startled bush deer and her three young fawns, who ran off so quickly that I wondered if I'd really seen them. A blister was beginning to form on the side of my foot, so I decided to rest momentarily on the rocks—still warm from the sun. I indulged the urge to spread out on the sloped granite, put my face to the sky, take a deep breath, and shut my eyes. A noise startled me, and I looked up. I could feel the silhouette of a man inside the shadow of the rocky outcrop. Scrambling to my feet, I saw Pa Bindi's warm and familiar face.

"Ehhh Sia Tokpombu," he said. "How is Joe Samuel?"

"E no bin dey." *He wasn't there.*

We stood together for a few hushed moments and beheld the view. Then Pa twisted his small frame and pointed to the thick forest behind us—the unfarmed land that had never been cut down. Tapping the granite beneath us, he described how we were sitting along the natural boundary of the protected forest. "Nobody farms beyond this rock," he said.

I assumed Pa Bindi was considering the danger involved in felling such trees, some nearly eighty feet. But that wasn't the reason he gave.

"Nar sacred land," he said.

Pa Bindi led me toward the highest—and more jagged—part of the rocks so I could better view the old-growth forest. Past the granite mound was an incline of thickening hardwood trees twice the size of the steel girders that held up bridges back home.

"The plants that grow here have sooo much powa. Nar plenty medicine de inside dat forest-o!," Pa interjected.

"Herbal medicine?"

"Here is where we can bury."

"Not in the graveyard?"

"The people who understand the forest are buried inside here."

I explained that, back home, we go to great lengths to wrench those worlds apart, distinguishing how we heal from how we die.

"Oh, but dis forest is our life. If we destroy this, we destroy our history; all of who we are will be consumed with it."

With so much mining going on beyond the chiefdom's borders, how could Bindi be so confident that this forest would remain protected?

"What if a road were built here?," I asked. "In America, many, many trees are cut down and many people are relocated to make room for new roads."

"Yes, the mining company can sometimes do that. Those are men with small minds."

"So, this land is protected?"

"It must be!," he answered. I watched his eyes track a flock of crows flying in the distance. Then, he said more ferociously, "No! Nohto anybody get foh build road inside dis forest." His voice was resolute in a way I'd never heard it before. "If we countryman poil (spoil) what holds us together, we will have nothing." He laughed at such implausibility. "The temptation of wealth may poison our leaders, but they know too that the real wealth is here. It's protected by law." He spoke as if it were as specific and pure a truth as the moon's rising.

As we approached the pond, I was surprised to hear women singing and laughing. I hadn't expected any spectators; only Pa Bindi and I were needed to harvest the fish. When the pond came into view, I saw the women from this morning gathered knee-deep in mud, slogging back and forth through it as they netted the large fish at the deep end and carried them back to their baskets on the walls of the pond.

"Ehh, Sia Besty," Sia Sam called with a wide, innocent smile. "We caught all di big-big fish. Dem pleeeeeenty!"

"Oh no!," I called back. "Yu no supposed foh walka inside di pohto-pohto." *You weren't supposed to step inside the mud.* "Sometime, yu foh don kill di pikinfish." *You might have killed their offspring!"*

A look of confusion clouded the women's faces as they trampled through the mud, crushing the new eggs and suffocating the young gills of the baby fish that would have repopulated the pond. I didn't have it in me to say more.

"Yes. We caught all the fish," Sia Sam said. "We have so many today from this dry pond. Tenki, tenki!"

She and three other women stooped and slung their big hoop nets through the mud again, making noises, looking for the baby fish the traditional way. I noticed a frog leap in front of the women. Frogs were likely to take up residence in this pond if there were no fish. Farmers liked eating frogs, too.

Staring helplessly at the scene, I understood that it was already too late to save the offspring or eggs of this brood. As the women counted the number of fish and began to portion them out, I couldn't mask my disappointment. Four months of work—one-quarter of my time here felt wasted.

Sia Sam cast a sideways glance at me. "Yu no gladi bak (again)?"

Pa Bindi, who'd been watching, said, "We shouldn't have walked inside the mud because it killed the young fish who could not yet be born."

I pointed to the water pipe to show Sia Sam how we had filled and emptied the pond.

"Dis nar new way di Peace Corps uman dey show we ow foh fish," Pa Bindi said. I wondered why "di Pa" was only telling the women this now.

"All of yu," Sia Sam called to the others. "Listen, Besty get foh learn we about something we no know." All eyes were suddenly on me. "Talk now," he said to me.

I shared with the women how the new "grow fishing" worked and saw baffled expressions wash over their faces.

As we walked back in a long line along the narrow trail to the village, I also saw embarrassment in their postures. I told Pa Bindi that I was surprised he'd recruited the women for the harvest. In our months of conversation, we hadn't discussed this.

"Women catch and cook fish," he responded, then let out a sigh. "Ehhh Besty, we de fall down and grap." *We fall and stand back up.*

Pa Bindi made plans to refill the pond in the morning while I rode my motorbike to Makali to collect new fingerlings for the fishpond.

"Our fish story," I reassured him, "go go before."

*Our fish story will go on.*

# CHAPTER 11

# Directions of Wonder

You don't see the world as it is—you see the world as you are.
—THE TALMUD

When I opened my door after a cloudburst had passed through, the entire Muslim side of the street was tucked beneath the arch of a newly forming rainbow. Moments later, a more dazzling second rainbow appeared above it. In haste, I began lugging one of my recliner chairs onto the front verandah, aware of how nice it would be to sit outside and watch—to enjoy the sweet earthy smell of the cool after-rain just gazing at the rainbow until it vanished.

By the time I finished wrestling the chair's bulky frame out the front door and swept up the goat kaka I'd managed to smear in the lugging, the rainbow had already been swallowed by the bright blue. During all my heaving and hauling, I was unaware that my across-the-street neighbors were watching the rainbows and watching me, too. Finda and Estelle ran from the direction of Pa Sorie's house and made a short play poking fun at my efforts, laughing and mimicking the way I scratched my chin, tied up my skirt, and heaved the chair: they even mimed the way I'd scrunched my face as I stepped over the goat kaka.

Finda leaned on my porch railing and pointed to Pa Sorie, an old man who, beneath the shelter of his own front porch, spent most early mornings teaching his grandsons Arabic on small slate squares before they set out for the Tikonkor Primary School. His gleaming long white tunic, the pink scarf he draped around his neck, and his self-possessed demeanor suggested he was the natural born teacher the children said he was.

"Pa Sorie, Amara, Tamba, Kai, Aminata—all of we been luk (look) you!"

I blushed. Even in the distance, I could see that Pa Sorie's friendly wave was full of his usual warm laughter. Whenever he and his wives watched me pass behind their house on my return from the stream, water splashing over the rim of the bucket I struggled to balance on my head, this Pa fell into a relentless round of laughter hiccups that sent the women and then me into bouts of hilarity, too, which made it even harder to hold the bucket steady.

I slouched back in my chair, admiring how free the girls seemed as they leaned against the iron railing of my verandah, waving their arms in the air for stability. But as I gazed into their steady blinks, I became unsettled by how thin the girls had grown compared with a few months ago when they had the soft, round look of the last harvest on their bodies. Now their limbs seemed longer, their eyes and teeth set more boldly alongside their drawn cheekbones. Farmers in Tokpombu made light of this expected hunger, calling it "Hungry Season style."

When I was their age, August meant corn on the cob, tomatoes, cantaloupe, plums, and watermelon, hamburgers and hotdogs on the grill, Dairy Queen Blizzards, all before we went shopping for our back-to-school clothes and supplies. I didn't know that people waited for a harvest like this.

Estelle and Finda both asked if I liked being "one grain," meaning by myself on the verandah like one grain of rice.

"Yes. Sometimes I like to be one grain," I answered. They didn't know the months it had taken me to muster the courage to work with farmers here and to sit outside like this, instead of secluded inside my house with my curtains drawn.

"Yu nohto sik," Finda said with equal parts curiosity and accusation, her eyes narrowing. In her world, only the elderly or ill—those who can't make it to the farm—sat alone on their porches. It was hard to convey this very American craving for physical space to be alone with one's thoughts. My hosts, both adults and children, felt it was their obligation to visit me and "humbug me" so I would never feel alone or abandoned.

Finda tapped my shoulder. "People here are afraid of someone who doesn't make conversation with others. They must be hiding something."

When Finda's mother, Ma Sando, appeared from around the corner, she reprimanded the girls for harassing me and told them she was heading to the farm. After that, she'd be checking on her ailing father, who had taken up much of her time and worry in recent weeks.

"Sometime, the rice go begin for dry," Ma Sando said with a look of new hope in her eyes, referring to the final stage of the rice plant before harvest. With last season's upland rice consumed, everyone was eager for the new harvest.

As Ma Sando crossed the street, I noticed how she appeared more tired than usual. When she was out of earshot, Estelle announced, "Sia Besty, we want to sweep for you." Like most of the village's children, these girls knew that any small chore could mean that I might offer them something to eat—leftover rice or yams, sugar cubes, a cup of powdered milk mixed with hot tea. Estelle patted her belly. "Sia Besty, hungry de pan top we," she said. *Hunger is on top of us.*

I told them I didn't have anything to share today. But the girls didn't believe me. My own full hips were the same size as a few months ago. Finda curled onto my lap. "Yu get," she insisted.

I shook my head. "I no get nutting," I said, clapping my empty hands. It was true. My shelves were bare.

She slid off my lap and tucked her hands into her armpits, glancing at me sideways. "Yu greedy."

"I am not greedy!"

Finda uncrossed her arms. "Yes. Yu nar greedy pawsin (person)."

She grabbed my hand and pulled me up out of my chair. Estelle held my other hand, and they led me back through my house to my supply room. Its door was slightly open and revealed the Ministry of Agriculture tools and bags of seed rice. The girls stood tall now, persistent as market women peering in at the twenty burlap bags of seed rice. They shifted their weight from one leg to the other, each pulling on the worn thin dress of the other. Finda pointed. There was enough rice inside this room to get the whole village through to the next harvest. She licked her parched lips, saying, "You no give we small?," and cupped her hands.

"This is seed rice," I told them. "It's for planting in swamps, not for eating. The upland rice will be ready soon."

Both girls turned their empty eyes up toward me. Their hunger wasn't starvation. Their bodies weren't of the guilt-inducing fundraising kind of images that convinced Americans to send checks or drop pennies in a jar at the store cash register. No one here was as powerless or broken as those media images suggested.

But this hunger, which could reduce two or three meals a day to one, was so close that it beat you down. It was hard to dismiss the girls' eagerness when my childhood hunger had been sated by running to the third drawer down in my mother's white Formica kitchen to grab a bag of Lay's potato chips or a tube of Pringles.

I shut and locked the storeroom door and ushered the disappointed girls outside. I asked if that meant not even fried plantains, what Sia Sam had been selling in front of Pa Bindi's house earlier that morning.

"Nobody bin cook foh we," Finda said. "Nar rice no more we wan foh eat." *We only want to eat rice.*

Yes, of course, it was always about rice here. I told the girls I knew where we could find both ripe and unripe plantains by the elder Sanusi's house, referring to where Finda's grandfather lived with their uncle Peter, his wife, Masa, and her children.

At that moment, a young man came sprinting down the hill from the direction of the Sanusi house, waving his arms and shouting. Finda, Estelle, and I watched my across-the-street neighbors nervously and warily surround the man, who pointed back up the hill. The man darted toward Finda and taking her hands, said, "Di Pa een condition dey change. Luk for yu mama. Cam wit am quick!" *Bring her to me quickly!*

Finda's face fell. She tilted her head as if to keep her world from spinning. While the girls made a breathless mad dash toward the forest trail, I followed behind several villagers heading toward "the Pa's" house with urgent footsteps.

More farmers hovered along the road at the foot of Peter's home. I was led to the Pa suspended inside a hammock that was tied between two beams on his front porch. Ella was beside him with a bucket of cold water, twisting out pieces of cloth and applying them to his forehead. As his granddaughter washed him, I watched Pa's eyes sink deeper inside the bones of his cheeks under the soft pressure of her hands. His long legs and torso filled the entire sack of the woven rope that cradled him.

Audible panting and footsteps behind me announced the arrival of Finda and Ma Sando, who took over the washing from her eldest daughter.

"Tuye," she said to the Pa over and over, her lips making a near kiss. It was a tender expression that conveyed empathy for what another endures. Pa Sanusi's eyes were so far back in his head, it was hard to know if he heard or understood.

Ma Sando saw the concern on my face. "Tuye," she told me too.

"Tuye," I repeated to her and then to her father. I fingered the diamond weave of the hammock's frayed rope, careful not to cause it to sway.

I remembered the day when I first met this Pa. It was between Christmas and New Year's in my first year. Finda, Ella, and I brought him a young coconut to drink. He was perched in his upright mahogany chair, his knobby elbows resting on his knobby knees, his long fingers curled up inside themselves, so all you could see of his hands were his knobby knuckles. He didn't shake hands like most men did, presumably from a lifetime of grasping a hoe, machete, or axe. I had the sense that it was more than arthritis that kept his hands so tightly clenched, as if letting go could unravel everything. He seemed to be the invisible ladder the people in this village clung to in order to lift themselves up.

Ma Sando offered her father a cup of water. But he said, "I no get thirst." I looked down at the Pa's hands. I thought I saw his grip finally loosening.

All around us now, the women had begun cooking, and the smell of rice and groundnut sauce filled the air. Finda told me they were making rice porridge for the Pa, though we both knew the Pa was beyond eating.

As word of Pa Sanusi's imminent death spread beyond Tokpombu, many other people began stopping by—farmers bowing their heads to Pa or touching him, then milling around in front of the porch or behind the house where the kitchen fire burned with cooking yams, enough for everyone who visited. I watched Ma Sando's brother Peter capture two Guinea fowl for the occasion, tie the birds' legs with a thin rope, and take a blade to their necks. He handed both dead fowl to Kumba, Ma Sando's younger sister, who carried the birds away.

The talk of the town was focused on one thing and one thing only—the Pa's unstable condition. It was clear that Pa Sanusi was a man everybody loved, and a man who loved everybody. When Mohammed's taxi passed, he slowed and stuck his head out the window, "Ow di sik Pa?" Before the week was over, even miners would find their way back to town to pay their respects to the ailing old man.

A few days later, Sahr Joe visited my house after sunset with a small jug of palm wine. We drank, and he leaned forward with his hands on his chin, "Dis Pa nar rice farmer who don plant coffee, cocoa, and palm oil inside all these hills. But ehhh, di old man is tired now." Joe took a few more slurps from his cup, fingering the red ants on top, then squashing them between his fingers and flicking them on the floor. In his loosened state and mine, it seemed to me that Sahr Joe was rehearsing his eulogy.

I sat there, knowing how little exposure I'd had to death and its rituals, and that loss wasn't something I regularly experienced the way everyone here did. I was nine when my maternal grandfather, Harry, died. My parents left us kids with a babysitter while they drove to Albany to inter him, as if to keep me and my brothers safe inside the bubble of a Norman Rockwell childhood. After my parents returned home, I rarely heard Harry's name mentioned again. Thirteen years later, I stood with my family in a receiving line, greeting mourners with pieces of torn black ribbon fastened to our clothing—a ritual duplication of the feeling that a life had been torn from ours. As with my grandfather, Grandma Lillian's name didn't come up much again. "Life was for the living."

But now I was here understanding that if you gloss over death, you also gloss over life. No one in my family visited the graves of the dead.

"The Pa was a disciplined man who worked every day! But now he will soon cross to the other side." Sahr Joe spoke with a melancholy that had a dirge-like quality.

I felt a strange shiver down my neck—as if in that very room, the dead were now gathering, filling up space around and between us, their omniscience the reason no one swept inside their homes at night.

"It would be for nothing to carry him to the clinic because he's already lived his life," Joe said. "Old people are like termite houses; they have more life inside of them than you've ever considered—boku-boku eggs! Each egg, each bug-bug, that is their wisdom."

"In America," I said, "we no lek foh age." *In America we resist aging.*

"Watin? Yu no lek old?" He screwed up his face in confusion like I'd just insulted someone.

"No, people even have procedures to take their wrinkles away." I pulled my face back to demonstrate what a facelift does.

"Ehh no!," he exclaimed, shaking his head as if this was the strangest, saddest thing he'd ever heard.

Back home, I explained, we were apologetic, not for being old, but for looking old. I shared a memory with Joe about how my grandmother dyed her hair red to cover the gray, the same shade as the lipstick she consistently applied after every meal without needing a pocket mirror. I would ask her, "Grandma, how do you know where your lips are?" She always answered, "When you've had your lips as long as I have, honey, you know where they are."

"One grandfather died before I was born," I told Joe. "My middle name, Joan, begins with a 'J' because his name, Joseph, began with that letter."

"Who is your other grandpa?"

"Harry."

"Udat get di name Harry now?" *Who is Harry's namesake now?*

"No one. All the grandchildren had already been born by the time he died."

"So, no one ebba repeat een name again?," he said, meaning his name had died in the family too.

"No."

Joe looked confused. "Here, when people die, we remember them at every ceremony, every libation." He also drew attention to the fact that here the dead are promoted. "They are even better than when they were alive."

"Nde-ble-sia," I offered, remembering the word I'd been taught for the ones whose names were forgotten but not their souls.

---

The fourth day was not like the three before. Ma Sando and Ella became consumed with caring for Ma Sando's father, so Finda and Sahr Kondeh spent most of their after-school days with me. When the three of us went to check on their grandfather's condition, Pa was no longer in the hammock but on a straw mattress on the ground. Ella and Ma Sando were still wringing out the cloth pieces in cold water and applying them to his forehead and chest, but less frequently than before.

Ella looked up at me. "E no dey eat. E no dey drink. E no dey talk." She added, "All of life is in the bosom of God. We all get foh ber." *We will all be buried.*

Since yesterday, the Pa had grown even thinner and more ashen. No more words were spoken between shallow breaths. The one hand, now resting on his chest was no longer brown but the gray blue of nightfall. Suddenly Pa Sanusi opened his eyes and smiled at his daughter and grand-daughter with stunning momentary alertness. "Ah gladi," he said in a barely audible whisper before his eyes closed again.

Ma Sando continued to place the cool cloths along his torso, all with the familiar synchronized movements she used when she pounded her clothes on the rocks. I couldn't tell if a tear fell from her face or if it was a bead of sweat dripping off her tall forehead. Either way, I was deeply aware that I was watching a man, a father, a grandfather die.

I was returning down the road when I heard the loud cries. I hurried back toward Pa Sanusi's home and found a community already gathered on the verandah. Ma Sando was surrounded by a swell of sisters, wailing with her. Several men, Peter, and the town chief among them, looked solemn as they arranged chairs for the people who would soon be arriving and paying their respects. The parlor quickly filled with women crying out, "No! No! Ehhh, Ehhh. Di Pa. Ehh." I listened to their guttural heaves, sounds from deep inside them. They lifted their empty hands into the air and fisted them on their way down, thumping the damp earthen floor beneath them. Finda and Sahr Kondeh stood on the edge of the property, close enough so that I could see their pained, teary expressions.

Ma Sando had once taught me the Kono-Mende word for child: Ndo. Ndo means "the one who will bury you." It wasn't until this moment that I understood this was a word that told the story of the proper order of a life. When parents have to bury a child, there is a phase in the mourning process where the men will dress as women and the women will dress as men, reflecting how the death of a child profoundly disturbs that order.

I knew Sahr Kondeh and Finda were watching not just the loss of their grandfather but a generation that had witnessed the birth of their new nation, who had breathed the fumes of colonialism, the hope of self-determination, and then perceived its downfall.

Years later, when my father died, the memory of Pa Sanusi's passing surfaced. There was comfort in seeing myself, now a grown woman with children, accepting the place of "ndo" to my father, now understanding the full measure of the word. Ndo is a universal word that names all our futures and gives a universe a home.

I offered my condolences to the family and headed back out onto the verandah where the men were still gathered. I overheard conversations about what needed to be done in the next few hours before the same-day burial—how the carpenter and tailor needed to be notified, and men selected to dig the grave, and other men to bathe the body.

That evening, when Joe dropped by, our visit was consumed with chatter about planting rice on our demo swamp. Before he left, he asked me what I was going to contribute to the seventh-day ceremony for Pa Sanusi.

"I can go to the Koidu market tomorrow and buy some rice for it."

He shook his head. "It has to be done today for the people coming to pay their respects tomorrow."

"I can go first thing in the morning and come back quick."

"It won't be enough."

I had never heard Joe tell me something wasn't possible. Our relationship had always been one of imagination and potential. "But then what am I supposed to do, Joe?"

He pointed to the storage room.

"Our seed rice? We can't just give it away!"

Sahr Joe ignored me and began walking with his lantern toward the storeroom as if to help himself. "Twenty tropenzpan go du (will be enough)."

"Twenty pounds of rice! How about just ten?" Standing behind him in the storeroom while my eyes scanned the eight different varieties, wondering which bag he would pull from, I pointed to the Roc 6 because I knew we had more of that than the other varieties. He didn't answer immediately, so I grabbed an empty sack from a pile in the corner and dipped the tropenzpan into the pile of grains. He shined the light into the new sack while telling me the Pa had been adequately bathed, placed in a box, and dressed in white.

"Nar di same dirty dehm get for ber we," he said. *We are all buried in the same earth.* I kept filling it, uneasy as I watched the more considerable bag slump as it grew emptier.

———

On the sixth night after Pa Sanusi's death, people began gathering for the twenty-four-hour seventh-day ceremony at his compound. A makeshift shelter was quickly assembled and set up in front of the house, with benches and a podium. The smell of burnt hair and skin caught the edge of my nose while a large goat was suspended over a fire between two poles. All night the men drank palm wine and bani (the chief's wine, *bamboo wine*), along with coffee and soft drinks. Rice was plentiful and served on large enamel trays. Praise for Pa was unrelenting. "Dis Pa sabi work!" *This Pa knew how to work.* "Dis Pa made a big-big farm for his family." "Dis Pa respected mortal man. "Dis Pa no ebba put bad word upon any person." It was well after midnight when I returned to my house to sleep.

In the morning, over half the village took their seats along the rows of benches under the shelter. Sunlight broke through morning clouds with its searing heat. Men took turns speaking from the podium, again offering praise and testimonials about the Pa. Hymns lasted until the sun bore down directly upon us. The elders sacrificed another goat and poured libations for the ancestors.

As the service wound down, there was talk of the Pa making his transition to yonda side, where his spirit was now "crossing the big-big water." By then, I understood that though Pa Sanusi was gone, he would live forever in the villagers' hearts and minds. Buried in the Poro bush, Joe had explained, the forest plants would consume his knowledge. "This burial will bring relief to the next generation," he said.

That Pa Sanusi's soul—his spiritual self—could be contained within the forest trees of the Poro bush pointed to the limitations in the ways that I had always understood death. The idea of our spirits, our knowledge—not only our names—forever being present for the next generation was a concept that made every moment before now a continuous knowing. *Before Before.* Remaining present in death, not just in our minds but in nature. Not ashes to ashes, dust to dust but soul grasping tree and tree grasping soul.

CHAPTER 12

# Felt-Tipped

Prejudice is a burden that confuses the past, threatens the future,
and renders the present inaccessible.

—MAYA ANGELOU

In early winter, when I received my mother's letter, I was filled with a sense
that the intense division I had felt between my life in Tokpombu and my life
back home had melted away. The part of me that had instinctively walled
myself off from the inevitable daily suffering here had retreated. I began to
accept that the frustration, loss, heartache, and greed belonged not just to
the village of Tokpombu, any more than their joy did. Through the months
of building our friendships, here wasn't someone else's so-called Third
World (now called "Global South") but all the world's creation—and my
inheritance too. Sierra Leone's diamonds had traveled to nearly every continent. Only recently, it now felt, were people brutally trafficked from their
ancestral homeland to a world without the intention of giving them the
full measure of their worth.

Then I opened the letter—on tissue-thin monogrammed stationery
composed with my mother's purple felt-tipped pen and read. "Today, we
are going to the golf course and having cocktails with the Levines at four.
Dr. and Mrs. Levine's daughter got married last month, and they are going
to show us the proofs from the wedding." And then, "Your father played
his usual Wednesday golf today while I took the day off to finish knit-
ting a cable sweater." I could feel beads of sweat forming on my neck, my
forehead.

Just as I was starting to understand that resolving conflict is more often about restoring harmony than establishing blame, that caring for the elderly is a privilege, not a burden, that I was finally orienting toward this life that I'd assigned myself . . . my American Express card-carrying, diamond-ring-wearing, Gucci-buckled "You're not going to take those Marimekko sheets to Africa" mother was coming to visit with my father! Oh damn!

I looked down at the letter and read aloud to Margaret, the Scottish nurse whose two-bedroom bungalow provided respite for Peace Corps volunteers living in the Kono District: "We are looking forward to seeing you. Have you heard of Dakar? We're flying there direct from New York before we take the next plane to where you are."

"Have I heard of Dakar!," I sagged back into the rattan chair in Margaret's parlor and rolled my eyes. "I had no idea this was something they wanted to do."

"You are fortunate then—to get such a nice surprise," Margaret said. "For how many weeks?"

"Not even. Just days. Six." I groaned.

"Well then, you're welcome to use my house as a base for the two days your parents are in Kono," she offered, "unless they are going to spend a night in the village."

I could not imagine my mother spending a night in the village.

Both Margaret and I recognized that more than two days upcountry would be challenging, especially now, with preparations for President Joseph Momoh's upcoming inauguration underway in every one of the country's sixteen provincial headquarters. General Momoh's "New Order" government was stirring considerable anxiety about the nation's future, and it showed up in the form of what everyone said was unprecedented hoarding and price gouging alongside already skyrocketing inflation. Sierra Leoneans were circumspect that the new President's bold promises to create a culture of accountability would amount to anything. Everyone I knew intimated that the October referendum election was simply theater, the transfer of power from two decades of impunity under Siaka Stevens and his APC party (All People's Congress) to his handpicked successor. "Same taxi, different driver," everyone said.

Margaret lifted her legs onto a stool to massage her feet. "This visit with your parents," she said, "it'll last a lifetime."

The next day, while trudging up the steep, rocky terrain with the women and children, including Ma Sando, I noticed how we seemed to move together as if all of one piece. I wondered what my mother would think when she heard the women here refer to each other without judgment as "dat dry one" (thin), "dat stout one," or "dat one who has 'fresh blood'" (recently gained weight), or a "pocket waist" (big hips). Back home, every aspect of a woman's figure got a grade on a scale. My mother and her friends' generation went on diets for weeks in advance of special occasions with the hope that they could fit into their half-size-smaller-than-usual dresses that hung in the back of their jam-packed walk-in closets, each outfit with its requisite heels—ready to walk onto the stage of men, cocktail parties, receptions, fundraisers. I knew the women would judge me for judging her.

Almost halfway to the farm we would harvest that day, we arrived at a small clearing where it was apparent someone had recently brushed away the undergrowth with a machete to access a spring, a clean and safe water source.

When it was my turn to drink, I bent over, cupping my hands full of the freshwater. Ma Sando and Sia Sam stood over me with their animated laughs turning into caterwauls over my loud slurps.

"Dis cold spring wata sweet!," I said.

"Ahhh, Besty. Wey yu go bak, yu go tehl yu people dehm ow we African dey drink cold cold wata from di dirty. *When you return you will describe how we are so poor we look for spring water from the ground.*

It seemed impossible not to see that this moment had presented itself for me to announce my parents' upcoming arrival.

Sia threw her hands in the air. "Ehh! Yu Mama!"

"Mi Mama *wit me Daddy.*"

The women seemed so uplifted by this news that when clapping and smiles erupted around, my apprehensions about the visit fell away momentarily.

"Yu Mama go enjoy village life wit we! We go mek big-big party for greet dehm!" *We will organize a big celebration according to our tradition!*

Soon after we reached the farm, several people walked over and presented me with a few plantains they'd just pulled off a tree, exclaiming, "We go learn yu Mammy ow foh cook swit fry-fry."

Of course, I knew my mother would never eat fry-fry (too much grease). Or rice (too much starch). She probably wouldn't even touch their food (too unsanitary). She wouldn't distinguish between street food you don't eat in foreign countries and their home-cooked meals.

Finda opened her arms wide. "We go mek big big feast foh yu people dehm! We go eat plenti. We go dance wit yu Mama tay di rooster dey crow nar early morning, way doklin." *We will celebrate until the dawn when the door to the day is clean!*

I doubted whether my mother would stay for a welcome party with dancing devils and men and women in grass skirts, their faces and breasts chalked white. I could already see her arms reaching toward my father.

Ma Sando sang as we harvested the rice, "Yu Mama wan foh meet we!"

I was struck by how all the women's enthusiasm was directed toward my mother. My father was the one with wide curiosity about the world, the one who had suggested we search the town's library for books on Sierra Leone and suggested to the librarian that the dearth of information was a problem. Though I hadn't any indication of either of them considering a visit, I was sure it was my father's doing, that he was the one who initiated purchasing the tickets.

I asked Ma Sando, "Why does everyone talk more about my mother coming to see me than my father?"

Ma Sando looked surprised. "Isn't she your Mama?" As if I were missing the obvious, where the sphere of women's power, respect, and influence resides. "Doesn't a mother give birth to her daughter? Doesn't a mother eat with her child? Doesn't a mother do all things with her daughter before she marries?"

Her voice held the tremor of a mother when she said this as if she knew there was never any guarantee any daughter would reach marrying age. And who would she marry? She snapped the seeds from the plant, making a short bundle in her hand. It seemed as if each plant, heavy with rice, leaned in—toward her.

All I could think was "you haven't met my mother."

I was raised in a world that did not fully allow for other people's experiences. My mother had no true interest in what was going on inside the continent of Africa. I saw that my mother and father were coming because they loved me, but not to see what I had come to love. I wanted to protect the dignity of both those I loved in America and those I had come to love in Sierra Leone.

I decided then that the best way forward was to keep the date and time of my parents' arrival vague, which was believable because transport from the capital city was always unreliable.

Later, near the farmhouse, I stared out at the side of the mountain, a once charred and barren-looking slab of fragile earth, now a lush upland farm. The beauty of tall golden stalks of country rice mingled with corn and the bright yellow flowers of okra, nearly iridescent among the greens and purple coba-coba (eggplant), the reds of tomatoes and cayenne peppers, and the orange of pumpkins.

Suddenly, Finda ran toward me, shouting gleefully that she'd pulled a tiny rat she discovered from the hayloft. "Look, Besty. I get arata!"

"Safulo!," I shouted. *Be careful.*

She laughed as she passed the limp rodent to her brother, Sahr Kondeh. "Leh we cook dis arata now."

But it wasn't a plain and uncomplicated "arata" to me; it could have been infected with Lassa fever, one of the "new rats," making human contact due to mining and deforestation. Their urine on stored rice had already led to the deaths of dozens of villagers in the region. Should I warn Finda? She was filling her belly with food, and I wanted to fill it with fear. It was a familiar dance. It might also save her life.

The small fire their mother had prepared in the kitchen hut was ready for cooking when we arrived. Minutes later, Sahr Kondeh came in with the wrinkled rat skewered on a long branch like marshmallows at a campfire. He had also pierced a few tree slugs on sticks. Once he fully cooked them, Sahr tore half for his sister and took the other half for himself. They chewed and sucked the bones.

"Dis swit lek sugar!," Finda taunted me, knowing she would never convince me to take a bite. Sensing my worry, she cried, "Dis nohto Lassa arata!" She said those ones were too stout.

Ma Sando called me over to join her for rice. She expressed concern that my parents would worry if I didn't gain some weight before their visit. Especially my mother.

"When will they arrive?"

I pretended not to know.

Through the tinted glass-paneled windows on the second-floor balcony, I stood watching my mom and dad descend the collapsible airplane stairs and walk across the tarmac into the shade of the Lungi Airport's arrival terminal. My heart lurched toward them in a way I hadn't anticipated. The security guards whisked my parents through the arbitrary barrier. A customs official collected my mother's suitcase, with the faint but unmistakable smell of her Chanel #5 drifting my direction. "Welcome! Welcome to Swit Salone!," a baggage carrier greeted her. "Nar helicopter yu dey take?"

My mother hugged me tightly but then let go. "What's he saying? Let's keep moving so we don't get too hot." She ran her fingers through her short black hair.

"He's asking in Krio if we are taking the helicopter."

"Well, I don't know where we're going."

"I'm sure she knows," said my six-foot-tall father, giving my arm a tight squeeze. I noticed the stubble of his beard and how his hair was grayer.

Agitated by the bustle of the unfamiliar chaos, my mother had to let go—and trust me. She looked at me, brows crinkled by the haze, her voice tired and disoriented by the crowd, the heat, and the jet lag. My initial jump toward her receded.

In my last-minute efforts to secure any means of transportation for my parents' visit to Kono and at a time when the government refused or was unable to pay for the delivery of fuel from the offshore tanker, I uncovered a wholly surprising silver lining to their trip: the Russian government's timely donation of two helicopters to boost tourism. This discovery meant that my parents and I could, for the cost of what a farmer here might earn in a year, avoid the unwieldy lines of the decades-old Chinese ferry and the haphazard peninsula crossing that had taken me three hours to navigate earlier that morning.

From the helicopter, I pointed to a small dot in the distance, Bunce Island, where tens of thousands of farmers had been captured, bought, and chained, bound for America's rice fields. The serenity of the harbor belied its actual history, just as in the ruins of this former slave castle, there is little more than archeological intrigue, so neglected then by mostly everyone even as the island has been steadily sinking for centuries.

In less than ten minutes, we landed on a heliport beside the five-star Mamy Yoko Hotel, a seaside resort with a well-known expat dance club named for a renowned nineteenth-century female paramount chief whose loyalty to the British during the reign of Queen Victoria conferred a "Silver Medal" on her.

"Welcome to Freetown," the pilot said to the passengers as they stepped onto a view of Lumley Beach, its beveled hills, and white sandy shores. "Thank you, Madam," he said to my mother.

My mother asked my father to take a picture of us at the shoreline before heading to Brookfield's Hotel. I'd explained how a night at the downtown government-run accommodation would save more time if we wanted to get upcountry. "On our last night, we can try to book a room here if you like," I said.

I loved the look on my mother's face when she was happy.

Early the next morning, we set out with Abdulai, a wiry middle-aged Temne driver who'd mounted two stickers, "Allah Gives" and "Jesus Saves," and a four-leaf clover with a leprechaun to the dashboard. He'd also dangled green and pink Mardi Gras beads and a miniature shuku blai (woven sweetgrass basket) from his rearview mirror. He was covering all bases. He provided a running commentary that proved the distraction we needed in our family dynamic.

"Tenki Tenki!," he said with more gratitude than the moment deserved. "You are thanking me. But your parents have come far from their own home to see their daughter." He looked at them through the rearview mirror. "They are the ones to be thanked."

I turned around to smile at my parents who were oblivious to our conversation as they stared out the window in amazement. I felt overwhelmed by the fact they were here. I understood that their effort to see me in Sierra Leone would bind something between us long into the future, though I didn't yet know what.

Abdulai popped in a new mixtape as we drove downtown, listening to Sade's "Diamond Life" and the beloved Cameroonian musician Sam Fan Thomas's latest release, "Freetown Titi (Girl) Collection" (from the popular album "African Typic Collection"), while gradually making our way along Pademba Road.

"We are many towns in this one town," Abdulai said, pointing out the sites to my parents. When I pointed out Pademba Road Prison, the driver said, "This is the most brokenhearted place in our country. Dem brok yu down to nothing inside those walls."

Quickly changing to a chummier topic, Abdulai told my parents, "I am always a fan of the Peace Corps. They are the only ones who eat the same food, speak our dialect, really live with we, the people. We have plenty of our own citizens who don't do that!"

Abdulai slowed his sedan and pointed to the famed landmark cotton tree, a more than 300-year-old kapok dating back to when freed Africans settled the town. "This is who we are. Anything that needs to be said about Sierra Leone can be understood if you understand this cotton tik."

We took an unexpected detour up a long and winding paved drive-way to Fourah Bay College overlooking the eastern part of city, on top of what is called Mount Aureol. Abdulai parked and exited the car, pointing my parents to the beautiful expansive views of Sierra Leone's vast harbor, obscured as they were by Harmattan winds. Turning around, he said, "Look at this tallest building." He pointed. "Kennedy built this for us; we admire him for that. He brought us your daughter and this monument to peace and learning. This is the legacy he left us." He paused for a minute. "He made us love America."

Abdulai got back into the car, regaling my parents with confessional stories of his misspent youth, how he'd squandered too much of his time preferring "young ladies" to books at Fourah Bay College, ultimately dropping out because he'd become a father and mining afforded more hope than a degree that could only make him a teacher, and an unpaid one at that. "Give me the name of one government worker in my country who is paid on time," he said. "Diamond money bought me this car. We all have to survive."

Driving back toward the city, descending the windy tarmac, Abdulai continued narrating; his lens was trained on Sierra Leone's history from colonial times to the present. He detailed how he believed the country had been bankrupted, how he blamed all of West Africa for the unity its leaders had promised each other but didn't deliver, and how all of them were crooks who got rich off the business of nation-building. "But what choice did they have?," he said.

My mother grabbed my arm in the back seat each time his voice rose, or she couldn't understand his words.

"What's he saying? I can't understand his thick accent," she whispered.

I held back from clarifying that he didn't have an accent because he's from here, just as I held back on responding to Abdulai's commentary. There was so much complexity in everything here. Away from the village, it was hard to know who the reliable narrators were. They were two different worlds.

We entered Mama Johnson's cookery beside the Peace Corps office on Lamina Sankoh Street, a restaurant with half a dozen empty tables, each with little plastic flower arrangements in tiny vases beside salt and pepper shakers. She was mumbling under her breath as she set a jar of pickled pigs' feet on a table beside pickled eggs, homemade ginger beer, and unrefrigerated soft drinks. According to her, she was the only one in Freetown who was staying open through the inauguration.

Mama Johnson had a strong profile and thick wavy gray hair pulled back. Her grandfather, Wallace Johnson, had founded Sierra Leone's labor movement, and his open-minded stance regarding women's rights put him at the vanguard of a new way of thinking in this country. "Many people say that my grandfather's premature death prevented Sierra Leone from realizing its potential," she said, referring to how her father died in an automobile collision in Ghana. My father shrugged with understanding. My mother said, "It's a shame,' her eyes never leaving the pigs' feet.

Mama Johnson handed my mother a stack of postcards with a photo of a recently erected statue of her grandfather. She said she wouldn't charge us because I was serving her country and wrapped the cards in old *Newsweek* pages. As we departed, she said that Sierra Leoneans are the most comfortable and happy here—in their own land. "We know it is a beautiful place. No one has to tell us this."

We walked out the door, Mama Johnson tapping my mother on the shoulder. "If you come back on Saturday, I will prepare fufu for you," she said, referring to the traditional Saturday Krio dish made from gluten-rich fermented cassava and served with sauces poured over its elastic mounds. "But fufu will make you sleep the whole day, and you might miss your flight. I will make coffee too."

My mom asked if I remembered the Johnsons, the neighborhood family who'd refused to buy a TV set. "That was so strange," she said.

"I remember them," I said a little harshly. The only TV I knew about in Sierra Leone was at the American embassy. Her comment seemed to fall from the sky.

We descended the crumbled cement steps, my mom in front of me, when a man with elephantiasis crossed the empty street. I saw my mom avert her eyes.

———

Margaret gave my parents and me a soft landing in Koidu. We ate bread and jam and stayed up late talking by lantern. My parents slept in the spare bedroom, and I set up Margaret's collapsible cot in the parlor. Privately, Margaret handed me a package she said was a gift to my mother and me from Dalia, her Lebanese neighbor. Inside were two beautifully sewn floor-length dresses with appliqué—one with a picture of a little girl and her dog (mine) and one with a bouquet of flowers (hers). The gesture nearly brought me to tears and a realization that while my mother would appreciate this sentiment, it was accurate to think that she would never wear this "moo-moo." I tucked it into my backpack, considering to whom I might gift it.

We were woken at dawn by the crackling loudspeaker bellowing the morning prayer from the new mosque across town in Koidu and, after that, the rattle of Amadou setting up his cigarette booth beside Margaret's front door. Abdulai appeared with a handful of bananas for Margaret, ready to resume his role as driver. He'd filled the tank with a gallon that Amadou provided. He said he had a secret stash to keep Margaret's generator going.

We all hopped into the car with me again in the front to direct us down the rutted, overgrown narrow twelve miles to my house in Tokpombu. My parents were so quiet even our breath was audible.

"Dis dust dey choke we," Abdulai said. *This dust fills up our lungs.*

We arrived at the village ready for Tokpombu but found that Tokpombu was not prepared for us. Abdulai parked close to the house, so my parents had only a few steps to take before they stepped onto the verandah (where even the goats were nowhere to be found) and followed me through the metal doors, and we entered the space I now called home.

My mother's eyes darted to every corner, and she held her arms close, looking almost relieved that the floors were swept, the rooms spacious. The Peace Corps house I'd described in my letters matched what she now saw in front of her.

We lingered for a while in the coolness of my house, me holding onto Two-Stroke until he squirmed out of my arms and bounded back outside while I gave them a tour: my kitchen, my bedroom, my storage room, and out back, my cookstove and my latrine and shower hut. I momentarily stepped away to see who might be milling around KT's house. I found only Mama Sia cooking in her cookhouse, accompanied by a few of her co-wives' children. Ordinarily, a vehicle would have drawn them to my house, but today was a harvest day, the community's last, and everyone else had assembled on the hill early that morning.

I called Abdulai and my parents to follow me because I had someone that I wanted them to meet. Mama Sia ducked through the wobbly metal door of her kitchen, wiping her hands, and then touching her right one to her heart to say, "It is a pleasure . . ." Dauda and Mohmmed clung to my leg, repeating. "Yu mamma! Yu daddy!" Kadiatu stood shyly behind Mama Sia in her school uniform, home for the day because she had a fever.

After a few minutes, Mama Sia returned to her kitchen, saying she would bring us a tray of food. I knew that this tray could take hours to prepare and that my parents would not be here when it arrived. A tension rose within me.

"OK, that's it. I've seen everything I need to see," my mother announced as if she'd just finished the tour of my summer camp bunk.

No one balked. Not me, not my father, certainly not Abdulai. We didn't meet the chief, my landlord, Ma Sando, my counterpart Sahr Joe, or Binah, the teacher. We didn't see my demo swamp or the waterside. We took one picture of my mother sitting on my day bed—the one with the yellow pin-striped (Marimekko) sheet. And that was *it*.

---

We arrived in Jaima without incident an hour later. We refreshed ourselves from the drive with warm sodas at Sia Gborie's shop when, suddenly, every shortwave radio playing up and down the main street of Jaima was turned up for "live coverage." Eyes turned toward us as the announcer declared that the space shuttle Challenger had exploded. "Dust is skewering everywhere. There is no way that any of the seven crew could have survived. We have lost Christa McAuliffe, the first teacher in space."

The entire street settled into stillness. A small crowd of fifteen or twenty drew close and began offering condolences as if someone close to us had just died. To my parents, "Ahhh. A teacher. We are so sorry, Ma. Ehh, Papa! We are so sorry, Sir." In the clamor, I heard someone say that it could be Sierra Leone's diamonds falling from the sky. "Our stones have been used to make America's spacecrafts!"

A man cried out, "By God's grace, it all comes back to we (us)!"

Amid the stir, my father drifted away from us, apparently engaged in conversations with various townspeople. My eyes tracked him as he stood beside a woman I recognized, Mariama, whose baby Gen was named after a volunteer. I could see blisters over her sleeping child's body and wondered what she said to my father. I watched her take a small cloth tucked into her skirt and dab Gen's eyes. Of course, this woke up the child, and loud shrieks turned to loud retching. Mariama held her baby horizontal to the ground while the vomit projected to the earth and made a little puddle. She unraveled her headscarf, placing it on the ground beside the pool she would clean once she'd settled her daughter. A moment later I heard Mariama's scream. "My head-tie! My head-tie!"

Holding Gen to her breast, Mariama said the missing scarf was where she stored her money.

My father asked me if this had happened a lot.

"Not a lot," I lied. "Some."

He pulled twenty leones from his wallet and handed them to Mariama.

"Tenki Papa," she said, bowing and kissing his feet.

My father stood there, looking dismayed and uncomfortable, and I felt helplessly proud. I knew my father was proud of me too.

"Wait a minute, you are going to leave and not allow your parents to meet one of its leaders?" I turned around and saw paramount chief Matturi, the 6′ 4″ larger-than-life general manager of the NDMC. He extended a firm and confident hand to my father to shake. Then he reached for my mother's hands and returned his hand to his heart. "Pleasure," he said. "I am so happy to meet you."

He was dressed in Western clothes. I noticed my mother looking up at his hat, Brooks Brothers, and looking down at his shiny shoes, Gucci.

When Chief Matturi invited my parents for a snack, Mrs. Matturi met us by her outdoor kitchen in a walled-off compound. She was wearing traditional clothes, a lappa wrapped around her and well-worn sandals. She called out to a nearby teenage girl to find oranges and fried potatoes for my parents to enjoy.

The paramount chief's wife asked about my parents' trip so far. She wondered about the layover in Dakar and described what life had been like for her when she accompanied her husband for cataract surgery in Washington, DC. New York was her favorite city, though. "Have you ever been to Tiffany's?" When she asked this, my mother seemed to come alive.

I recalled watching my mother peel potatoes one evening when I was in sixth grade.

"What are you thinking, Mom?" I asked.

"I'm not thinking; I'm peeling potatoes so we can have dinner on time."

"Do we have to eat at six? Can't we eat later than six? I'm not hungry."

"Yes. Dinner is always at six. Your father always walks in the door at six. Your brothers are hungry."

"But I'm not hungry."

"Betsy, I'm getting dinner ready now. Can you please just let me peel the potatoes? Go on, scram!"

I closed my eyes and folded my arms the way Jeannie did, from the TV show *I Dream of Jeannie*, and funneled myself into the genie bottle.

At 8 p.m., after homework, I watched *The Waltons*, a show about a large churchgoing family who lived on their namesake mountain expressing romanticized American values.

Living on a mountain in the Gorama chiefdom, I was beginning to realize how my younger self had seen my mother caught between both archetypes—Mrs. Walton's stereotypical maternal strength and generosity in conflict with the submissive but provocative world of Jeannie.

Only now did it occur to me how much my mother's attitudes were rooted in conflict between these opposing forces. Coming to Sierra Leone to meet swamp farmers was never on her to-do list. It surprised me all those many years later when my sixteen-year-old son told me one day that visiting me in Sierra Leone was one of the highlights of her life. Maybe she had felt something that I felt.

On the day I hugged my parents good-bye, I photographed them sitting with the Sierra Leone national soccer team, who were dressed in uniform, the colors of their flag, and on the same plane as my parents, via Dakar. I overheard snippets of pleasant conversations between my parents and this team of twelve as I exited the airport doors and back into my life.

Months after my parents left, while sitting with my friends on the back stoop with our lanterns turned up bright against the moonless night, Ma Sando admitted that she was disappointed she'd missed my parents' brief stop in the village. Sia Sam, Gbesay, Kumba, Pa Bindi, Sahr Binah, Chief Lahai, and Sahr Joe all echoed the same feeling.

I wanted to tell them I was angry at my parents. But by then I knew that anger is a symptom and never at the bottom. This is what Sierra Leone was teaching me; there is always some other hidden vulnerability not being expressed.

Mama Sia quieted everyone. "Dis Mamy bin cam foh see een daughter! *This mother came to see her daughter!*

She continued, "Di Mamy no cam foh meet any of we." *The mother didn't come to meet us. She didn't want to experience our tradition—for our community to prepare a party to honor her.*

Sia Sam offered, "Sometime, een nar get nar hand Mamy." *Maybe she is a get in the hand Mamy.*

"Wetin get nar hand?," I asked.

"A person who holds on too tight!," everyone answered, laughing.

"Lajeelahh! Oh, we get dat kind of Mamy here boku! Nar foh hold yu heart." *We have many mothers here like yours.* Hold your heart—remain steady.

# CHAPTER 13

# Good Morning, America!

In God We Trust.

—UNITED STATES CONGRESS, 1864, ALLOWING IT TO BE ON A COIN

A day with a spiritual element that distinguished it from the other days of the week, Fridays in Tokpombu reminded me of the traditional Jewish Sabbath. On this day of rest, no one left their house in the morning to plow, plant, or do work of any kind unless it involved a communal village chore—filling potholes, clearing footpaths, pulling weeds from the waterside. Instead, villagers visited neighbors; created music on keleis (slit log drums), shekere (beaded gourd), and balanges; played warrie (a carved wooden board game); gathered to perform ritual ceremonies. And sometimes they met to discuss village affairs.

One Friday almost two years into my stay, the village assembled to deal with the theft of some sheep. An itinerant laborer was proclaimed guilty, but Chief Lahai signaled for everyone to wait before he could be led away. "May God give Sia Besty a long-long life, plenty pikendehm (children), bless all those who came before her," he said. "Ray came to live with we, become a brother to we all, become one of we, and he built we a fine church. People have come from all sides of Gorama to pray inside this church. Our Christian brothers and sisters, as well as our Muslim brothers and sisters."

"It is a fine-fine church," someone in the crowd called out.

"It is a fine church," the chief echoed, "but Ray built it with a thatched roof. We all know that a thatched roof after three years can begin to leak," he continued, looking right at me. "Yu are one of we now. Yu have lived with we for nearly two years. We are begging yu, 'Mek we no put disgrace *pan top of Ray's efforts.*" *The church needs a zinc roof before the next rainy season.*

All around me, people nodded. "I am not a Christian, but I am a man of God," said Pa Sorie. "This church is the only one in the many little villages along this road that everyone can see. It should have a proper roof. So, duya, we dey cry belleh." *This complaint is from our hearts.*

I doubted anyone knew that their constant pleading for a metal roof had carved a place in my heart. But a genuine shift had taken place in me, as if all the closely welded parts of this community—what made it whole—had finally sunk in. Most everyone around me said they whole-heartedly believed in the God brought here by "yonda people's Jesus" reli-gion. Farmers perceived no contradiction in combining these "new" spir-itual abstractions and practices with the "old." Their amulets for good health and good harvests, what everyone wore or buried or hung on trees, stood easily beside the churches.

Now I announced to everyone I had already written a letter to the Jesse Lee UMC church in my hometown, asking for funds to repair the roof. The funds had been transferred by Pastor Walter H. Everett in Connecticut to Bishop Bangura in Freetown and then to a bank in Koidu, where it was waiting in an account. My hometown congregants looked forward to a "sis-ter relationship" with the village and planned to send letters, books, and supplies.

When I shared this news, cries of joy erupted.

The following morning, I was called by my neighbors to gather with community members along the mainline to witness the thief's punish-ment. Led by several men carrying sticks, he walked trance-like for five miles, from Tokpombu to Kangama, the chiefdom headquarters, with metal anklets clanking, his bound hands clasped around a broom. Onlook-ers jeered, and children clapped and sang, "Tiefy! Tiefy!" as he walked past, naked except for several old snake skins draped over his body.

Sahr Joe was sitting on the iron railing of my porch when I returned to my house.

"How you see we justice system?," he asked in earnest. "Once a man has been shamed like this, it's in the memory of the people."

The following Friday, men scrambled up and down the rickety peak of the church, tossing dry, crackly branches down to the earth as they dismantled the old church. Children caught the branches for their mothers to use for kindling.

As I worked alongside Kumba, the youngest and most stylish of KT's four wives, both of us gathering water for Ma Sando so she could prepare food for the village laborers, I complimented her on her indigo batik top. Kumba smiled and waded closer. When our buckets were filled with water, she set hers down to hoist mine onto a kata (the cloth pad where a bucket or basket rests on your head). Slowly, I lifted my chin from my chest as far as it could extend to balance the bucket. As always, the water bounced forward and back when I took my first steps, so I had to keep moving to the undulations of the water and not my own pace until it became a rhythm, something I could control.

Kumba cheered, "Ehhhh Besty," as I navigated tree roots and rocks, my eyes fixed straight ahead. The simple joy of mastering a task so foundational to everyone's life here unexpectedly caught me, and I was overcome with a rush of sentimentality about my time here. Maybe it had to do with my age and inexperience then, but also Pa Sanusi's death, the harvest that followed, and so many other little things too. What had led me to appeal to church members in my hometown whom I'd never met was about more than the church roof. Where I once felt coaxed, I now felt free. In abiding by the continuity of effort, I found new parts of myself that reached not just across geographic borders but across those in my mind.

As I was getting dressed, Kumba arrived at my door with the batik print I'd admired and placed it on the day bed. "Dis nar foh yu." *This is for you.*

"Wait me," I said and dashed into my bedroom, returning in a moment with an armful of skirts—denim, khaki, and plaid. "Us (Which) one yu want?," I asked. I wanted the gift exchange to be fair.

She declined my offer and said, "You can wear it on the day we celebrate the new roof."

After she left, Ma Sando came to my door, offering me a portion of the food she and Mama Sia had prepared for the laborers. I showed her the top that Kumba had given me.

"Oh, e lek (like) yu," Ma Sando said, smiling. "You are like family. If yu get, we all get."

The blue Mazda pickup truck with high wooden slats and a newly painted slogan on the back, Rasta Man, "One Love," seemed fitting for my journey to purchase the zinc for the roof. I climbed in along with more than a dozen other people, and an hour later, twelve miles down the road, the wide-faced, barrel-chested Officer Kamara shouted, "All man get foh climb down." He and three other officers stomped the periphery of our vehicle. When Kamara spotted me, all formality fell away. "Where's your motorbike today, Sia Tokpombu?," he asked, leaning his head through the slatted sides. When I told him I needed a new spark plug, he replied, "You should have told me. I could have had one sent to Tokpombu—*no problem.*"

Kamara approached the driver, "Ow many passenger you get inside dis vehicle?" He stomped out his cigarette while waiting for an answer.

"Nineteen, sir."

The sergeant blew a shrill whistle, signaling the other officers to begin conducting their search. He ordered the passengers off the lorry. The official reason was a search for smuggled diamonds. But everyone knew that the "checkpoint business" was a trap to take money out of passengers' hands.

"Dis permit business nar waste of time," one passenger exploded. "Here is where we were born!" Everyone ignored him, including the officers who, like Sahr Joe and the teachers, may not have received their salaries from the government.

The inspection, while brief, was enough to arouse anyone's temper. When the sergeant shook his head to indicate the passengers were free to board again, the driver slid a small stack of leone notes into Sergeant Kamara's fat hand. As he lifted the gate, he called to me again through the slats, "Next time you have a spark plug problem, send me a message, and I will have one delivered to you in Tokpombu." I sometimes wished I could just blend in, be one of and not the stranger. But it was impossible.

As we drove toward the Koidu bus station, a woman named Masso asked me when I would be returning home.

"In four months, pas Christmus time," I answered.

Behind me, I heard whispers. "White man dey come, white man dey go. Dem dey forget we." *Westerners come to help us. After they return to their homes, we are forgotten.*

Then Musu said, "My brother went to America ten years ago, but nobody no dey ebba yehri from dat man dey." *It's been a decade since anyone has heard from my brother.*

I suggested that it wasn't easy being an immigrant in America.

Musu dismissed the idea. "The sun always comes out twice. *If you do something terrible to me today, tomorrow it will be my turn.*"

Beside me, a man complained that the country had filled up with too many strangers who didn't care about the village man. He described the influx of many new ethnic groups: Indians, Chinese, Lebanese, and Syrians. "Mortal men fasten to diamonds like bees to honey," he said.

Another man stated that only the Lebanese profited from the diamonds and tried to make Sierra Leone look like Lebanon while "we yone" government makes Lebanese men the chief of any place they decide to live in the country. He said he had a "sorry heart" knowing that his children would not be able to farm like their ancestors. About three miles from Koidu, he pointed to the last patch of savannah and told me this was the NDMC boundary line. Without any signage or change in the terrain, the diamond compound's vast holdings were indistinguishable to me.

Entering Koidu, the driver slowed to a crawl to accommodate swarms of other vehicles and pedestrians. Corrugated stalls leaned into one another like card houses that gave way, a few blocks later, to rows of large concrete storefronts with garage door openings, the owners' names painted in block letters above: Basma, Bahsoon, Farid. These Lebanese shops were the wholesale departure-and-arrival terminals for every foreign good in the city. The man beside me said, "When families came here, they carried only one suitcase. But now . . ." He pointed to the Lebanese shops and cursed.

Don't most fleeing immigrants arrive in a new country with only one suitcase, I thought. When the Lebanese first showed up, they were escaping famine and persecution. That was four generations ago, in the same era that my family fled persecution in Russia and Europe to reach America. Was America not my home?

Then the man said something stark. "Our government loans money to the Lebanese instead of to its own citizens. We have given the Lebanese man the upper hand. This problem is Sierra Leone's fault. For this, we pay bribes at the checkpoint. And so, too, we have a checkpoint. They are not paying the police enough to do their job."

I registered the "we" in the complaints, how stems of betrayal and sorrow makes the seeds bitter.

After climbing out of the truck bed and exiting the lorry park, I headed to the bank, avoiding the occasional mangy dog or chicken, bicycle or motorbike, and sometimes holding my breath at the stench of raw sewage. The usual crowd of beggars was staked out in the tiny parking space in front of the Barclays Bank. One thin bare-chested man cried to me, "Please, gimme money foh God een sake. Ah get foh feed me fambuldem. Ah dey beg yu."

Just then, a stout man with a gold watch and leather shoes exited the glass doors and announced to the group, "No humbug this Peace Corps woman wit you beg-beg business." The man apologized to me and didn't drop anything into the tin can.

I entered the building and the assistant manager, "Zainab Taylor," whom I had met when I first set up my account, greeted me from behind a plexiglass counter as I took my place in line. "You can come to my office." Once again, I was being given preferential treatment.

Zainab leaned over her desk, red fingernails counting the stack of leones I would use to purchase the roof. In only ten months, the value of the leone had declined exponentially—from 3:1 to 47:1 leones to the dollar.

When I left the air-conditioned building and stepped back into the claustrophobic humidity, I walked through an aisle of a now-dozen beggars, dropping a leone note into every hand or can. "If nar me get, you all foh get," I said beneath my breath. *What's mine is yours.*

I walked to Father John's compound, a compact, whitewashed ranch where Peace Corps volunteers were always welcome. "Betsy!" he greeted me in the lilt of his native Dublin. "You've timed your visit perfectly; I've got someone here for ye ta meet."

In his living quarters, I encountered a middle-aged American man holding a teacup and a camera strapped across his chest.

"This is Mack, and he's one of yers, from the colony." Mack beamed his sunburned face at me, so I reached to shake his hand. "Me man Mack here has quite a story ta tell about his time here in Sweet Salone" (which was how many Sierra Leoneans refer to their homeland with fondness).

"You're probably not gonna believe it," Mack said. "My church back home raised twenty grand to build a clinic here that turns out not even to exist."

"Really?," I said.

"Yea, I came to meet everybody and to get some video footage of the project to bring back home, and there was nothing to see and no one to meet."

I tried to act surprised at the size of such a lie and theft. But I wasn't.

"We got the letters of thanks, progress reports, and even photos of the construction, the whole nine yards—two years of it. But it was all fake, a scam. All that money just went into a bunch of people's greedy little pockets."

"Or some individual's pocket," Father John said.

I'd heard all this before. Everyone here had. Those without political connections were the only people who got caught for any wrongdoing.

I reached into my bag to give Father John the cash to arrange for the roofing supplies he planned to buy from his Lebanese neighbor. I said, "That's horrible. If it's any consolation, this kind of thing happens here a lot."

"You mean stealing is normal here? Lying is normal here? Taking people's hard-earned American buckos is normal here?"

Mack didn't know what I was gradually beginning to understand—that every organization brought with it its own corruption. Even the venerated Peace Corps. The year after I left, allegations of corruption within the Peace Corps would lead to firings and dismissals. All I could think to offer to Mack was "mortal man business no easy."

Mack looked at John. "The only reason I'm still in this godforsaken country is because of this one true man's hospitality."

Father John responded with a passage from Genesis: "And God looked upon the earth and saw it was corrupt."

I could see the gears turning in Father John's head. He offered for Mack to videotape the work of placing a permanent roof on the Tokpombu church.

"Sure!," Mack said, "I'd like to visit a real village and a real African church, and for all the trouble, I may as well give the folks back home something to feel good about."

I felt uneasy, the way I felt when I told a small lie. Making his church members in Virginia "feel good" wasn't top of mind for me. On the other hand, I was thrilled by the novel opportunity to have a videotape of life in Tokpombu—a permanent record of village life—for all of us.

Satisfied, John said, "You never know with whom or how the Lord conspires."

———

The following Monday, John's Lebanese neighbor, Marwan, pulled into the village in a brand new, air-conditioned flatbed pickup. His apprentices were a tangle of muscled young men wearing sun hats and tank tops.

Marwan asked where his men should start unloading the piles of zinc pan: here on the ground, or—maybe inside my house. He wanted to know if I had a storeroom for safekeeping. I didn't like the intimation that the farmers in this village who had pleaded for this roof might steal it—though it was possible.

"You can leave the zinc here outside for now so everyone can see it's arrived," I said.

When Father John's blue Toyota arrived with Mack's sunburned arm hanging out the passenger side, the neighborhood children who'd gathered on my verandah applauded and shouted cries of joy. I'd prepared them for the filming adventure. Mack stepped down and slammed the door, his expression anything but joyful. "Hello folks, Kushe y'all," he said before hurrying into my house with his equipment, assisted by his doting driver and Marwan.

"You gotta restroom somewhere?," Mack asked.

"A latrine," I said, and led him to the backyard, pointing to the mud-brick dwelling.

Mack handed me a plastic-handled bag. "Here's a gift. It's got some local university hospital scrubs I would have passed out to the nurses at the clinic, but since there's no darn clinic. Wanna put 'em on for the videotape?"

I laughed and told him I wasn't a nurse.

"You gotta put on those scrubs," he insisted.

I found Mack's urging manipulative. Here he was offended at having been lied to, yet he wanted me to participate in his own lie.

"Are you asking me to pretend I am a nurse for your congregation back home?"

"That works for me," he said.

I disappeared to change in my bedroom and returned feeling (and looking) like someone going into an ER. I saw my deference, how it felt to be desperate to want something for this village, and the ridiculous lengths I was willing to go.

With Mack now filming, we entered the church and then took a tour of each mud-brick home in New Town and Old Town. We stopped at the blacksmith's, the palm wine bar, the carpenter's, and the home of the town chief. Nearly every village child straggled behind us, along with a few goats. Mack was a spectacle everyone admired—the important stranger with the big bird mounted on his shoulder, who had hastened the arrival of the zinc pan roof.

Mack was enjoying himself. "This is amazing. I feel like a celebrity!," he said.

But there was one person who didn't like Mack's celebrity. Or his camera. A man in his twenties stood on his porch beneath a clothesline sagging with a row of shirts and pants. As we approached, he covered his face and said, "Ah dey ask leh yu no tek me picture." *Do not take my picture.*

When Mack continued to film, he became angry. "You will take this picture to America and mock us," he said, not realizing that he was still being filmed.

We kept walking, and Mack kept filming. We reached the demonstration swamp, where Sahr Joe had cleared away the stubble of harvested rice plants to make room for next season's plots—when I would no longer be here. Mack followed Sahr Joe as he described our project in animated detail, his voice choking with emotion as he told all the work he, Ray, and I had done to improve swamp farming. Sahr Joe finished his monologue with his hand on his heart. "To you, my dear friend Raymond," he said.

Mack clicked off the camera and slapped Joe on the back. "Fantastic. You were a natural. That was just great. You have a job in Hollywood if you want it."

"Thank you, sir," Joe said, looking pleased, though I couldn't be sure Sahr Joe even knew what Hollywood was.

"Raymond go see dis," I told Joe. I told him I would make sure he got a copy.

"Ah gladi," he said.

As we turned back toward Old Town, I thought about how many days I'd spent inside these plots, how every inch of this muddy soil now felt personal. Mack continued to film each person we encountered. By the time we returned to my house, I could hear Ma Sando directing the women to pull up their lappas because the man with the camera might come around the corner any minute and take their pictures to America.

Mack filmed the church that would soon have its new zinc roof. All this, I thought, so that a tiny church won't require seasonal repair and everyone who passes by will see this shiny reminder that, even in the worst of times, something bright and new could appear on the horizon.

By late afternoon we found ourselves on KT Sonda's front porch. Mack corralled as many children as he could onto the twelve crumbly steps. They all complied enthusiastically, laughing and giggling as each made room for the next to squeeze into the camera's viewfinder.

"Okay," Mack said, "when I say 'Go,' say, 'Good Morning, America.' Ready? Set? Go."

The children stared at the camera and then at Mack with blank faces.

Mack repeated his instructions, this time more insistently. Finally, they repeated in a chorus with the same self-confidence they always had when instructed to speak in call and response at school.

"Good Morning, America," they said in full force.

Mack smiled. "That's right. You got it now."

At the day's end, my house was packed. Fifty people had elbowed their way inside to see themselves on a TV monitor not much bigger than a boombox. My house had never been this full. I enjoyed seeing this eagerness, the universal giddy waiting-for-the-show-to-start excitement. After Mack was sure no one else would be entering the house and that the windows were clear for those who couldn't get in but still wanted to watch, he pulled the generator cord, which turned on the monitor with a spark and a sudden ringing thrum. Suddenly there we all were: walking, talking, living, breathing. Everyone was mesmerized. When the "show" ended with the refrain, "Good Morning, America," no one clapped. No one knew to clap.

CHAPTER 14

# Strident Cry of the Weaver Birds

To trace something unknown back to something known is alleviating,
soothing, gratifying and gives moreover a feeling of power.

—FRIEDRICH NIETZSCHE

When a tall papaya tree was uprooted just twenty feet from my house at
two a.m., its trunk collapsing the metal roof of Mama Sia's mud-brick
kitchen hut, I lay awake as if I were a tree limb holding on, determined not
to let the deafening wind or rain dislodge me from my own four sturdy
walls. This rain was no ordinary downpour. It was the sort of downpour
that is sometimes called "the devil with pitchforks."

Over the last year and some months, I had seen how the rain was a
harbinger of disease, even death. Back home, the slightest bacterial, viral,
or parasitic infection could be abbreviated by a sterile gauze, a Band-Aid, a
stitch, a shot, or an aspirin. Here in Sierra Leone—where there was no easy
access to clinics and little money to pay the expenses; where the climate
fluctuated between drought and saturation; where infant and maternal
mortality rates ran among the highest in the world and life expectancies
among the lowest—villagers relied on roots and herbal remedies.

Mae Jemison, our Peace Corps doctor, who would later become the first
female African American astronaut, had warned us about the risks of living here, although not only because of bacterial or viral infections from
untreated water. Dr. Jemison's list was long: malaria; typhoid, dysentery;
hepatitis; schistosomiasis, a parasitic flatworm; hookworms; roundworms;
pinworms. Though infrequent, there were still incidents of leprosy, polio,
and cholera. Naturally, too, she'd lectured about unplanned pregnancies

and venereal diseases from sex without condoms. HIV/AIDS had entered our lexicon along with syphilis and gonorrhea and were included in the advisory. To those of us posted in Kono, Dr. Jemison gave specific warnings about Lassa fever.

Yesterday afternoon, when the dark clouds had gathered, the farmers had hollered to each other across their verandahs, "Dis rain get foh be vievie!" (*violent*). It might wash away the newly transplanted seedlings, including the rice Sahr Joe and I had painstakingly transplanted in our demo swamp.

In the now clear morning, I gathered my overflowing buckets and joined a few families who had already begun to roam the village, collecting the debris scattered in everyone's yards. We shared a collective shudder about how quickly the road had become uneven, rutted land strewn with debris. I wondered aloud how long it would be before a transport vehicle could pass through.

"It will be one week," Amara Mara said, standing beside me, scratching his arms.

"It will be well past that!," his brother, Amadu, contradicted.

Wanting to be helpful, I deposited an armful of branches beside Ma Sando's kitchen, with its thatch cover leaning on one side. A moat had formed around its raised platform. My friend looked discouraged but appreciative of the gesture and later delivered a pot of boiling water to my house to make tea.

"By this hour, those with zinc pan roofs will be worse off than those with thatched roofs," Ma Sando said. While corrugated iron on a kitchen roof didn't leak as often, its replacement cost was heftier.

Just then, we heard the noise of a stick clanging the metal rim of a tire—the summons to church. As I stepped outside onto my verandah, my legs suddenly began to itch then burn. I looked down and saw a cluster of red marks where fire ant secretions were beginning to sear the top layer of my skin, something that could quickly become infected in this humidity. I ran to a nearby bucket and splashed the rainwater on the bites, which momentarily relieved the pain. Ma Sando looked down at my leg and offered a startling perspective. "Yu foh gladi it wasn't a Champion," she said. Champion spider secretions leave scarring and produce more painful burning sensations.

In the church, the preacher, O. K. Pessima, thanked the women who'd sprinkled water from the rain-filled containers on the dirt floor to keep the dust from rising. "Those with metal roofs and without ceiling boards or mats," he said, "must talk loudly to God during the rainy season, but the ones with thatched roofs will hear themselves. God," he said, "uses different tongues for each of us, but everything is God."

As we exited the church, fragments of a bright blue sky seemed to warm the congregants. Everyone was talking, smiling, and looking up at the sun. The children were having a field day with the puddles. It was proving to be the kind my mother called a "good to be alive day."

Ten days later, my gratitude dissipated into fear. What started as a low-grade fever quickly shot up. Mild nausea turned into a constant need for the outhouse. From my chills, I knew this was no common parasitic infection like my previous cases of giardia and worms but malaria and, quite possibly, a chloroquine-resistant strain.

When a new round of belly cramps gripped me, I fought my way through roaring, ankle-deep floodwater to the outdoor latrine. Lifting the cover, I saw more than the usual crowd of cockroaches, each the size of my big toe, clinging around the hole. As I vomited, the pounding inside my head was undifferentiated from the pounding of the rain on the roof. My neck felt strained from the countless contortions of my retching, and my throat was scratchy. My belly was sore, my knees knocked, my feet throbbed—but it was all one collective pain. Back in my house, I fumbled through my Peace Corps medical kit and found a thermometer to stick under my tongue: 103.5. I swallowed four more chloroquine and four aspirin and fell into bed. All movement and light blurred.

This was the malaria that killed hundreds if not thousands of Sierra Leoneans every year, millions annually worldwide. This was the malaria on my mother's list of why I should not go to Africa.

For the next five or ten days, my temperature fluctuated between 101 and 104, and my sleeping hours were more lucid than my waking ones. Dreamy hallucinations (a well-known side effect of quinine) had me reaching back into the past, running in a loop like sad songs. There had been so many of these sad songs since I arrived about people I knew here who became sick and whom I feared would die. The danger of living in the tropics, where there were no doctors, nurses, or medical infrastructure, had revealed life's true fragilities.

But there was one particular memory that looped hauntingly over and over and would not ease throughout my fevered state.

———

*I only just had returned from a two-week-long agricultural in-service training and a seaside vacation. In total darkness I rode with only a slight wind behind me and the moon just a sliver above. My motorbike's narrow beam pierced the shadows as I rolled through the valleys of the Nimini Hills. The contour of a road I'd learned so well told me when I arrived at Tokpombu: the slight incline and a sudden drop. Even when driving in daylight, I had waited for the downhill feeling that signaled home, a shelter plus the land it sits on—where I once felt like a stranger, I now felt like a friend.*

*For the spiders in my house, my reentry must have felt apocalyptic. As I stumbled about searching for matches, my body careened into one after another giant web. In the dampness, it took half a box of matches to get one lit, and when I finally managed to ignite the wick of my lantern, I saw that every corner of the room was crisscrossed with gossamer. After nearly two weeks without the daily whap of my broom, every room had become a spider's haven.*

*I cranked the window open to let in the fresh air and slept soundly under my mosquito netting until there was a knock. Ma Sando entered, with Bondu toted on her back. "I've made this fry-fry for you," she said, setting a tray full of crispy cassava pancakes on the table. There was a strain in her voice.*

*"Sia Tokpombu, yu toma (your namesake) no well. Bondu Besty sik."*

*I touched Bondu's warm, flushed, and now bumpy red one-year-old skin smeared with clay, then grasped her hands and leaned in close to her head, stroking it. "We all go help you to mend," I said. "No worry. No fraid."*

*I, of course, was terrified. I lifted Bondu's whimpering and sweaty body from her mother's arms, a listless girl I barely recognized. "Ehhh, Bondu Besty," I sang, looking into her eyes, so red and weepy.*

*Only last month, Ella, Finda, and I had practiced walking with little Bondu. We couldn't believe how quickly she'd gotten the hang of it, letting go of our hands and heading off with her willful spunk, her plump, lively limbs flailing toward a family of goats until she'd stumbled and let out a shriek.*

"What's happened? When did my toma become sick?," I asked.

"The time after you left," she said, referring to my recent return from two weeks of travel on the other side of the country.

"Sometimes, nar measles," Ma Sando said.

But without a diagnosis or medicine, it was only anyone's best guess. I felt guilty and told Ma Sando I should have come back sooner.

She looked confused. "You didn't cause this sick. Everything is God."

Even when people died here, no one concerned themselves with a diagnosis, the cause of death, only the death itself. Her outward calm unnerved me. Bondu was her baby!

I pulled Bondu Besty's toes like I always did, as if this could be the one right touch to return her to the smiling, growing girl she'd been. I noticed her mother tied new cowry shell amulets to a healing string around her ankles and wrists.

Ma Sando looked at me and asked, "Yu go help me carry and go with Bondu nar di clinic in Jaima." Her question reinforced my fear and guilt. She'd waited for me to take Bondu the twelve miles to the clinic because she had no money to pay for her daughter's treatment.

Of course, she had waited. In villages like this one—where there were no trained first responders, nurses, or doctors (and maybe less than fifty in a country of what was then 3.5 million people), where one in seventeen women died while giving birth, where one in thirteen children died before their fifteenth birthday—it was inevitable that I would become an extra link in the chain of survival. Requests for me to help with any one of many wants and needs—a roof, school fees, medical fees, transport costs—were routine. My monthly stipend was stand-in enough; if I gave up batteries and cut back on coffee and sugar cubes, there was always enough left to help.

I gazed at my namesake, not thinking about medical costs, only time. How much time did Bondu have before she became dehydrated, unconscious, or had a febrile seizure or encephalitis kicked in? Frantic, I turned the key on my motorbike. Right now, I have to take Ma Sando and Bondu to the clinic! I didn't care that Peace Corps rules prohibited me from giving rides on my motorbike.

Just then, we heard the rumble of an engine coming from the direction of Old Town. Then, the world went silent.

———

I heard only the drizzling rain when I first awoke. I vaguely remembered Sahr Joe's wife, Sia, standing in my living room and saying, "Yu no look well at all." Now, warm sunlight poached the room, and I heard the weaver birds' strident cries in their arboreal nests tucked into branches of KT's mango tree. The loud bird cries, which indicated where I was in time and space, made my head pound. I knew I needed to try to stand up and take more aspirin and chloroquine pills, two every six hours instead of the once-weekly preventative.

This was the chloroquine developed by IG Farben, the notorious Nazi chemical company, with the hope of saving the German Afrika Korps from deadly malaria in World War II. How ironic that chloroquine was now going to keep me, a Jewish woman in Africa, alive, just as it had saved millions after the Allied forces had stolen the secret formula from the Germans.

There was a loud knock, and then Finda walked in and presented me with a bucket of fresh water. Her mother followed behind her with a ceramic bowl of warm water full of leaves and tree roots. Ma Sando dipped a wash towel into the mixture and, after wringing it out, placed the warm cloth on my forehead, but I began shivering.

"Lek dis. Du am so," Ma Sando said. She then packed an herb and clay mixture around my head, neck, shoulders, and chest. After my friend left, I heard the village children gathering beneath my window. They said they wanted to see how Besty looked with medicine on her body.

"We hope e no go die." *I hope she doesn't die.*

"Shhhh. You will make Besty afraid. E dey sleep. Don't wake her."

---

*I was revving my motorcycle when the gleaming black Mercedes approached. Quickly, I turned off the engine and, running close to the road, gave a friendly wave. It worked. The driver rolled down an automatic tinted window and leaned his head out. "Eh, Peace Corps?" he said, surprised. "Wait for me now." He rolled the window back up, pulled close to my yard, parked, and got out with two other men.*

*The men, maybe in their mid-forties, greeted me with fetching smiles. They were dressed in button-down shirts and creased linen pants and smelled of fancy cologne. The driver wore a loose, chunky gold bracelet. When we shook hands, I noticed how soft they were, nothing like a farmer's hands.*

*"You are a teacher?," they asked.*

*"No. I work with farmers," I said and showed them my calloused hands. The men found me and my response entertaining and laughed for longer than I was comfortable.*

"Look at her, she's a real country girl now," they said.

They were amused by my living here in this remote village—a young American woman. Then they asked for Ray and recalled how he was experimenting with new rice varieties in the demo swamp they'd just passed. The driver turned to his friend and said, "Ray is the yellow man with straight yellow hair. The one who helped make that church."

"E dohn go back nar America," I offered. He returned to America.

"Ehhh, so you replaced him?"

"Yes," I answered, aware that I had engaged them enough to lead them closer to Ma Sando and Bondu who were quietly standing along the side of the house a few yards behind us. I desperately wanted them to give Ma Sando and Bondu a ride and I understood that this could be the difference between life and death for Bondu Betsy.

"My namesake has fallen ill," I told them, and then introduced them to Ma Sando.

When they laid eyes on her, the expressions on their faces changed. Their demeanor shifted from propositioning me to concern. Undoubtedly, these men were fathers too. "Lajeelahh!," the driver said.

All three men hovered around Ma Sando taking stock of the limp baby in her arms. They rubbed Bondu's forehead and grabbed her foot, looking at her mother. "Do you want to go to Jaima or Koidu clinic. We foh make haste."

"Jaima," Ma Sando spoke.

I scanned the car. The black leather back seat was stacked high with briefcases and rice bags (likely to feed miners). "So you will transport my friend to the Jaima clinic?"

"Yes, where those German nurses stay," the taller of them said. He turned to his companion. "You know, where Phillip's girlfriend works."

"Yes. I know them, too," I said.

"OK. Leh we go now," he said.

It was so easy. Too easy.

Once Ma Sando and Bondu were in the back seat, the driver turned to me. "They have people in Jaima to stay with?"

"Yeees," Ma Sando spoke up. "Yes. My man is there." Her reply was the first and only time I heard Ma Sando speak of her older three children's father, a miner. Bondu remained limp in her mother's arms. It was haunting to see her so still, her eyes droopy. As the car drove away, I was relieved.

That night, Sahr Joe, Sahr Binah, Musu, Tamba, and Bondu Betsy's father visited my house. No one was overly excited by the good fortune of a ride. At the same time, no one disparaged the men whose wealth was the corridor to an unattainable world.

"Nar God," said Bondu's father. More hmm's from Sahr Joe, Binah, Musa, and Tamba.

It went on like this for a long time; it was reverence—acceptance and awe, in keeping with the Kono tradition. Then they stood up, shook my hand, and left.

Their visit helped me settle. I slept well.

The next day, every motor in the distance—motorbike, lorry, or private vehicle—invoked hope, then disappointment. I worried all day. Everyone who passed me in the village noticed.

"Eh, Besty," they said. "No worry. Everything is God's time." But this didn't comfort me. My thoughts raced to how I could stay here if Bondu died. My grief would be unbearable.

The following day, there was still no word. I realized that at twenty-three, I was the only one here who had never seen a child they loved risk death or die. Every mother here told you how many children she'd given birth to, their names, who lived, who they buried. Often, I'd heard Ma Sando say that Bondu was her eighth child. "Two dohn die."

Finally, I heard the galloping rattle of a lorry approaching, the gear shifting into neutral, and the brakes squealing. The driver pulled up, and Ma Sando was the first passenger to step out of the fully packed truck. I hoped for a smiling Bondu behind her. Instead, Ma Sando waited for a woman to hand her Bondu, bundled up with three or four layers of cloth, her face hidden behind the folds. Babies here always seemed overly swaddled to me. Mothers told me they wrapped them like this to prevent dusty wind from blowing in the babies' faces.

The first thing Ma Sando said to me was, "Sorry ya," apologizing that she had not sent me a verbal message with a lorry driver. She explained that the nurses had kept Bondu hydrated overnight with "a drip."

"But now Bondu dohn bettay small small. Tenki. Tenki."

Still, I could see the concern in her eyes had not let up.

———

"I no put fish head because yu no lek am," Ma Sando said with a chuckle. It was the second week of my being in bed. She entered and placed the rice porridge tray mixed with lemon and sugar on the bench beside me, peering into my face. She could always tell when I was gloomy. She directed me to drink the brewed roots because they would soothe and cleanse my blood. She fixed the pillow behind me.

I was overcome with exhaustion, and my tears overflowed for the first and only time in my stay.

Ma Sando put her hands together and said, "Try foh eat." And then, as she stood, she remarked, "Just as men aren't as likely to become vexed when their stomachs are full, women's heartaches can be dulled with a full stomach."

Later that night, feeling a little better, I crawled under my mosquito net and wondered how I got this malaria.

———

*Two days later, Ma Sando visited again. "Sh Sh Shhhhh," she murmured as she rocked Bondu.*

*"Is she going to be OK?," I asked.*

*She pulled what looked like a Chinese origami fortune wrap from her pouch, except inside each fold was a tablet and Roman numeral instructions on how many to take three times a day for the next week. "Dehm gimme medicine for Bondu," she said.*

*I asked to hold my toma (namesake) in my arms. "Shhh. Shhh," I said, shuffling and singing as her mother had. After a few minutes, I noticed a spider in one of the webs in the corner of the room. I walked toward it, singing, "The itsybitsy spider . . ." I thought I saw Bondu's mouth turn up, the beginning of a smile. Ma Sando asked me if the spider's head was pointing up or down.*

*I leaned forward to get a closer look. "Down," I said. "Why?"*

*"No kill' am. That one is good."*

*I looked still closer. "Yes, the spider's head is definitely looking down. Good luck, then?," I asked.*

*"Yeeeeees! This spider means good luck for Bondu."*

*I smiled, and the corners of Ma Sando's mouth turned up slightly too.*

———

Malaria marked my time in Sierra Leone with a before and after. Strangely, the time and space of this illness recovered a sense of my commitment to being there. I'd spent the first year learning the language and navigating the culture. In my second year, I found a rhythm. My heart was less distrustful and more resourceful. By gaining more fluency in the language and culture—the village's community practices, institutions, relationships, and rituals—I had also gained a better awareness and understanding of the people I was working with, which meant I could be more creative in my efforts to serve. Or so went my logic.

Instead of preparing to wind down and begin my transition back to America with a resume and job applications and all that those things implied—securing a privileged life, conforming to the expectations for a twenty-four year old of my suburban upbringing—I devised a way to extend my Peace Corps service for a third year. This assignment involved a move to Sierra Leone's southern district capital, Moyamba, 200 miles south of Tokpombu, a region populated by Mende and Sherbro people rather than Kono and Mende. I would be working for the Moyamba Disabled Blacksmith Apprenticeship Program, among some of the country's most marginalized youth—boys with polio—in a residential school where they would have the chance to read, write, and secure their well-being and future by applying their upper body strength to make farming implements.

I knew this new position would be far different from working for sustainable nutrition in a remote village. There would be surprising, unknown, and unexpected challenges. But I believed the foundation I'd built so far and my willingness were now embedded.

I learned about the program's founder, Mustapha, and how he founded the program from an ad in Di News De, the monthly Peace Corps volunteer newsletter, which was mostly heavy on comics but light on news. There had been an open slot for a position helping with the daily management of the residential boys' program and finding markets for the machetes, axes, hoes, and buckets the apprentices were making. Mustapha was also a polio survivor. He received training as a village blacksmith with the rare support of an uncle who had taken him under his wing. Mustapha decided early on in his life that, if given a chance, he would take in boys with polio but less fortunate than himself, those who were abandoned by their rural farming communities and forced to resort to begging on the streets of Freetown or Koidu or some of the other provincial capitals.

Mustapha wanted to train these young boys so that they would have the same opportunities as he did to become productive, literate citizens with valuable skills. His aspirations to counter the superstitious beliefs of the communities who had cast them out when they contracted the disease, fearing further damage by presumed wickedness or the actions of witches, devils, or angry ancestors, had inspired me.

The blacksmith workshop, funded partly by Catholic nuns, was a cement room with bellows beside small fires in stations with an adjoining dormitory. The boys, some of whom crawled on blocks, while others were fortunate to have had surgery allowing for braces and calipers, spent eight hours a day pounding and scalding pieces of scrap metal (old railway ties left by the British). I quickly grew accustomed to being there but would occasionally take the six-hour lorry ride to visit my beloved friends in Tokpombu.

Ma Sando and Bondu Betsy surprised me by visiting me first. They arrived in Moyamba in the middle of March while Mustapha and I were salvaging the last of the scrap metal and sorting through the remaining bags of donated bulgur to determine how many meals we had left before our supply ran out. Their arrival was announced by one of the four apprentices, Mohammed #3, who sped with his crutches to the storeroom.

For the next three days, I hosted my friend and her three-year-old baby in my new home, cooking in my outdoor kitchen. I introduced her to my new neighbors, Mustapha's family, and my apprentice friends, who were all delighted to meet a member of the village I had told them about and came to regard her as their big sister. Ma Sando learned nearly everything about my life in the town. We visited the well-regarded Harford Secondary School for Girls and met the missionaries who ran it, and the other Peace Corps volunteers who lived in Moyamba. Treating Ma Sando like a member of my family felt like a natural expansion of the feeling I had when I lived near her in Tokpombu.

When it was time to leave, I escorted Ma Sando and Bondu to the lorry station, passing a few markets along the way, selling used clothing, shoes, and local crafts. I reimbursed her for the expense of the lorry ride and paid for her return trip. I added as many extra bills as I could afford to the wad she tucked into her bra. Ma Sando surprised me as I waved good-bye through the window, calling out, "I don't have shoes for Bondu."

I hurried back to the market area and rummaged through a pile of plastic sandals of varying sizes set out in front of one of the stalls, picking out a pair of tiny pink ones. I returned breathlessly to the lorry and reached through the window to hand them to Ma Sando, the engine puffing black smoke.

"Besty ehhh, leh God bless yu! Tenki! Boku tenki! Bondu gladi!" But I knew it was she who was gladi.

I walked back toward the blacksmith workshop, thinking how uncharacteristic it was for Ma Sando to ask for anything, and wondering why the shoes mattered when it suddenly became clear. Ma Sando could make our having seen each other credible through these shoes. They were evidence that I cared and that I was like a sister, an auntie, and a loyal friend. I thought about how she too had been the woman who had held me up and kept me from stumbling. And even when they no longer fit, I knew someone in Tokpombu would be wearing those shoes.

## CHAPTER 15

# Be All and End All

Peace is not the absence of war, it is a virtue, a state of mind,
a disposition of benevolence, confidence and justice.

—BARUCH SPINOZA

I spent the last week of my stay in Tokpombu walking up and down the rows of houses in Old Town and New Town, saying good-bye to KT and his four wives, to the blacksmith, the Monserary family of palm wine tappers, Chief Lahai, my counterpart Sahr Joe, his wife Sia and their son Raymond. I visited Pa Bindi's pond and the village of Tembeda. I said good-bye to all the students and teachers at the Tikonkor Primary School and to the guava granny. Sia Sam, Sahr Binah's wife, and I made one final batch of cassava cakes together while I toted their baby, John. I attended a final service in the UMC church beside my house. And I made a final trip across the hammock bridge to meet the old chief who had repeated what everyone here had said: "No forget we."

These final days, filled with intimate good-byes, felt like an acknowledgment that we'd all given to each other the best of what we could offer. It all felt strangely peaceful until now, on this last night, the final sunset of my stay.

Ma Sando called into my parlor to announce that she'd prepared my two favorite dishes: cassava leaf stew with the beans we had shelled that morning and a side dish of dessert-like punkie soup (pumpkin). She said it was a "good luck way" to begin a new journey. Outside, on the back stoop between our homes, we shared a large tray with her children, the rich sauces ladled over heaps of red country rice. I knew this was rice from a stash she stored under her bed and that the new crop wouldn't be ready for harvest until after I was gone. This crop that had brought about my arrival and nourished my staying was now going to send me on my way.

"Besty dey go tomorrow," Ma Sando said. "We are family."

We ate mournfully, with lumps in our throats. After tossing the leftovers onto the ground so that the chickens could peck at them, the children nudged their heads into the nape of my neck and my chest, holding onto me a little more tightly. I watched them all scatter in the direction of KT's, except Finda. She had quietly entered my house unnoticed until the sound of her deep sobbing grew audible.

I couldn't conceive yet how I would hold onto these memories, the depth of feeling that came from being in this valley, especially at this hour when the sun became a crimson awning all across Tokpombu, the fragile green clearing they had shared with me, melding into the hills that surrounded it.

I jiggled my lantern to check whether I needed to replenish the kerosene, aware that an eagerness was taking shape inside me, though its contours were murky. Thoughts about the life I had postponed, rejected, or didn't understand pricked me. I wondered whether it was possible to resume that life. Here, I felt loved and seen. This made all the difference.

During my three and half years in Sierra Leone, I'd transplanted thousands of rice seedlings, moved them from one location to another, closely observed how tiny roots are always left behind, even when the new roots form healthy attachments in their new home. Still, I didn't fully realize that unbound roots hold the consciousness of separation in the soil of both lands.

After I left, there would be no way to call, write, or be in touch regularly. I pulled a box of matches from my skirt pocket, tilted the lantern's glass shade, and ignited the wick to guide me back inside my house, and quickly shut the door. I found Finda curled and shaking on my day bed in the dimming light. Her sniffles turned to whimpers and then little snores until eventually her breathing was calm, her tearstains blotting one of the inkblot centers of the flowers of my sheets. I touched her soft face, turned the wick down to a dim glow, and set the lantern on the cement floor beside her.

When I glanced across the room and caught sight of the duffle that I'd stuffed with my belongings beside the front door, I let out a heavy sigh. It would be winter when I arrived back home, the streets and houses would be illuminated early to offset the darkness. There would be shopping and comfort foods, overworking, punctuality, and materialism. I would be coming home to a life I had never created. I had never looked forward to the short days or darkness of winter, January and February always drawing me inward. Now I had another reference point for understanding how things move us forward—in literal seasons, rainy to dry, planting to harvesting.

Nothing stopped the farmers here. Not their corrupt leaders, not the anemic efforts of the international aid community, not the relentlessly encroaching diamond industry, not a leaky roof or the impassible road after a tree had fallen or a mudslide, not an illness from preventable diseases or death. Much of what I didn't fully understand—the rituals and customs, their different understanding of God, magic, witches, and ancestors—had provided a canopy. They were all arrangements and patterns of knowing and thinking that echoed the cadences of the forest—its inhaling and exhaling—producing one collective breath and, within that, a voice. It had been a breath wide enough to include my own voice too.

Ella, toting Bondu on her back, and Angela and Sahr Kondeh burst into my house looking for Finda. When the baby woke up, we took turns trying to console her. I lit a candle that Finda and Ella and I had once made from the dried wax of imported store-bought candles. They had shown me how to pour the remelted wax into the hollow stem of a leaf and we'd set it on the bench, where it had remained all these months.

Sahr Kondeh suggested we play a final game of Pick-Up-Sticks, but Finda, who'd just awakened, only hurled the Pick-Up-Sticks on the floor and wept. When Bondu saw her sister's twisted face, she too began bawling. All I could do was hold Finda and promise that my leaving wasn't forever.

"How could I forget you!," I said over and over. "I will never forget you. We will see each other again. From the bottom of my heart, I promise." I repeated what her mother said earlier: "We are family."

Soon Ma Sando entered and sent the children away, telling them it was time now for sleep. The sight of her third-born daughter folded and whimpering in a ball at the exact spot that Two-Stroke always slept elicited a smile. I'd given Two-Stroke to Marwan, the Lebanese shopkeeper who'd sold us the zinc pan for the new church roof, now securely in place, who'd asked if he could adopt the cat to keep mice out of his coffee store.

To cheer Finda up, I reminded her of the day a chicken had entered my house and laid an egg on this very bed. "We cooked that egg and ate it!," she exclaimed.

This is how everyone learns here: if one person remembers, everybody remembers.

"Sine soma," Ma Sando sang as she left. "I will see you both tomorrow. Sleep well."

And we did see each other the following day. Then, not for fifteen more years.

---

Four years and four months after I left, this community of farmers whose shared interests and collective purpose had inspired me saw their future overtaken by tragedy and atrocities. The same rope the children had pulled on in Mama Sia's story to shrink the middle of the greedy spider had frayed too much to pass along its lessons. We only see clues in the rearview mirror. Or perhaps, we trample on generations of ideas that we ourselves don't spawn.

In Tokpombu, I encountered village-based traditions founded on giving its members a voice—a way of problem-solving and collaborating, open discussion for the betterment of the community, which was part of a long-standing cultural heritage of nonviolence and restorative practices. An essential aspect of this was the critical skill of listening, understanding, and respecting. Routinely, I saw elders gather, taking turns debating and weighing in with an entire community invited to watch and see how so that they would know the ropes when their turn came.

The chaos and terror came instead.

On March 23, 1991, eleven years of civil disorder and chaos ignited in Sierra Leone when widespread attacks began in the country's Eastern Province. What later became known as the Rebel War, or Blood Diamond War, displaced half a million people and resulted in the deaths of an estimated 75,000. The numbers may be more.

Decades of kleptocratic rule by Siaka Stevens and his handpicked successor, General Joseph Saidu Momoh, whose transition was referred to as "same taxi, different driver," had plunged the country into economic and social turmoil and, finally, total collapse. The initial perpetrators of the violence—the Revolutionary United Front (RUF)—were not members of any obvious political faction; they were, rather, criminal bands relying on kidnapped child soldiers, competing for loot in a disintegrating nation at a time when many innocent people could barely make a living. When they attacked a town, they obliterated it—burning homes, schools, and clinics. Their unimaginably brutal and vicious tactics resulted in some of the worst atrocities of late twentieth-century warfare. Attacks took place under the banner "Operation Pay Yourself."

The RUF and the banditry that evolved around them preyed upon the same innocent people who had been preyed upon by the government. They employed hideous methods to turn loyalties, drugging young boys with "brown-brown," a mix of gunpowder and cocaine, and then forcing drug-crazed child soldiers to kill their relatives and chiefs in front of the whole community. Often, these young soldiers were then ordered to carve the initials RUF onto the chests of the forced initiates. The RUF also forced girls into domestic and sexual slavery. While many of the boys were recovered and sent to rehabilitation centers after the violence ended, the girls, who were abducted and sexually terrorized, had few such formal programs to help them reintegrate and were often stigmatized as "junta wives" and the mothers of children who were born of rebel fathers.

Only the kamajors, local Poro society militias, successfully protected their villages by taking matters into their own hands. The rest of Sierra Leoneans, rich and poor alike, Christian and Muslim, and representatives of every tribal and ethnic group in the country, steered wide of the fighting, fearing the violence that had already touched every family since every family had members swept up in the violence.

At first, there was no prominent leader in the RUF. But gradually, Foday Sankoh, a high school dropout, itinerant photographer, and former corporal in the Sierra Leone army, emerged. Unlike most of the rebels, he had some experience with revolutionary campaigns. He had attended one of Muammar Gaddafi's training camps in Libya for would-be insurgent leaders in Africa. In the 1980s, he'd escaped to Liberia, where he forged a relationship with Charles Taylor, also an alumni of the Libyan training camp and now Liberian warlord.

After successive military coups and democratically held elections, the international community latched onto Sankoh, a rebel leader whom they believed could negotiate a peace that would halt the brutal massacres. But the RUF, government soldiers, and even UN peacekeepers all continued to plunder and sow carnage against civilians, swapping the country's diamonds for drugs, guns, and other military supplies. Stockpiles of abandoned weapons, too, were now more readily available on the black market after the collapse of the Soviet Union. No one in the industrialized world prioritized putting a stop to the terror. The flow of Sierra Leone's diamonds, however, persisted.

Finally, with pressure from the international community, led by British Prime Minister Tony Blair, the violent derangement and mania halted in 2002. By then, the innocent citizens of Sierra Leone no longer had any governance, law, order, or civilization. It was difficult to participate in conversations with my American friends that bought into approximations of stereotypes of modern Africa to explain the senseless carnage, as if all the pieces of this could be understood in one sitting. Corruption. Drugs. Diamonds. Guns. Children. Saddest of all were the childhoods stolen by war, how the country's most innocent victims were also its perpetrators. Some of them were my friends.

In 2002, the first modern international tribunal and the first court since Nuremberg, called a Special Court for Sierra Leone, was established jointly between the United Nations and the government of Sierra Leone to put the marauding rebel soldiers on trial. After nearly a decade of court proceedings, Charles Taylor was eventually found guilty of planning, aiding, and abetting crimes committed by the rebels, making him the first head of state to be indicted, tried, and convicted by an international court. Sankoh died awaiting trial.

For many Sierra Leoneans, the Special Court was only the tiniest seed of accountability, justice, and reconciliation that would allow for a tranquil life the brutal war had destroyed.

After such a war, nothing can be as it was.

———

Before starting graduate school in New York in the fall of 1991, I indulged in a weekend poring through old photographs of my Peace Corps days in my childhood bedroom in Connecticut. I sat on the emerald-green carpet and took out shoeboxes of pictures of Sierra Leone that I kept stored in the closet. America was four months away from President George H. W. Bush's Operation Desert Storm, and yellow ribbons were tied around neighborhood trees to honor the brave American soldiers driving Iraq out of Kuwait while New York City's streets were packed with students protesting the military actions.

My mother sat downstairs watching television and smoking a cigarette. My parents had separated, and the shame burned in her so intensely that she sometimes said it would have been better if there had been a body to bury. In a letter to her three children, she described herself as "a discard, left only being a mother, displaced and alone." This was a reality she could never accept. She had married Mr. Right: he had decided she was Mrs. Wrong.

I am still reckoning with the circumstances in her life, expectations for assimilation and the construction of a self that allowed for the creation of such emotional distress, the dis-ease of her perfectionism knotted and bound in the unrealistic expectations of success, obedience, and beauty that America's "cold war" toward women has insisted upon. Or why my mother bought in. My mother's use of the word "only" when referring to her role as mother—*my mother*—stung.

Flipping through the photos, I was surprised to discover a stack of images of Freetown that weren't mine yet were strangely recognizable. Then I remembered where these photos came from. Two American tourists, Brad and Barbara, had asked me to mail an undeveloped film roll to their address in California when I returned home the following week. I had forgotten.

My hand shook as I picked up one of the now almost five-year-old photos. It was 1986 when we'd been a party of six, and it was after midnight. Alex's Beach Bar was getting ready to close. George, the owner, said it was a great night for swimming, and he was right. The tide was low, the moon bright. Brad and Barbara, two visiting Lebanese businessmen, Hadi and Youssef, a Canadian volunteer, and I ran with abandon toward the deserted beach.

The flashing lights of an oil tanker glinted on the water. I stripped down to my underwear and dove in last. We bobbed, splashed, and laughed.

When we found ourselves too tired to swim, we rested on our backs and stared blissfully into the starry sky.

"See, those ships out there waiting? It's because the government isn't, in fact, a functioning government at all," Hadi said. "All of us should get the hell out of here before this place blows."

This judgment matched the cynical buzz circulating in Freetown that the country was on the edge of institutional breakdown. Among the expats, including many frustrated aid workers and missionaries, there were murmurs that they should fold up shop and leave Sierra Leone to the upcountry people, Krios, and Lebanese to sort out their desires for their security and their land—to reimagine themselves on their own.

"Sierra Leone should be running itself after all these years," Youssef said. "Momoh is weak. He's not up for the job." Of course, at that time, the Lebanese in Sierra Leone weren't even citizens. Even after nearly one hundred years, these families held considerable sway and power in the country, but no official vote.

Hadi ranted about the billion-dollar extraction industry sucking the history of this land down the drainpipe as evidence of everything going wrong. But the Lebanese were part of it, just as the men like KT had been part of it—because everyone was a part of it.

"Any way you look at it, this country is going down. The whole country is in a blackout because those government fuckers won't pay their fucking bills!"

My mind turned to the village as it often seemed to do. I was weighted down by conflicting emotions over three years of irreplaceable life experiences on land and with people I loved and was now abandoning. While standing chest deep in the water, the blast of a horn interrupted my ruminations. I saw a tunnel of light and heard another overpowering blast. What was happening? I squinted at the beach where seaweed outlined the shore and where two jeeps were now parked. In the distance, soldiers were standing with their arms crossed and their legs solidly planted on the sandbar. I heard a husky voice call through a megaphone, "Duya. All man foh reach di shore. We get foh arrest yu now."

Barbara and I swam toward each other. Panic consumed me. According to the soldiers, we had violated the curfew (one I didn't know about) and therefore broken the law.

Hadi called, "Don't worry. These guys are a 'one bullet per year for practice!,'" implying that the Sierra Leone army, so reduced and dismantled by former president Stevens and now General Momoh, wouldn't waste their bullets on any of us.

I spotted the others making their way to dry land and followed them. Not complying wasn't an option. I squatted and remained covered by the sea while Hadi and Youssef negotiated something I couldn't hear with the soldiers, who then gave us the all-clear.

"We are friends now," Youssef called out to Barbara and me.

The searchlights dimmed and then went dark. Hadi walked into the water with our clothes and handed them to us. He said that the soldiers were just patrolling, looking for an opportunity. Dawn was imminent. We walked toward the soldiers who by now were laughing at the situation they'd created. One of them asked Youssef if we had a camera to take a picture so they might have a souvenir of this moment. Barbara and Brad dug around in their packs.

"Everyone—head to the jeep, *now*," Youssef said.

"Snap di picture," the squadron leader said. And then we intuitively arranged ourselves for a photo op, six of them and six of us. The soldiers sculpted their bodies around the jeep. One of them had climbed on top of the roof in a dance pose, resting his elbow on the arm of his weapon. Another had put his arm around Barbara. Three others had picked up their guns, strapped them over their shoulders and knelt in the "front row" pointing.

I was still too jittery to join in their fun, and my clothes were wet. So I volunteered to take the picture. I peered into the lens, focusing on their playful faces smiling at me through the viewfinder.

"Ready aim, snap," the one with blue cap shouted without any danger in his voice.

I clicked.

In that split second, what could have been a deadly encounter, guns pointing toward the camera—at me—turned into just another straightforward request by a Sierra Leonean to have their picture taken by the stranger. How could I have not seen anything but their smiles?

I looked back at this moment for the first time, a tremor through my body. My childhood bedroom, with its Marimekko cornices, window shades, curtains, and bedspread meticulously in place after all these years, was proof enough of the care I'd received—money, protection, education—which had brought me to Sierra Leone. I had to acknowledge how bound and deep this web of privilege extended. Knowing the privileged Lebanese men who could pay the bribe to protect us was also to know a hierarchy that lined up as neatly as the waves at the low tide.

At its core: privilege is the value that one person's life is more important than another's. How differently things could have gone in that moment on the beach that night and, more importantly, how quickly a life—an entire world—can change. It was irrefutable that the privilege of being American and living here allowed me to carelessly misplace any sense of danger in my life—because I could.

A whole country had agreed to keep safe those of us who came to stay, even those who were ambivalent. We were welcomed as "the stranger" hoping we could make a difference. Before. Before. Which means, in effect, everything is still possible—everywhere. If you go, you hurt. If you hurt, you feel. If you feel, you are connected forever.

Ma Sando would frequently say: "Everything is God and the ancestors."

———

In June 2002 the war was officially over, and George, Stella's Peace Corps boyfriend and now husband, came to visit my house after his first return trip to his homeland since the war began. George, who now called himself Braima (the family name he reclaimed), and I both found ourselves living in Durham, North Carolina, working in the same schools, within the same community—like before.

All morning, I felt jittery anticipating his arrival. Braima was bringing a cassette recording he made of Ma Sando when he found her in a refugee camp on the outskirts of Freetown, where most of the people who'd fled Kono for Guinea during the war had returned. The camp was along the route he traveled on his way to see his own family members. I felt both dread and excitement—as if, with the delivery of this singular recording, all the years of waiting and wondering were going to bring long-awaited answers.

As soon as Braima walked through the door, I offered him a seat at my pine kitchen table where a pottery bowl was filled with oranges. "Please, take one," I said, as Braima set down the recorder, a stack of new photos, and three small multicolored shuku blai baskets, a gift from Ma Sando.

"If you could see the potholes on those roads to your village! Sista! The size of swimming pools! All those charred homes, buildings. Lorries left on the side of the road where they burned." He looked down at my tile floor. "It's going to take a long time to rebuild."

Braima said it felt like he didn't have a home anymore. Like his childhood didn't exist, as if it were all gone. He's taken hundreds of photos with the hope that he can reach beyond the stereotypes his students in North Carolina have of a war-torn African country. He told me he's taken pictures of children preparing food: fetching water, pounding, and winnowing the rice, collecting firewood, and cooking on their outdoor stoves. "This way, they'll see how children are starting to get back to their normal lives—to become children helping their parents again. Not drug-filled, gun-toting, crazed soldiers."

As an artist-in-residence in the schools, he paints a picture of the rich childhood he experienced in his homeland through drumming, telling stories, tie-dying cloth, and teaching recipes. Braima maintains that involving young children in the arts to bridge links between Africans and Americans more profoundly connects them to an interwoven history between two continents. His grandmother always told him, "Remember your food." He tells his students how a new world is born each time a story is told. As Braima began peeling the orange I reminded him not to eat the goat's part. He smiled.

I loaded the cassette he brought me into the recorder. I hadn't yet learned to handle the truth of the last twelve years, what happened to Tokpombu during the war, and what happened in my family. A decade after my return from Sierra Leone in 1989, I decided to move to Durham, North Carolina. I was seeking more of the America I wanted to live in, with its newly integrated schools and neighborhoods, where the civil rights movement seemed to have gained a foothold. I worked with new immigrants and for a newspaper that covered those stories. Stella and Braima had made their home and family in Durham too. During these war years, I thought a lot about obligations between parents and children, and what makes a good friend. I married Jim, who valued my experiences, and we started a family together.

I heard the crackling sound of the recorder, then the steady breath of my friend who cooked for me long ago. Ma Sando. Six thousand miles away, she took a long, deep inhale, the sound we make before we speak our truth.

"Ay Besty!" and then her words: "Ah tehl God tenki, Ah still dey alive! Di war dohn dohn." *We are all here. The war is over.*

Nearby on the hutch are photos: Ma Sando and her children. Ella. Kadiatu. Finda. Bondu. Sahr Kondeh. Their faces, full of bright smiles. I looked down at the new photos Braima brought. These people were only vaguely familiar: Ma Sando's eyes are sunken into her face long and thin; her daughters Finda and Kadiatu are carrying their own babies now; Sahr Kondeh, who was twelve when I left, has gray hair at twenty-five. A memory of Sahr Kondeh washing my motorbike flashed through my mind, his fawning over it and telling me that one day, he wanted to ride a motorbike like this and travel everywhere when he grew up. When I told him I knew that feeling, he looked at me and said then, "of wanting to freely go somewhere?"

"Yes. *That.*"

I glanced around at my freshly painted kitchen. At the other end of the room, my two-year-old son napped on a futon, next to a plastic potty that sings when you pee in it and a CD player on which I played Putumayo lullabies from around the world. Through sheer floral curtains I looked out of windowpanes facing a stone wall gleaming with springtime gladiolas, purple, yellow, and orange. I saw my daughter Lilly going up and down her green plastic dinosaur slide while the air conditioner's soft breeze lifted the cafe curtains.

Ma Sando launched into a string of sentences in Krio, but I couldn't understand them as I did before. I paused the tape. "Braima, I can't make out all of what she's saying."

"She was weak when she was talking. It was hard for me to make out her words too." He paused. "I love my people, but my country is spoiled."

Braima leaned back on his chair. He explained how he felt his dignity in being able to go home after the war, to make a proper send-off to the family members who had died. What he didn't say though is that some of his family member's whereabouts remained unknown.

"Would you ever want to live there again?," I asked.

His gaze was unwavering. "Sista, my mother never gave birth to me so that I could be buried here in America—a poor man without family support in a white man's country!" For the next half hour, he started and stopped the tape, translating Ma Sando's account.

"Oh, Besty, there were so many who wanted to kill us." Her voice cracked.

I felt sad and helpless.

"Anybody on the road to the diamond fields could be killed, amputated, raped. Anyone in the way was sacrificed."

At the barrie, I thought.

I remember the jolt I felt in 1999, holding my nine-month-old daughter in a grocery store line, and seeing the *New York Times* Sunday Magazine headline: "SIERRA LEONE IS NO PLACE TO BE YOUNG." Below it was a picture of two child soldiers packing semiautomatics, AK-47s retrofitted for children by greedy weapons manufacturers and from abandoned black-market stockpiles created by the fall of the Soviet Union.

Ma Sando's voice cracked again. I felt my throat constrict, thinking about how frail she sounded. I tried to picture the village empty or taken over by rebel bandits. I can't.

"We traveled through the bush paths trying to avoid rebels. . . . We left without a single belonging. We spent nights sleeping on the forest floor. My heart been like a drum inside my chest. All I could think about was death, waiting to die."

I couldn't conceive of Ma Sando's spirit so broken that she'd welcome death. Ma Sando was the one who could always lift those around her, as she did me. Ma Sando never projected fear, or anxiety, only the steady movements of a survivor.

"The rebels were carrying guns, looking for the kamajos or government soldiers to kill."

Braima paused to explain that kamajos, as Poro warriors, had mobilized during the conflict, trying to protect their chiefdoms.

"Sometimes the government soldiers who told us they came to help were also rebels. Sobels were on all sides—everywhere."

Braima clarified, "Soldier-Rebels."

These fighters were little more than groups of individual children with fickle loyalty, whose affiliations had more to do with access to food, drugs, and women than anything ideological. You were on their side if you were fed rice in the morning by a band of rebel soldiers. If you were fed rice by a band of government soldiers in the evening, you were on their side too.

I thought back now to how the government of Sierra Leone had consistently stolen from its citizens. The gradual process of government dissolution during General Momoh's presidency was only an extension of what his predecessor, Papa Siaka, had slowly sawed away at, having cut the support beams of the country one after the other. He did everything terrible to his people until they could do everything terrible to one another.

"We carried each other on our backs; some disguised themselves as grandmothers, terrified that they were going to take our children away from us."

In my head I recited the names of Ma Sando's children: Ella, Finda, Bondu, Kadiatu, Sahr Kondeh, Mohammed.

I had read all the news I could find on the war. I knew about the failed peace initiatives, including one infamously negotiated in Togo by the Clinton administration. Jesse Jackson was the "Special Envoy for the Promotion of Democracy in Africa"—placing the so-called northern rebel leader Foday Sankoh in charge of a new commission to oversee Sierra Leone's diamond fields in Kono. The commission also made him vice president. A Sierra Leonean friend later made the analogy that Sankoh holding office to end violence was like bringing a member of the Ku Klux Klan into our government.

The strategy of the Clinton administration and the Congressional Black Caucus unintentionally accelerated some of the world's worst humanitarian, human rights, and international law violations in Sierra Leone. While there was never going to be an easy path toward solving the country's political problems, this particular illiteracy of the region proved fateful. The world has never provided appropriate economic and political commitment or resources to the needs of particular African nations, including Sierra Leone.

When powerful foreign governments, even well-meaning ones, lack insight and experience and yet impose their ideological perceptions on people who are vulnerable and at the mercy of their power and prestige, it's likely to end up in chaos—economic, political, and social. When the RUF entered Freetown on January 6, 1999, intensifying the same brutal tactics they employed upcountry, America didn't prove nimble enough to redress their failed policy.

President Kennedy understood Sierra Leone's potential at the moment in its history when it needed that understanding. His personal diplomacy and recognition of African nationalism and independence turned him into a beloved hero. Sierra Leoneans exalted Kennedy as the father of the Peace Corps, a patriot, a world humanitarian, and a friend of the African people. Subsequent presidents appeared unable to recognize their moment or chose to ignore Sierra Leone's growing disarray, not as a country or people but as a troubled failing state on the brink of disaster.

Even so, nothing I had ever read or heard about this Rebel War or Blood Diamond War compared to this recording. For the first time, I could picture its civil conflict—the village empty or taken over by rebel soldiers. Haunted faces on my friends. It was terrifying.

I stopped the tape to check on Lilly. "Mommy, if you pick 'em they die," she said, referring to the handful of pansies, the pretty flowers she is holding tightly in her hand.

Motherhood is like this, the strange overlap of thoughts, that life of every kind can expire quickly. I asked Lilly if she wanted to come inside and reminded her to stay quiet until William awoke from his nap. She was four.

"No," she said and continued her climbing and sliding.

"I'm here if you need me. I can see you."

"I know," she said.

When I returned, Braima turned the recorder back on.

"Oh, Besty, I will make punkie (pumpkin) soup for you! I remember how you liked punkie with rice too much." She also recounted the first time we made cassava leaf stew together and how I had added tomatoes to the pot. "You are not supposed to add tomatoes to cassava leaves." She laughed, and in my home, I smiled too.

I was relieved to hear Ma Sando laugh, a portal to the life rhythm we shared, pausing at the same time to look off into the distance before standing to fold clothes or gather water or pound rice.

"Everybody wanted to get to Guinea, where we were told there were refugee camps for Sierra Leoneans. The vehicles were so overloaded with passengers trying to board, piling on top of one another, it didn't look safe. In the struggle, I got separated from my children. I arrived in Guinea alone. Day after day, for two years, I kept my hope up of seeing them on the next vehicle, but that day never came."

I stopped the tape and stared straight at Braima. "Jesus-Allah," is all I could think to utter.

He rocked forward and backward, forward and backward, forward and backward. Minutes passed.

My son woke up and began crying inconsolably. I picked him up to console him. I pressed "Play" again.

"The Guinean soldiers were also merciless and hostile to Sierra Leoneans, especially the children. In their eyes, every young person—boy or girl—was a rebel. At the camp, the only way for any of us to survive was to collect wood in the wild and sell it for money. This became everyone's daily routine, young and old. We searched for wood in the grass like wild animals, hopefully to trade for a cup or two of rice. All this time, I kept thinking of my children. Some nights, I dreamed they were all dead."

Ma Sando's voice faded to a whisper, though, instinctively, I covered my son's ears.

"Eh Besty. That time was hard. We were so tired. Finally, when I was on the verge of giving up, there was news of a nun making our case to President Kabbah, speaking out against our constant harassment and mistreatment. That day we left Guinea for Sierra Leone to come to Waterloo began *gladi*. But the soldiers at the checkpoint stripped us of everything. They said that because we did not bring anything into Guinea, we couldn't take anything out. Many people died because they refused to part with their plastic tarps. The soldiers shot them dead in front of all of us."

A tarp—the only thing between them and seven months of rain.

Braima made a point of telling me how suspicious everyone had become of any Sierra Leonean. "Any healthy adult or child could be seen as a rebel."

"In the camp here, we have single rooms with metal roofs. They give us bulgur and vegetable oil to cook with. It is here that I learned more about Tokpombu. Who were the dead ones and who survived. Thanks to God, my children are all alive. This is a miracle from God."

There was a silence, followed by the sound of her breath. When she resumed speaking, she spoke even more softly than before. "John, my brother, lost two of his children. He was shielding them from soldiers when they shot him too."

"Ehhhhh Besty! Sia Tokpombu. Braima delivered your letter, and the money. I was so close to death. Now I am so gladi. You have no idea how gladi."

"We will all be going back to Tokpombu. We are going to properly bury those who have died. We are trying to rebuild everything, I am so gladi you found me."

I leaned back in my chair and closed my eyes. I could still picture the stream bank where we fetched our water, and where a stone might sit forever. Many seasons have come and gone and the stone remains. But it is the stream, not the stone, that Ma Sando's voice evokes. The water flows to all of us. Our connections are threads in a worn but still useful bedsheet washed and beaten on the stones of a stream.

CHAPTER 16

# Perception

Love does not begin and end the way we seem to think it does.
Love is a battle. Love is a war. Love is growing up.

—JAMES BALDWIN

It is November 2013, and Lisa, Lilly, and I deplane and walk in lockstep, the still, damning swelter of the evening heat constricting our breath until our lungs made sense of how we might inhale in this new climate. We skipped across the tarmac of Lungi Airport to a slow but orderly line snaking toward a renovated and modern municipal structure that was only hazily recognizable from decades past.

The war had been over for as long as it lasted. It was the beginning of the rice harvest. I had invited my now fifteen-year-old daughter, a high school sophomore, to join me—to meet my friends from long ago who survived three rebel attacks on their village, living in a refugee camp or on the run as child soldiers, porters, some of them bush wives. Those three years in Tokpombu had been my experience, not my child's. It was "my before." But I recalled Ma Sando telling me, "Doesn't a mother teach her child all things?"

A few years earlier, I'd worked as the director of a nonprofit, War Child USA, which had its headquarters in Peterborough, New Hampshire, close to where my family now lived. The organization was part of a worldwide network supporting programs with marginalized youth in conflict zones—street children in Iraq, girls unjustly incarcerated in Afghanistan, and child soldiers in the Democratic Republic of Congo and Sierra Leone. The organization's local fundraising efforts and the programs we initiated fortified my conviction that while young people—especially children—can easily be recruited into conflicts, their agency over their future, their lifespans, isn't predetermined despite the trauma. The more invested I became in the harrowing stories of these children, the more I understood how much easier it is to find buried diamonds, to get lost in the digging up of the whole world for our own shortsighted purposes, rather than to repair it.

A friendship grew with Lisa, my son's kindergarten teacher, during those years. She had lost a son to violence during his senior year in college in Maine. His younger brother and his girlfriend witnessed the whole terrible thing—how he tried to break up a fight but was murdered by a knife through his chest.

Watching Lisa calmly redirect six-year-old boys like my son from pretending with their fingers or sticks to kill the bad guys was both reassuring and unsettling. I'd shared with her that when I lived in Tokpombu, I had never seen young boys play pretend war. Lisa had asked if there was room for her on my trip to Sierra Leone. She said she wanted to meet the mothers like her—the ones who had lost children to violence. It convinced me that what ties any of us together is a longing for continuity, which stands at the core of everything—especially our grief.

With our carry-on luggage in one hand and our passports and World Health Organization vaccination cards held tightly in the other, we were directed by the customs official toward the baggage claim, where a bus shuttled passengers between the airport and Tagrin Bay, the northern landing spot where the ferries dock, a ten-mile drive. Speedboats called "sea taxis" now provided relatively effortless passage into Freetown. Flip phones and iPhones, with their varying tunes, corresponded with the snatches of Krio melodies: "Yes. Nar me." "I'm on the way." "Yes, everything is good."

In the bus ride crosstalk, the familiar voices of men tossing invigorated opinions in Krio created a bass that flowed beneath the rhythms of chatter. "It will end up being a waste of time!" were the final words I overheard before the bus ground to a halt, and screechy doors opened. More ringtones.

I slowed my steps when I saw a barely detectable sign that read "Tagrin Bay." It was little more than a stake in the ground. Even so, it was something to mark the history of this crossing—a trace of the markets of human horror at this very oasis.

It was already late, nearly 10 p.m., when we lumbered across rickety scaffolding that provided a dock and descended a set of stairs until we found ourselves cradled in the well-lit cabin of a boat of considerable size with café-style seating and a television mounted to the wall blaring *CNN Breaking News*. A middle-aged Sierra Leonean man with a shaved head seemed to be staring at us with his arms folded as if trying to deduce something.

The man abruptly uttered, "You Americans are obsessed with guns."

I told him I'd been a Peace Corps volunteer in the mid-1980s.

"That's interesting," he said.

With the headlights of the boat careening toward the pier, I glimpsed the three of us in the window's reflection. Gusty winds swelled deep inside me. It called to mind the breeze when it caught the outer reaches of the forest canopy in Tokpombu.

On the Freetown side of the peninsula, we followed another ramp, this one covered and dimly lit, to where a band of boisterous vendors, porters, taxi drivers, and family members converged. I watched Lilly's and Lisa's movements closely, wondering what these sights and pungent familiar smells of roasted palm and diesel fuel, cigarette smoke and cheap cologne meant to them.

We emerged onto a congested street searching for our hosts, Lorelei and Kim, expats living in the city, relatives of former Peace Corps volunteers. They'd offered us a spare room in their rental, a third story walk-up that gave us a soft two-day landing before the ten-hour drive to Tokpombu.

By late morning the next day, we had already begun exploring: the city's narrow, gutted streets teeming with lorries, automobiles, motorbike taxis, wall-to-wall pedestrians, and colorful markets. There were piles of seeping garbage and people excavating what they could from its smoking mounds. I held fast to Lilly's hand as we dodged stray dogs and puddles of urine.

Punctuating the vibrant scenes of hardship, resilience, and ingenuity were beautiful, tie-dyed colors and the warm greetings of passersby.

We strolled down a cul-de-sac, stopping at Tambakula, an eye-catching all-women's art cooperative where twenty or so weatherproof booths were set up beneath temporary construction. In the women's friendliness, I sensed a familiar welcoming and connected cultural landscape. Still, I imagined that beneath their bright-eyed and eager smiles were private reconciliations of their harrowing wartime experiences—deprivation and trauma.

After a war, renewal and survival can look the same.

On that morning, we were their only customers. We bought some beaded jewelry and batik cloth.

From there, we taxied to Lumley Beach to enjoy a meal at Alex's beachside restaurant bar. During our ride, we saw billboards and hand-painted murals that advertised telecommunications networks: Africell and Sierra-Tel instead of Coca-Cola and Fanta of the prewar and pre-internet days. This too: bold signage, infographics, and pictures promoting contented nuclear families, vaccines, reproductive health, and birth control ("Wear a condom!"). Even the rusted shacks lining the streets had themselves become billboards with window posters and flags of Sierra Leone. "Stay in school," "Say no to unwanted sex," "Report rape."

Yet even to Lilly it was evident that these bulletins for changing mindsets were at the same time advertising the pressing stress of being a child in Freetown, youths coming of age without formal education, few opportunities to earn a living wage, and a lack of the customary support of village life.

"Everything in life is trying," I said to Lilly, just as Ma Sando, Pa Bindi. Sahr Joe, and so many others had said to me.

After our late afternoon meal, we took a long walk on the beach flanked by rows of buildings, the charred remains of houses neglected after the war, which were side by side with new and incomplete McMansion-style construction. My recollection of Freetown's landscape held lush mountains, empty beaches, green spaces, and few billboards. Now, foundationless construction had overtaken the hills, buildings planted on earth without roots to hold them, making it easy to imagine how easily life can slip into the sea. After all, the leone's value had sunk to L510.000.00 per dollar.

Again, the past merged with the present when by extraordinary coincidence we ran into someone from before. One moment, he was a strange face. The next, he was my old friend who lived on one side of the church in Tokpombu while I lived on the other.

"Besty. Is that you, Besty?"

"Sahr Pessima!," I blurted.

In this country of now close to seven million, a man from the village of 400, 250 miles away, stood in front of me, twenty-five years later.

Sahr pulled out a flip phone and tried to ring his mother. He wanted to tell her about our chance encounter, but she didn't pick up. "You have to climb a hill for a reception in Tokpombu," he said. "I left a message. She knows you are coming."

We wandered the bright sandy shoreline for another hour, searching for shells and watching the tide go out. A group of runners—Sierra Leoneans and expats—zoomed past. Lisa struck up a conversation with a man lugging his boat onto the sandbar.

"My son liked deep-sea fishing," she said.

We listened to the fisherman's animated complaints about the vast Chinese commercial trawlers illegally scraping the offshore seabed, tanking his would-be-catches, and destroying the ancient breeding grounds for millions of fish. "Praise God, we are trying, small-small," he said, holding up a compact but lively red snapper for us to inspect.

On our third morning in Freetown, we were introduced to twenty-something-year-old Joseph, the designated driver of the Jeep Overland I had rented. In the brisk early morning hours, we began our journey to Kono. Immediately after exiting the compound walls, Joseph put the pedal to the metal.

"Is someone chasing us?," I said mildly. My grandmother Lillian, Lilly's namesake, used to ask me this when I drove too fast.

"You don't like fast?"

"Not so much," I said.

Joseph eased up a little on the gas pedal and told us about his life. He said he still hoped to get his high school diploma and attend Fourah Bay College and sometimes worked at an internet cafe where customers could rent computer equipment by the hour.

"I didn't have so much schooling when I was a boy," Joseph said. He was referring to how he came of age amid one of the most brutal wars of the late twentieth century, but he said it so matter of factly that you might have thought he was describing this interruption the way you would spotty internet service. Sometimes it's hard to understand what is being said because we don't know, haven't lived, don't have a reference point for what we are hearing.

On a newly paved forty-seven-mile stretch heading upcountry, complete with three tollbooths not seen before in this country, compliments of China, the tarmac suddenly stopped, jolting Lilly awake. We found ourselves bouncing over the grooves and potholes Braima had described—reminders of the grenades and rocket launchers that had punctured the earth.

As we moved through towns and villages, Joseph pointed to the burnt houses and rubble that would have to be removed by hand. He explained that grieving families were still searching for the bones of loved ones lost during the war. "We are taking time."

He told us that the spirits of the dead still exist inside the rubble, and it called up the women in Tokpombu who had instructed me not to sweep the house at night for fear of a similar ancestral disturbance.

The day was growing hot. Joseph turned up the dial on the air-conditioning and the volume on the CD, which played a Krio song called "Mariama." It was a catchy tune about young love and a miner pleading with his girlfriend's family to allow them to marry. We drove past green fields of swamp rice with stalks that bent from the weight of its seed in their arc toward the sun. "Mariama" became our theme song, and we teased Joseph that he played the track so often that there must be a Mariama waiting for him somewhere.

Along the way, we were waved on at checkpoints by camouflaged soldiers toting machine guns until the final one, where we were stopped by two officers who instructed us to roll down our windows and then poked their heads inside.

"I'm going to where I lived as Peace Corps. This is my daughter," I said, turning and smiling at Lilly to provide some reassurance. She smiled back, but I could see that she was bracing herself.

"So, you are bringing your daughter to meet the village!," the officer said in the friendliest way, switching to English.

I dug out a book of photos I'd brought from home and gave it to Joseph to pass to the officer on his side—the one who had declared himself in charge. The officer's formal and stern demeanor suddenly melted away. He called for the soldiers clustered in a nearby shelter to look at the pictures. One soldier remarked that the children looked "stout and carefree, not like today's children." The one in charge handed the book back and signaled us to leave.

Joseph accelerated quickly. Unexpectedly, I teared up. It was the same Sierra Leone, and yet.

We sped past Makali, a town I remembered for its Lebanese shop with ice-cold Star Beer and the tilapia fingerlings I had scooped into plastic containers for Pa Bindi's fishpond. I was surprised to see the Chinese fish station still intact.

Joseph remarked that the demand for fish farming was growing because freshwater fish were disappearing. It was the same fish story as before.

We were all relieved when we finally arrived at the Shine On and Stay Hotel—our base while we made our four daily trips to Tokpombu. Joseph was eager for a high time in Koidu, the former diamond boom town. Lisa, Lilly, and I were ready to eat, wash, and sleep.

We met Tiffany, the hotel's owner, an African American from California whose love for Sierra Leone had planted her here. Shine On and Stay had become a popular venue for aid workers, people in business, and local big men, and created an intimate international hub for conversation and collaboration. As she handed us our key, Tiffany mentioned that we could visit the school she had helped to create. "Muddy Lotus," she called it.

We unpacked and re-sorted all our bags full of greetings in a room equipped with traditionally woven cotton blankets, air-conditioning, and netting. We carried supplies for newborns, bedsheets, towels, headlamps, and a variety of school supplies, as well as our personal belongings. I looked forward to the morning when we could go into Koidu to buy bags of rice, fresh fish, palm oil, and Maggi, just like I sometimes did before.

We woke up to the smell of smoke and the sounds of birds, brooms, and pestles thumping into mortars, outdoor kitchen routines gesturing toward breakfast preparations. They weren't just patterns of sounds transporting me back to village life—they were intractable morning rituals for the generations of women who sustained the lives of everyone here.

There was a moment when Lilly and I got into a tiff. She wanted to wear khaki pants with Converse high tops to our village reunion. On this first day, I wanted her to wear a dress, specifically an African batik dress we'd packed from home—one she'd willingly worn before. It took only seconds for us to become ankle deep in a battle of wills.

I described to Lilly how I was sure what she wore would hold meaning for the women in the village. "When you are somewhere when they walk on three sticks . . . ," I said. We follow different rules in different places.

I confessed that at this moment, I cared more about pleasing Ma Sando than I did Lilly. We reached a standoff. Then Lilly conceded. She slipped the dress over her head with an exasperated sigh. "Are you happy now?," she said.

"Yes." But I wasn't just happy. I was grateful and proud.

After a complimentary breakfast, we reunited with Joseph, who was already waiting for us in the carport. He helped us load up our gifts and complimented Lilly on her dress. "Mi small sista de look fine today." Lilly smiled.

We approached Koidu, our music blaring, windows open, feeling celebratory. Suddenly, a distant, overly worked gray mound began to eclipse any former sense I had of this city and its warm embrace. The shadows cast by the hill's awning over the lowland plateau, some of it clearly gauged by vast open pit mines, didn't reveal a mountain in the usual sense. An immense slag heap, some hundreds of meters of sand and gravel, and rock high, stood reconfigured. My first thought was that this monumental destruction could only be a billboard for suffering, yet it was so much more.

I had seen the landscapes change here before. Slash and burn methods used in shifting agriculture routinely left bald scars on the land that were eventually covered over with the new green growth of rice seedlings. Occasionally, there were landslides from the accidental felling of too many trees. But as we drove closer to the city, I became acutely aware that this moonscape was permanent. For the generations of young men who chose a different gamble from their parents' labors, mining instead of farming, the seduction of diamonds had become one long and soul-emptying process. And yet, its continuation was allowed—even after eleven years of a Blood Diamond War.

As this waste of extraction grew more prominent as we drove closer, I felt a strange desolation. It wasn't just this massive, demolished mountain that penetrated the skyline in front of us like mountaintops blasted for coal. It was the full measure of how a complicit world seems not to notice or care, so overcome as we are by the richness of a diamond's symbol on a loved one's finger. When the world's consumers became aware of the diamond industry's entanglement with the so-called blood diamond trade and how diamonds fueled rebel movements and their allies to topple weak governments, the industry responded by formulating a patchwork scheme to provide better oversight. But this so-named Kimberley process, established in 2003, was not positioned to address the broader and more entrenched risks to human rights that the diamond trade poses. A diamond will never be able to tell you of its heartache: the children who died from waterborne diseases; the malaria, Lassa fever, cholera, and Ebola that results from disrupted ecosystems; the families and communities decimated in the course of a purchase.

In my lap, I clutched the pages of the well-worn yellow notebook I'd carried with me—the one Ray had given me, with its maps of the chiefdom, the names of farmers, and descriptions of the land they'd cleared and plowed, planted, and harvested. I suddenly recognized the continuity this book had provided all these years, a bridge between my then and now. It was still guiding me.

We drove past children standing along the roadside, waving at our vehicle. Women carried oranges in trays on their heads beside men carrying machetes and sometimes briefcases. I delighted in watching Lilly and Lisa wave back, enjoying the warmth of these greetings from total strangers. In ways I didn't expect, new outlines of how life could renew so fully here began to appear. It wasn't barren like the view of the mountain. It was warm and inviting yet also unfamiliar. Perhaps another reminder of how Sierra Leoneans, like citizens of every war, had become a diaspora in their own country, left to pick up the pieces. And, in the healing, there were new things.

In Koidu, the old roundabout suddenly emerged where the Barclays Bank once stood, along with the Ministry of Agriculture—a dilapidated charred remnant—and even Margaret's little compound, abandoned and covered in foliage. We passed a secondary school, "on vacation because the children are helping their parents harvest," Joseph said.

Lisa, Lilly, and I ventured about the premises. Lilly spotted a geometry problem on a chalkboard and said, "We did this same problem in my school!" Lisa noted Einstein's equation: $E = mc2$.

Walking through the city, we saw many shops boarded up. There wasn't access to perishable foods; the vast market field was mostly abandoned. We had few options for purchasing our gifts. Joseph suggested cases of soda: Coke, 7 Up, Fanta, Orange, and Grape. This notion bothered me— imported soft drinks without nutritional value rather than local supplies. "Why shouldn't they drink what the rest of the world drinks?," Joseph offered. With ambivalence, I loaded the Jeep Overland with the cases instead of bags of rice.

———

The police officers in Jaima stood in a shelter much larger than the depot-sized one I recalled. They approached us, grinning. "Who are you?" "Where are you coming from? Where are you going?" They requested that we step out of our vehicle.

I told them I was Sia Tokpombu and introduced my daughter and Lisa to them.

"Ehhhhh," they cried. "Yu are talking Krio!" They asked if I had been a Peace Corps, the person they were expecting who was coming back to meet the village.

I told the men that Lisa and I were teachers and that three generations of my family had passed through this checkpoint—that my mother and father had stood here on the day the space shuttle *Challenger* exploded, and now my daughter, Lilly, was standing here.

My daughter's eyes were fixed on the same verdant mountainous terrain where I'd ridden fearless and alone on my motorbike. To handle the challenging rock-ribbed terrain, Joseph had to slow to a snail's pace. We craned our necks when we heard the noise of a motor popping as it accelerated past us—a motorcycle taxiing a sandal-footed bony older woman wearing a flowing Nigerian lace cotton gown who held tightly to the driver's ribcage. Motorcycle taxis were a thing now, accessible to everyone, young and old.

"This is our tomorrow," Joseph said. "Our future." It was so rare for elders to leave the village when I lived here, and now they had the flexibility of a motorbike for their comings and goings, especially on the market or clinic days. This simple change for women felt momentous.

We bucked and bounced along the narrow, canopied road, passing a tractor coated in a film of dust. Someone had secured a prominent weathered-looking "OBAMA" printed umbrella to the side mirror. I understood the umbrella to be a nod to our being here at this moment.

We stopped in Moimondu, where we encountered a weekly market closing now that the sun was directly overhead and the heat bore down. Women were folding up tables and placing their unsold produce into bags to carry back to their villages. A young man introduced himself. He said he was the town chief in Tembeda, Joe Samuel's great-grandson. He knew about our swamp work—the rice plots we'd built and the fishpond. A lump formed in my throat as we locked eyes.

At the final six-mile mark of the twelve-mile trip down the rock-ribbed road to Tokpombu, I lost myself wondering whether any of it had mattered. Then, moments after we cleared the last hill beneath the Jeep's wheels, I was filled with a vivid sense of the Pentecostal church members swaying and losing themselves in spoken tongues; of Finda dancing toward my house like sugar spilling from a sugar bowl; of the community paying their last respects to Pa Sanusi.

A small crowd was waiting diagonal from the crumbled remains of my former house, now swept into one smooth flat surface. Ma Sando was the first person in the group that I recognized. She was warm, smiling, and visibly nervous, her eyes looking in all directions. Ma Sando wore a gold-plated pendant around her neck with a lightweight sweater buttoned at the top over a camisole. She had dressed for the day!

I was nervous, too, as we climbed out. We all were.

"Ehhhhh. Besty. You dohn remember we! I gladi!" was all Ma Sando said.

"Yeees, we are here," was all I could manage.

I loved saying, "We."

With a crowd beginning to swell from every direction in a circle around us, their playful, familiar Krio and Kono filling our ears and my heart, I felt outside the bounds of anything I knew how to understand. It wasn't just happiness or a longing fulfilled; it wasn't just bittersweet because I left and their way of life fell to pieces, and now I was returning. It was all that, and it was lighter and heavier than that too. The earth vibrated with feet, and everything felt quick and dizzying.

I held onto Lilly's hand.

"Ehhh, Besty. Aw di bodi?" What is still said to determine whether your health is well enough to work.

"Ay de try, small small." I am trying, little by little. "We tehl God tenki."

"We also tell God tenki. How is your mama?" Ma Sando turned toward Lilly. "How is your grandma? And your grandpa?"

I told her that my father had died in 2009.

"Oshea." *I'm sorry.*

A community had come to greet us with open arms, and the drums, singing, and dancing quickly began. I moved my feet awkwardly at first. But then the women threw up their arms and began to sway and move their feet, and so did Lisa and Lilly in her batik dress, and then, allowing myself to join in the merriment with total freedom, we all danced—as a powerful single unit. Recognizable expressions began matching faces to names I'd carried in my head all these years. Maurice, Patrick, Musa, Sorie, Kumba, Bintu, Hawa.

There, in the middle of the red dirt road, mud homes that had been burnt to the ground were now rebuilt with the old tin roofs repurposed for doors and windows. A crowd of children formed a new circle of clapping and dancing, each taking turns in the center of a ring to perform "her dance" while the men accompanied us with drums, hollowed wood covered with the skin of a goat. The women's leader paused, grabbing a drumstick from one of the young men. She showed him the proper rhythm with one hand on his shoulder and another on the drum. "Don't do it like this. Dis way, ya."

When I lived here, every young man had known how to beat a drum, not how to hold a gun. For a decade, the children had lived on the run, hiding in forest caves to evade death or capture or injection with drugs and gunpowder to force them to take up arms. Even if they made it safely over the border to neighboring Guinea, they became trapped in a refugee camp. The transfer of knowledge had been disrupted.

The women began to sing the Kono Bondo song, and I joined in repeating the still familiar words. "The light has changed; the light in you, Besty, has changed." Next, they substituted the name Lilly, adored for being my daughter and admiring her dress, and then Lisa, adored for being a teacher who'd come all this way to meet them. As we sang and clapped for each other, I felt a shift taking place inside me—as if the feeling of being small and insignificant could be silenced by the will each of us had to lift the other up.

Sahr Binah tapped my shoulder. He was proud to tell me that he was still teaching at the primary school in Tikonkor. Binah said the guavas at Tikonkor were not ripe yet, remembering how much I loved them. I could see the shape of his jaw wasn't right due to a war injury.

Amid all the initial merriment, the heartfelt greetings, the dancing, the singing, I couldn't help the wedge I felt between my heart and lungs at seeing the remains of my former Peace Corps house. During the war, rebel soldiers had set it ablaze. Only the concrete foundation and the metal railing of the front porch were left. The crumbled remains in the photos had been swept clear.

Our dancing and singing came to a final halt when we arrived at the court-barrie. The town chief, Patrick Lahai, the now-grown son of Chief Lamin Lahai whom I had known, ushered us onto the new wooden benches—the original also having been set afire like all the homes in this village. I watched the adult faces on children who'd once drawn crayon pictures in my parlor and were now the leaders of this village. I found echoes of their parents, Maurice, Patrick, Sorie, Bintu, and T-Boy, in their gestures, many of whom did not survive the war.

We stayed at the court-barrie for the whole of the afternoon. Lisa, Lilly, and I were invited to sit at a table in front of rows of benches. My legs couldn't stop shaking beneath the table. I felt the tears streaming down my face. A ceremony on our behalf was beginning in earnest. This was a tradition for guests—the way it was always done, with pride.

Speaking through a megaphone, Sorie, a large man with a round belly, the son of the Old Pa Sorie, introduced himself as the town speaker. He recited a Muslim and Christian prayer to honor both religions. He asked everyone to take time in the next few days to speak of their lives: their hopes for educating their children, of safely going to bed and waking up each morning with enough to eat.

When it was our turn to speak, Lilly, Lisa, and I presented the customary kola (a caffeinated nut with a waxy membrane) to the few remaining elders. Through a translator holding a megaphone, I said, "He who gives cola gives life," to the little boys and girls now grown. The acknowledgment of this tradition sent the crowd smiling and laughing. Then, more seriously, Pa Lebbie said, "More than anything material, which was appreciated, you brought your own daughter to meet us. We thank you, Sia Tokpombu. And we thank you too for bringing us a teacher."

Sorie and Patrick asked Lilly to speak. She described how she'd grown up hearing about the Peace Corps, about the time her mother had lived in West Africa. Lilly told everyone that she'd heard me speak Krio to our Sierra Leonean friends and sometimes to her and her brothers, William and Lucas, who weren't here but would also hopefully visit one day. "But now," Lilly told them, "Krio seems more real, and you are more real, and after only a few days in your country, I can feel how special all of you are to my mother and why she loves you so much. And so, I love you too."

There was standing and vigorous applause. A few of the same women who had once taught me when to stand up and when to recede here stepped forward to hug my daughter.

Knowledge has no worry.

Chief Patrick announced again through his megaphone that it was time for the children's presentation—nearly fifty patiently waiting pre-schoolers. "Preschool" was a new concept in Sierra Leone. Twenty-five years ago, the elders of this village sat on their porches telling stories to children, teaching them the songs and rhythms of daily life, while their parents went off to the farm and their older siblings walked the mile down the road to primary school. Now, there were not enough surviving elders to provide this care. So the village had decided to convert the vacant but still standing church into a school for young children. It was the only building the rebels had not destroyed during the war.

I could never have imagined this church providing something more important than the imposition of Western values through religion. It was now providing a softer, gentler meaning—a place for the community, for their children to stand up and fearlessly shout their names, to learn where they've been and who they might become; a place of healing.

Five of the children were called upon to stand and sing out their names for us, along with their parents' names, how old they were, and where they lived now. "My name is Kumba Sonda. I am five years old. My parents' names are Kai and Angela. I live in Tokpombu, Gorama Chiefdom."

The fundamental human right to safely state out loud who you are and where you come from never felt more important. As if all life depended on it.

Ma Sando and a few others placed a traditional striped gown made from country cloth over my shirt and skirt as the ceremony wound down. I turned to Lilly. Our eyes met as I placed the matching hat on my head.

At the end of the ceremony, we promised to return the following day—and the day after and the next day after too. Then a DJ turned the amplifier up full blast, and we all danced for hours.

Early the following day, we went to the school, and Lisa taught the children some of the clapping, singing, and hand-holding games she had taught my now thirteen-year-old son. Later, Ma Sando repeated to Lisa and me how her brother John had died protecting his children.

"The rebels fired their guns at him."

I translated this account to Lisa, who reached for her hand. "My son died a protector too," she said softly.

Lilly, Lisa, and I spent the next few days visiting the school, my old demo swamp, and the graves in and among the pathways to the rebuilt mud homes. At one point, I stole away to walk to the far side of KT's once reigning house at the foot of the village, where the graves of KT, Mama Sia, Gbesay, Kumba, and Fengai lay. I placed a stone on each grave—what I do for my father each time I visit his grave and according to Jewish tradition. Stones: the permanence of memory.

As the days wound down, one of our last acts was to distribute the gifts we'd brought from home. We passed out an assortment of soccer balls Raymond had donated, hoping that surviving Gorama United Soccer club members might resume their tournaments. Binah and Maurice Sonda, who bore a striking resemblance to his father, told us that their old soccer club was one of the first things they'd organized when they returned home. Gorama United Part Two, they called it. The men were overjoyed by the gift.

I also presented the village with two bound volumes of photographs I had taken between 1984 and 1987. Inside the front cover, I had inscribed, "Thank you Tokpombu, Gorama, for making your home my home when I lived here. . . . I did not forget."

Neither did Ma Sando, who led me to visit with an old man who wanted to see me but was too weak to participate in the festivities. I sat with him beside his bed in a dark room with a dirt floor. He cried out from the pain, and when it eased, he turned his head toward me and smiled. Ma Sando described the day's events, how my daughter was there, and how a teacher sang songs inside the old church.

It was as I remembered. No one was ever left out.

Midwinter, after our return from Sierra Leone, shortly before Lisa was diagnosed with an inoperable brain tumor and became too ill to teach, Lilly began volunteering in Lisa's kindergarten—the two of them singing songs with children seated together on wooden benches the way they had in Tokpombu.

One night, long after my family had gone to sleep, my phone pings. It is a text from Finda. She is now living in The Gambia, where she's found refuge after the war. Finda was barely a teenager when she lived on the run as a "rebel wife," a euphemistic term for what she calls being a sex slave and birthing three children under terrifying and merciless conditions. Ma Sando had given me her number when I visited, and we'd been in touch ever since.

Texts from Finda are invitations to talk, and the connection tonight is clear, so I put on my jacket, slip into my boots, and step outside, not wanting to disturb anyone's sleep.

She begins our conversation the way she always does, reminiscing about our time together in the village. "Eeeeeh God! My country was full of sweetness then."

Finda repeats the same story I heard many times before: how she escaped the rebel stronghold, along with ten other "bush wives" and their children after the guard who stood patrol over the stream where they were washing clothes stepped away momentarily. I listen, looking up a waxing moon, starlight blocked by its luminescence.

She details how they ran for the next three days, afraid to even stop or lay down until they reached the rebel-held town in the east. She tells me about the son she had birthed who had been stolen from her, how soldiers had named him "Long Life" because even after days of being left to die, he didn't, so they gave up and returned him to her. She describes her daughters' disfiguring burns too, but without describing the circumstances. The story of her torture is disjointed. "Now-now," she tells me, "only Jesus" can help her. She has joined a fundamentalist church that helps lift her from the pain and promises to deliver a better afterlife. "The old ways no longer suit me," she says, implying the anguish of remembering, of looking back, is still too painful.

Finda says that she still has many unanswered questions she wants to ask her mother." Yu no know how many questions I get foh mama."

It's taken me a while to realize her questions are the same as mine. Of course, they would be.

"What has my mother been thinking all these years!" She says this as a statement, as if laying the groundwork for all future questions. "All she does is cook another pot of rice." If not rice, then potatoes or yams as if it has to be this way—as if there is only this one way of being.

Switching back to the war, she says, "We told them we were market women, and they never questioned us." "Those rebels were nice."

I stare at the nearly full moon, considering all the nights I spent with her and her family in Tokpombu, how together we beheld the night sky. "It's so bright tonight," I tell her as if there was never an interruption in our conversation.

Finda recalls walking with me and Sahr Kondeh when the moon was full, not needing lanterns to light our steps. "It's really the same moon," she says.